The Scuttling Gourmet

Third edition (2010)

A guide to wholesome nutrition for rats

·Alison Campbell

Published by Shunamite Publishing
alison@shunamiterats.co.uk

ISBN No. 978-0-9566232-0-1

Cover design and photographs - Alison Campbell
All internal photographs by the author unless otherwise acknowledged in the text.

Printed by Reeds Printers, Southend Road, Penrith, Cumbria, CA11 8HJ

CONTENTS

This book is dedicated to Tabitha; matriarch of the Shunamite Rats.

"Mother of all my dreams…
My dreams with expectation
Growing."

From the poem, *Tabitha*, Alison Campbell, 2003

TABITHA

Your final breath
Breathes winter's icy chill
Into this heart of mine
Still beating.
Eyes flame of hope
Burns low with weeping.

Where is your living now?
Searching the empty pain of loss
I find you waiting
In every flash of midnight eyes
From shadows watching.

Mother of all my dreams...
My dreams with expectation
Growing.

Memories dance and play
Within this empty space
That is your leaving,
And I am wondering
Just who owned who?

I search the time
Of our belonging
As hopes flame grows,

And find you...

In my hearts remembering
In every graceful turn
And silent wandering,
Bin-raiding,

Fostering,
Mothering
In every friendly lick
Love growing.

You owned my heart
Each soft, soft footfall
Planted gently there
My heart yours for the breaking.
And in that yielding
I know your life was mine
For celebrating.

Alison Campbell, 2003

Facing drawing: Jenna

"Knowledge is the
food of the soul."

Plato

ACKNOWLEDGEMENTS

I would like to thank all those who have contributed to the content of this book through their ideas, reviews and recipes. Special thanks go to Alison Triggs, Jemma Fettes, Lilly Hoyland, Lloyd Allington, Laura Elfleet, Beri Instone, Andy Murray and Stacey Cochrane for trawling through pages of draft text to comment on the content and presentation - and to challenge my assumptions. I think that between us we did a good job!

My appreciation also extends to Kate Baker-Pretty for her gorgeous illustrations, which I concluded were simply too delightful not to carry over from the 2nd edition.

I extend my gratitude to Annette, lilladysez and Trudy for letting me use their photographs, and especially to Neil, who happily baked a selection of Scuttling Gourmet goodies in order to produce some perfect pictures.

The front cover photograph was made possible by Shunamite Tinkerbelle tendencies (AKA Belle); thank you little one for representing our special 'flavour' of rat-kind, the thing I call tabiness.

And finally I extend my appreciation to my special and long-suffering family who put up with zillions of hours spent researching, revising, designing and typing, not to mention my lack of grace at being interrupted!

INTRODUCTION

The third edition of *The Scuttling Gourmet* is essentially a new book with an entirely new approach. Only the first chapter and Appendix one remain from the second edition and even then, chapter one has undergone extensive revision. It is possible that in re-writing I have neglected to include information from the second edition that you found particularly useful, and if that is the case I would ask that you contact me so that I can rectify the situation in the future.

I have written this edition to the best of my ability, within the knowledge and understanding that is currently available to me, and have tried not to be prescriptive. Rather, I have aimed to provide a sound knowledge base that will allow you to come to your own informed decisions about feeding your rats. Each section has been referenced to enable you to read more deeply into any subject that interests you, but this is not a scientific review and often unreferenced information is included. Where this is the case I would seek to reassure you that (regardless of referencing) all of the content has been researched and is as accurate as possible. However, there may sometimes be issues with interpreting information gleaned in a laboratory setting, and applying it to the practicalities of feeding pet rats.

The chapters in this edition are organised according to specific aims in feeding our rats, depending on such variables as stage of life, health and reproductive status. Since all feeding aims (see page 15) are not necessarily compatible, you may wish to begin by working out your own priorities in feeding your rats, but remember that these are likely to vary from time to time, or as your situation changes. Once you have determined your aims in any particular situation, you should then be able to easily choose the chapters that are likely to be the most relevant source of information.

If you are seeking the answer to a particular question you will be pleased to discover that this edition has been indexed, making retrieval of precise facts or advice much easier.

Online sources of supplies are included within each section in this edition, as are the details of useful supplements. Frequently asked questions are answered in the general text, and indexing will enable you to find the relevant sections.

I hope you enjoy the new format, and find the information more accessible and retrievable at a later date. I am always keen to hear comments on the content and layout, suggestions for improvement, and discrepancies in the text. With this in mind my email address is included on page 2.

"Good food is a celebration of life"

Sophia Loren

CHAPTER ONE - OVERVIEW

Factors that affect nutritional requirements
Quantities
Nutritional requirements
Aims in feeding your rats
A balanced diet - complete food versus variety
Understanding major food groups
    Protein
    Fat
    Carbohydrate
Vitamins
Minerals
    Calcium and phosphorus
    Sodium, chloride, magnesium and potassium
Trace elements
    Copper
    Selenium

Chapter one
General principles of
rat nutrition

STARTING AT THE BEGINNING

When it comes to considering the nutritional requirements of the pet rat we need to realise that there is no 'one size fits all' response. Each rat is a unique individual whose particular need for nutrients will be influenced by many factors that will vary throughout its life.

These factors might include:
- Genetic differences
- Stage of life
- Reproductive status
- Environmental factors
- Activity levels
- Gender
- Illness

GENETIC DIFFERENCES
Most of us have seen genetic differences at work. Sometimes, although a group receives the same diet, one rat will become obese while the others remain slim and fit. This is probably the result of many factors, some of which are inherited differences.

STAGE OF LIFE AND REPRODUCTIVE STATUS
The nutritional requirements of an individual rat will vary considerably throughout its life, depending on age, breeding status and health. Young, growing rats, breeding does and stud bucks will have higher requirements for many nutrients - throughout this book, diets designed to meet these extra needs will be referred to as those that support *reproduction and growth*. Adult rats thrive on diets that are lower in protein, many micronutrients and calories, and as they age they may also benefit from a diet designed to protect kidney health - these diets are referred to as *maintenance* and *kidney friendly*.

ENVIRONMENTAL FACTORS AND ACTIVITY LEVELS
Rats kept in low ambient temperatures require more energy (calories) to

maintain their body temperature, while a warm environment often reduces food intake, as does social conflict and environmental stress. Varying levels of activity lead to differing energy requirements; a rat kept in a small tank or aquarium, with few climbing opportunities, will obviously use less energy than a fit rat kept in a large cage with lots of time free-ranging.

GENDER
Males and females may have varying requirements and tolerate different levels of specific nutrients in their diet. For instance, does are generally more active and less likely to overfeed and become obese (though some will). Males do not tolerate high levels of protein as they age, due to their predisposition to kidney disease, while females are more likely to develop mammary lumps and pituitary tumours if overfed, because of hormonal factors and their general predisposition to these types of tumour.

ILLNESS
Sick rats generally have high energy requirements as they may be using up calories in laboured breathing, fighting infection or supporting a large tumour. Many other nutrients may also be needed in greater amounts, such as protein, vitamins and minerals. Surgery can increase nutritional needs for the period of recovery and healing, while neutering can lead to a rat putting on weight more easily and if intake is not controlled, to obesity.

QUANTITIES

One of the common questions asked by rat owners is how much they should feed their rats. Some sources quote a weight of dry mix in grams per rat, which I have seen range from 14g to one third of its body weight - so about 150g for an average 450g rat! The truth is that this question can only be answered by trial and error for your own unique colony of rats. Try imagining how difficult it would be to answer the question, "How much should a human eat?" and you begin to comprehend the difficulties.

"How much?" (in terms of volume or weight) is also affected by difference in the weight and volume of all of the many and varied foods that you might choose to feed your rats. For instance, if you feed lots of fresh food, then the overall volume of diet must be increased to account for the weight of water in the food. Likewise, you will need smaller volumes when a food is primarily comprised of small, dense grains and seeds. The working answer to this question isn't even constant for a single group of rats, as it will vary with fluctuations in health, season, environment, age and activity levels. The following plan will help you to establish how much to feed your particular group, but remember that needs vary with time.

This approach is not intended for very young rats (up to about 8 or 9 weeks), who should generally have food available at all times.

- Feed once a day only and at roughly the same time - a useful time is after their evening activities, so late evening.
- Feed the amount that you think they are likely to eat in a period of about 20 or so hours.
- Take a look in the dish after their active morning period and really there should only be a little of their least favourite foods in the bowl, as they will usually eat very little during the day.
- Look again at what's left about 20 hours after the time that you fed them. This will coincide with them becoming wakeful again. By now there should be nothing edible left in the bowl – just food dust and empty husks.
- If you look in the morning and there is no food at all, you need to give a little more next feeding time.
- If you look 20 hours after feeding time and there is a lot left to eat, you need to feed less (reduce by the amount that is left).
- If you have rats that stash you might take a week or two to get it right. Check the cage carefully at cleaning time for uneaten food of any type. Reduce intake until there is no uneaten food lying around the cage when you clean out.

There is an expansion of this method, other means of reducing intake, and the need to alter the quantity of food given as growth slows (and eventually stops) in Chapter 9.

NUTRITIONAL REQUIREMENTS

Published lists of nutritional requirements for rats offer average values that will not apply to all pet rats, in all circumstances, and they were formulated using laboratory rats kept in controlled environments that are very different to those our pet rats enjoy. Many of the values relate only to reproduction and growth, with maintenance levels not being available for all nutrients. Laboratory diets are often purified, which makes the nutrients more readily accessible to the rat. For these reasons, it is more important to adhere to the principles of a healthy rat diet, than to try to feed precise levels of nutrients that are exactly in line with the available data, such as the list of requirements published by the National Research Council [NRC] - see Appendix 1.

WHAT ARE YOUR AIMS IN FEEDING YOUR RATS?

This might seem like an obvious or simple question, but in reality there are many answers and what you end up feeding to your rats will have to meet your personal aims. Not all aims are compatible when it comes to choosing appropriate foods and each of us should try to be clear about why we are making our food choices.

The aims that we might have in feeding our rats include:
- Health - protection (a healthy immune system), prevention (of illnesses like tumours and kidney disease), treatment (of illnesses like diabetes, hormonal imbalances and kidney disease). Chapters 7 and 8
- Longevity - may be improved by slight 'under feeding' and slow growth as well as feeding for health. Chapters 7 and 8
- Growth - rapid in kitten-hood, then slow and steady with some spurts. The tail can offer clues as to how well nutrition is meeting a youngster's needs. Chapter 6
- Reproduction - high protein, calorie and calcium requirements, as well as many other nutrients. Chapter 6
- Weight management - loss, gain and maintenance. Chapter 9
- Vitality and condition - fitness, showing. Chapter 10

- Pleasure - variety, taste, smell, texture; also increases amount eaten. Chapter 11
- Interest and enrichment - games, treats and scatter feeding. Chapters 9 and 11
- Personal ethics - food sources (free range, organic), vegetarian and vegan diet. Chapters 2, 3 and 7

Your aims will be unique to you as a rat owner and once you are sure of what they are, you will be more able to choose an appropriate diet for your rats.

A BALANCED DIET

As soon as people begin to talk about nutrition, it is generally only a matter of time before they move on to a "balanced diet". In the pet food industry this balance has sometimes been achieved by creating homogenised pellet diets for our animals, and for some species this is entirely appropriate. However, when feeding rats, I believe that 'balance' should be interpreted as feeding a diet that is varied enough to provide overall balance, rather than trying to find a diet where every mouthful contains the same balanced nutrients (but also the same flavour, smell and texture).

WHAT'S SPECIAL ABOUT RATS?

Like us, rats are opportunistic omnivores, who naturally eat an extremely varied diet. They also seem to derive a great deal of pleasure from eating. This may be in part due to their sophisticated sense of smell, which is far superior to ours.[1] Smell and taste are closely linked in the appreciation of food and rats use smell to modify their food related behaviours. A rat's taste preferences will move naturally from sweet (prefer), to salt (like), to sour (dislike) and finally to bitter (hate/avoid), but such is the power of smell that they can socially transfer food preferences, depending on what another rat has eaten.[2] This effectively means that food preferences can be modified and re-learned and the easiest way to get a reluctant rat to eat is to house him with other rats who enthusiastically eat anything!

I hope that we are able to free ourselves from the notion that there is a choice to be made between health and boredom. Anyone who has owned a rat will know the pleasure that food brings:

- The anticipation of excited, eager bodies produced simply by the smell or sight of food.
- The dancing bodies hanging from the cage bars at teatime.
- The optimistic searching for that special treat, followed by the finding of a place of solitude to savour and enjoy.

This description that Abi wrote when her rats were sampling the liver cake detailed on page 285 is perfect:

"They sat and ate it with their little eyes closed and their little ears all laying down on their heads as if 'indulging' bless 'em!"

It is well within our grasp as rat owners to feed for health *and* enrichment. Once you have understood the principles of a healthy rat diet, you can use them as a measuring stick to decide whether a particular food is a useful addition to their diet or not. Fresh and unprocessed food is often full of micronutrients, enzymes and even useful bacteria, that for the most part dried, heat-treated and extruded food simply cannot supply to the same extent. Processing food into extrusions and pellets is also used as a means of disguising cheap, low quality 'fillers', which can reduce the nutritional content further. Variety mimics the natural diet of the rat and taking this approach enables us to feed good quality ingredients that have undergone little or no processing.

I would caution against the attitude that I hear so often: "If it's good enough for me, it's good enough for my rats." Certainly, other than mango and citrus for males, if it's non-toxic to me then it's non-toxic to my rats, but the vast majority of western humans eat all sorts of things that are high in fat, salt or sugar. What may take 40 years to take a toll on our human health will very quickly show in the health and condition of a rat. Perhaps we ought to turn that one on its head and say, "If it's good enough for my rats, it's good enough for me!"

UNDERSTANDING MAJOR FOOD GROUPS

PROTEIN

Protein is required for the health, growth and repair of body cells, tissues (for example muscle, bone, nerves and blood) and the hormones that are required to regulate body systems. The National Research Council quote a requirement of only 5% protein for maintenance, and 15% for growth and lactation. These values are based on studies where the diet fed contained a purified, highly digestible protein source. With non-purified dietary protein sources (sometimes called crude protein), it is estimated that requirements are likely to be higher, because not all of the protein ingested is digested and absorbed into the body.

Adult rats, other than those who are pregnant or lactating, require a diet with around 10%-14% protein. Bucks may be less tolerant of high dietary protein levels as they are more prone to kidney disease. Extra protein within the body is broken down and detoxified in the liver, and excreted by the kidneys, which can accelerate the rate at which damage occurs when the kidneys are diseased. However, too little crude protein (probably less than around 8% for maintenance) may lead to a deficiency in essential amino acids, which are vital for the health and repair of body tissue. While it is often stated that too much protein can lead to 'protein scabs/sores', I am not aware of any documented evidence for this. This topic is discussed further on page 210.

All proteins are made up of amino acids. In rats there are 22 amino acids (including two that are rare and produced as needed within the body), but there are more than 100 amino acids found in nature. 8 of these 22 are considered 'essential' to both rats and humans, though this figure is higher for kittens and human infants. In reality all 20 are essential (i.e. the body needs them to manufacture all the many and various proteins it contains), but those that aren't called essential amino acids are the ones that the body can manufacture itself. The other 8 *have* to be taken in the diet otherwise deficiency occurs.

If a protein includes one or more of the essential amino acids then it can only be manufactured when the required amino acids are present at one time. If any are lacking, the body cannot manufacture the protein and if the deficiency of the essential amino acid continues, then a protein deficiency will occur, despite overall adequate protein intake. Imagine each essential amino acid as a different coloured Lego brick. To make a particular protein there will be a unique pattern of different coloured bricks, joined together in a specific way to create the final pattern (protein), and if one colour is missing the final pattern cannot be made. For this reason all humans and rats need to take in foods containing *all* of the essential amino acids on a regular basis.

Only protein from animal sources and a few plants (such as buckwheat, soya, quinoa and hemp) contains all of the essential amino acids. The plant sources often have a limited amount of at least one of these, and need to be combined to provide a good quantity overall. Soya, for example, is low in two essential amino acids (methionine and cysteine), but these are found abundantly in other plant material, so for vegetarian and vegan humans it is enough to combine a number of plant sources of protein (including soya), to provide enough essential amino acids for reproduction and growth. However, there are a number of studies which suggest that this is not necessarily true for rats during certain phases of life, and that due to their rapid rate of growth, they may actually require animal sourced protein to support reproduction and infant growth. This does not have to be meat or fish, as the proteins supplied by egg and (or) milk will suffice. Indeed, rats suffering from protein deficiency (not only the total quantity in the diet, but also lack of specific essential amino acids) may cease to ovulate, reabsorb their litters, or give birth to stillborn babies, and live babies may suffer from stunted growth.

Rapidly growing and lactating rats need approximately 23 to 28% protein to cope with the increased demands made upon their bodies. Pregnant rats (and those about to become pregnant) have increased protein requirements, and some of this should probably be from animal sources. Interestingly, rat milk contains up to 20% protein in comparison to human milk at only 7%, which reflects the rapid rate of growth of young rat kittens.

It should also be remembered that some protein sources are more easily digested and processed by the body, meaning that certain proteins are more useful than others in terms of higher protein yield and lower toxic waste products. Egg white is considered the purest protein in this regard, with almost 100% availability and little of note in the way of toxic waste. The rate of absorption of a protein into the body during digestion also varies. For instance, egg is absorbed at a rate of around 88% - compared with beans at only 48%. The actual amount of protein in protein-rich food varies too (weight for weight), with chicken and soya having the highest protein levels by weight, then tuna and other meats, with egg having one of the lowest.

Consideration of the role that protein plays in kidney disease is important when feeding rats, as almost all rats will have a degree of deterioration in kidney function as they age. The implications are greater for male rats due to a male-specific protein that is found in the rat kidney. A high protein diet in humans who have healthy kidneys will not cause or hasten kidney failure, and this also appears to be true for rats. However, the protein type does seem to be significant, for instance, rats fed primarily soya as a protein source were shown to have lower levels of kidney degeneration at the same age, compared to those fed primarily milk protein.[3] This effect was much greater for male rats in particular, and resulted in increased longevity on the soya based diet.

Feeding a diet that is protein-rich to a rat who already has deterioration in kidney function may accelerate the rate at which the disease progresses, and where the disease is advanced will certainly increase uraemia, making the rat feel more unwell. In terms of this effect, not all proteins are equal, with soya and egg proteins having a less detrimental effect, and meat or cow's milk proteins accelerating decline. In addition, the quality of meat protein is important, with good quality muscle proteins having a higher protein digestibility than connective tissue and reclaimed 'meat'. Higher quality meat protein will therefore have a lower toll on the liver and kidneys than meat by-products and derivatives, in terms of detoxifying and excreting waste products.

FAT
Fat is a useful high-energy source and also contains nutritional factors (essential fatty acids), which are important because they are found in all cell membranes and because they are the precursors of prostaglandins. These hormone-like chemicals are short-lived and need to be produced constantly within the body. They are responsible for regulating virtually every body system, including the cardiovascular, immune, and nervous systems.

Essential fatty acids can be split into two groups: omega 3 and omega 6, with sources seeming to suggest that both of these are required in a rat's diet. Omega 3 fatty acids are thought to have a particularly beneficial effect on cardiovascular health, which includes maintaining normal blood pressure and a reduced risk of stroke. It seems to be generally accepted that it is necessary for optimum health, to encourage the intake of omega 3 fatty acids at the expense of some omega 6 sources.

Good dietary sources include:
- Omega 3 – walnuts, oily fish, soya, flax seed/oil.
- Omega 6 – vegetable oils, animal fats.

Omega 3 fats and vegetable oils tend to be liquid at room temperature and are generally polyunsaturated fats. Saturated fats are those that are solid at room temperature, and include (non-fish) animal fats and coconut. They are considered by some to be unnecessary as part of a balanced diet.

A healthy rat diet is low in fat, around 5%, and because of the nature of their typical diet they do not tend to have the same problems as humans in relation to cholesterol and related cardiovascular disorders. However, if a rat is fed a diet that is high in saturated or polyunsaturated fat (or both), it will be more prone to high blood pressure, tumours, obesity and related disorders.[4,5] Obesity is a particular concern in rats, as it is responsible for an increased risk of mammary tumours, pituitary tumours, bumble foot, strokes, and diabetes (amongst other illnesses) and reduced longevity. High fat diets have been shown to have a negative effect on reproduction and the growth of nursing kittens, with reduced fertility and increased likelihood of neonatal death.[6] One study demonstrated a significant reduction in the activity, endurance and cognitive ability of rats after only nine days on a high fat diet.[7]

One group of fats that should probably be avoided, are those known as partially hydrogenated trans fats. These are unsaturated fats that have taken up extra hydrogen to become more saturated, and include vegetable oils that have been converted to harder 'baking fat'. Some of the soya bean oil used in feed manufacture is partially hydrogenated. There is a strong link between dietary hydrogenated fat and increased risk of heart disease[8], and although rats are not prone to this illness this is primarily because their diet generally remains low in total - and harmful - fats.

CARBOHYDRATE
Carbohydrates are high-energy nutrients and include starches and sugars. High carbohydrate foods are often low in fat and are from plant sources such as grains, cereals, vegetables and legumes. These foods should make up the bulk of a rat's diet (approximately 75-80%). They supply the body with energy for everyday activity, growth and reproduction, but if fed in excess they will be turned into fat and so lead to obesity.

Fibre is also a carbohydrate but it is largely indigestible to non-ruminant animals, and does not supply a meaningful amount of energy or nutrients to the rat. However, inclusion in the diet has been shown to have a number of positive benefits including enlargement of the caecum and colon, where fermentation and bacterial activity occur. This activity produces B vitamins that are then passed out in the faeces and become available to the rat through the practice of coprophagy (eating faeces). Bacterial fermentation also produces essential fatty acids that are then absorbed. In addition, fibre can improve transit time, reduce pressure in the colon (and related colonic diseases), reduce weight gain, reduce the occurrence of mammary tumours and extend lifespan. However, high dietary fibre intake can reduce the amount of minerals absorbed from the intestine.[9]

A rat's natural diet will generally contain adequate fibre from plant sources, especially unrefined grains, which can also help with weight control as they require more energy both to de-hull and to digest. Whole grains, or those that have undergone minimal processing, should generally comprise part of a rat's diet wherever possible.

Sucrose (refined sugar) is best avoided as it can cause obesity, metabolic disorders and tooth decay, and fructose (fruit sugar) is also likely to cause problems if given in excess. However, the nutritional benefits of giving some fruit in the diet seems to outweigh these concerns.

VITAMINS

Vitamins are micronutrients that are necessary for the maintenance of health and vitality. Rats are unlikely to suffer greatly from the majority of vitamin deficiencies (though potentially they can), because of the nature of their diet. The exception is vitamin D which will be lacking in any rat diet that has not been supplemented with the vitamin. Some concern is often expressed over lack of vitamin B_{12} in a largely vegan diet; however, rats can recover this - and other B vitamins - from bacteria in the gut, by coprophagy (eating their own faeces), so are unlikely to become deficient. A diet that is high in whole grains, herbs and vegetables, with some seeds and fruit is extremely likely to contain adequate amounts of the other vitamins and rats also have the ability to make and store their own vitamin C.

VITAMIN A
Sources: carrots and other red, orange, yellow and dark green vegetable, eggs and liver. It should be noted that not all sources contain retinol, which is the storage form of vitamin A in animals. Plant sources tend to supply the carotenes - primarily beta carotene - which is converted by the rat to retinal (the active form of vitamin A).

Needed for: vision and the synthesis of a hormone-like growth factor for cells. It can be stored in the body and rats are unlikely to become deficient on a diet that includes some vegetables and herbs. Vitamin A is added to all generic rat and rabbit mixes.

Toxicity: can occur as a result of chronic overdose (for instance through the overuse of supplements) and results in thinning of the coat, dry skin, fatigue, weight loss, anaemia, bone fractures and diarrhoea. Problems have been noted in humans at twice the recommended daily dose.

VITAMIN B GROUP (except B_{12})
Sources: whole grains, legumes, meat and fish.

Needed for: immune system health, cell growth and reproduction, red blood cell development and healthy skin. B group vitamins cannot be stored and excess is excreted by the kidneys. Rats are unlikely to be deficient as grains are a rich source, and these vitamins can also be recovered by coprophagy.

Toxicity: will not become a problem since excess is lost in the urine. This is important because high dose vitamin B supplementation is potentially useful in preventing and treating hind leg degeneration.

VITAMIN B_{12}
Sources: fish, meat, shellfish, liver, eggs, dairy and marmite. Some processed foods are supplemented with B_{12}.

Needed for: DNA and fatty acid synthesis. B_{12} is not stored in the body and excess is excreted by the kidneys. Deficiencies are possible, and more likely for vegan and some vegetarian rats - but B_{12} is produced in the intestines by bacteria regardless of dietary intake, and can be recovered by the practice of coprophagy. For this reason deficiencies are probably rare, but some dietary vitamin B_{12} is recommended, especially where litter trays are used and cleaned frequently.

Toxicity: will not become a problem since excess is lost in the urine. This is important because high dose vitamin B_{12} supplementation is potentially useful in preventing and treating hind leg degeneration.

Vitamin C

Sources: green leafy vegetables, herbs and berries. Rats can manufacture their own vitamin C.

Needed for: building and maintaining body tissue, fortifying the immune system, and is a powerful antioxidant. Antioxidants have a major role in the prevention of cellular and nuclear (DNA) damage, which is the common pathway for ageing, cancer and a number of diseases. Vitamin C cannot be stored and excess is excreted by the kidneys. Deficiency is unlikely, though elderly rats do become less efficient at manufacturing their own, however, studies suggest that high dietary intake could still be beneficial in terms of supporting the immune system, regardless of the ability to make vitamin C themselves.[10]

Toxicity: will not become a problem since excess is lost in the urine.

Vitamin D

Sources: eggs, liver and oily fish.

Needed for: bone health, parathyroid function and immune system health. Vitamin D can be stored in the body but because of the nature of a rat's diet deficiency is *likely* unless feeds are supplemented. All commercial rat and rabbit food is likely to have vitamin D added, but those who feed straight grains will need to add their own. Rats can manufacture vitamin D as a result of exposure to sunlight – but due to their natural habits this will rarely occur. Window glazing screens out the necessary UV fraction from sunlight. Further discussion of vitamin D can be found in Chapter 7.

Toxicity: unlikely but could occur as a result of chronic overdose (usually through the overuse of supplements), but problems only occur at many times the recommended daily intake. Signs of toxicity are due to raised blood calcium (hypercalcaemia) and include loss of appetite, nausea, excessive drinking and urination, weakness, itchiness and ultimately, kidney failure.

VITAMIN E
Sources: whole grains, nuts, eggs and green leafy vegetables.

Needed for: its antioxidant properties, protecting cells from free radicals and oxidation. Vitamin E is stored throughout the body and deficiency is unlikely.

Toxicity: very unlikely.

VITAMIN K
Sources: green leafy vegetables.

Needed for: the process of blood coagulation (clotting). Vitamin K is stored in the liver and deficiency is unlikely if some fresh vegetables are given.

Toxicity: extremely unlikely.

MINERALS

Minerals are needed for all normal body functions, and for cellular health. There are two groups of minerals: macro-minerals, which occur in all living tissues in substantial amounts, and trace elements that occur in much smaller amounts, but are still essential to health.

There are six macro-minerals:
Calcium	Phosphorus
Chloride	Magnesium
Potassium	Sodium

CALCIUM AND PHOSPHORUS
The requirement for these two minerals is closely linked and high levels of dietary phosphorus (P) will reduce absorption of calcium (Ca). Both of these minerals are needed for bone growth and bone health, calcium for

blood clotting and functioning of the nervous system and muscles, and phosphorus is needed in cell membranes and many biochemical reactions in the body. Excessive amounts of calcium have been implicated in the calcification of soft tissue (especially in the kidneys).

Recommendations for growing rats are for approximately 5g of Ca per kg of food (0.5% of diet) and 3g of P per kg (0.3%) and to support lactation 6.3g/kg and 3.7g/kg of food respectively. Optimal maintenance is around 3g of Ca per kg food, which is relatively hard to achieve on a typical grain based rat diet and supplementation should probably be considered. It can be assumed that phosphorus requirements can be easily supplied by a rat's diet, and too much phosphorus is more likely to be an issue that too little.

Lactating females pour large quantities of these minerals into milk to feed their babies (as much as 200mg Ca and 140mg P per 24 hours). However, studies seem to show that there is a dramatic increase in the absorption of these minerals from the intestine during the lactation period and this, along with a general increase in food consumption, will usually be enough to compensate for increased requirements (assuming that the diet contains sufficient Ca and P in the first place). Since calcium is often relatively low in a rat's diet, supplementation during pregnancy and lactation is strongly recommended. Vitamin D is also required for the uptake of Ca in the body and levels of this nutrient need to be adequate or deficiencies of both may occur. A supplement like Calcivet offers both calcium and vitamin D in the same preparation. Dark green leafy vegetables such as dandelion and kale offer excellent Ca to P ratios in a bio-available form, meaning they are well absorbed into the body. Daily green leafy vegetables can help to support requirements during pregnancy, lactation and the rapid growth period. The merits of specific greens in relation to supplying calcium requirements is discussed in more detail on page 133.

From observation (not research), deficiencies during the rapid growth phase of young rats seem to be reflected in their tail development (other bones will be affected, but the effects cannot be seen so easily). Thin, square (matchstick) tails are often seen in large litters where dietary needs are not fully met, though dietary changes, particularly increasing calcium and giving good quality fats and sufficient calories, can usually change the structure and shape of the tail to the normal cylindrical effect. A rat's tail will often become thinner and squarer in old age and illness, which may be due to demineralisation of the bones, as well as generalised weight loss. Further discussion regarding calcium and preventing deficiencies can be found in Chapter 7.

Reduced intake of phosphorus is closely linked to maintaining optimum health in rats with chronic kidney disease. This subject is considered in more detail in Chapter 8.

SODIUM, CHLORIDE, MAGNESIUM AND POTASSIUM

Excess of the other four macro-minerals are generally tolerated well by the body, and levels need to be artificially high before problems occur. In a varied rat diet deficiencies are extremely unlikely, and would certainly lead to very sick rats.

High salt (sodium chloride) diets may exacerbate high blood pressure and kidney disease, but salt is generally tolerated quite well by the species. Of course it is not necessary to add salt to any cooking that you undertake for your rats and most rat owners choose to feed their rats a low salt diet.

Magnesium absorption is greatly affected by the amount of calcium and phosphorus present in the diet. If dietary calcium and phosphorus are very high, magnesium absorption tends to be reduced. Magnesium has been found to have a protective effect against the formation of calcium crystals in the kidneys, and low levels are known to increase the risk of kidney and bladder gravel.

Potassium is often considered to be an issue for older rats and those with known kidney problems, but this is unlikely to be the case. The type of kidney disease that rats tend to suffer from results in excessive urination and this actually causes the loss of potassium from the body. Too little potassium in these circumstances is more likely to be an issue than too much, and will result in muscle weakness.

Trace Elements

Trace elements are needed for healthy cellular function but in very small quantities only. Examples are: copper, iodine, iron, manganese, selenium and zinc. Some (like iron) can cause problems when given in excess. All will cause symptoms if absent from the diet, but as only small quantities are required, a healthy varied rat diet is generally adequate, and if feeding a variety of fresh fruit and vegetables these elements will almost certainly be provided.

Foods that contain good levels of minerals

Calcium - green leafy vegetables (kale, green cabbage, broccoli), dandelion leaves, carrots, peas, yoghurt, sardines.

Phosphorus - whole grains, meat, fish, nuts, seeds, grapes, raspberries, kale, cabbage, carrots.

Magnesium - raspberries, elderberries, endive, nuts, soya, whole grains

Potassium - meat, fish, grapes, almonds, potatoes, celery, kale, bananas.

Sodium - cherries, peaches, kale, carrots, tomatoes, celery.

Iron - meat, fish, eggs, whole grains, pulses, dark green leafy vegetables, asparagus, cherries, apricots, raspberries, redcurrants, blackcurrants.

Copper - seafood, liver, kidney, heart, nuts, sesame seeds, legumes, kale, blackcurrants, redcurrants, potatoes, asparagus.

Zinc - seafood, meat, dairy, apples, pears, kale, carrots, asparagus, whole grains.

Selenium - brazil nuts, tuna, oysters, cashew nuts, sunflower seeds, chicken, liver, lean beef, eggs, garlic, green vegetables, whole wheat bread, whole wheat pasta, soya and oats.

COPPER

Copper is required for a number of functions including the synthesis of haemoglobin, the development of bone and elastic tissue, and the correct functioning of the central nervous system. It is also needed for pigment formation which gives coat colour, and for this reason is often commented on in relation to rats. A lot of texts give 5mg/kg as the requirement for rats, and this would be supplied by a mixed grain diet, however, minerals are never absorbed in their entirety and a higher level of up to 15mg/kg is probably needed in practice. This is especially true where the diet contains good levels of insoluble fibre as this tends to reduce mineral absorption in the gut.

Symptoms of deficiency include increased susceptibility to infection, stunted or slowed growth, anaemia, laboured breathing, weakness, skin sores, oedema (fluid in the body tissues), paling, thinning, or coarse coat, infertility and cardiac problems. There is an more information on copper deficiency in Chapter 7.

COPPER AND RATS (Ann Storey)

"I never used to take much notice of the mineral content of the diet I fed my rats. I mostly looked at the protein content and I never fed supplements, because I was of the opinion that a good diet should not need them. The basic adult feed I used to feed was a rabbit mix supplied by a rabbit fancier from Doncaster. Sometime in the mid '90s he gave up and I started buying from a local supplier. Within a fairly short space of time my adult agoutis and blue agoutis started to get wide, pale circles of fur around their eyes. This was especially noticeable with the does. I started to feed SA37, a commonly available supplement, but it made not the slightest bit of difference. I read up all the rat stuff I could find but the only information I could find was about biotin deficiency. However, in this case the rats lost the fur around the eyes and the coat was greasy, which my rats didn't suffer from.

Like most animal lovers I had read James Herriott's vet books and remembered the story of the copper deficient cows, which had pale eye circles. Okay, I thought, it is worth a try. As the mineral supplements available at the time didn't even mention copper, I decided to use copper sulphate which is the way the feed companies add it. According to Modern Trends in Laboratory Animal Diets edited by A. Steele-Bodger, 1987, a copy of which happened to belong to the toxicologist I used to share an office with, rats require 15mg/kg copper in their diet. My rabbit food contained 5! Within three weeks of feeding this extra copper the eye circles disappeared.

Shortly after this Burgess, brought out Supa Rat which contained enough copper and I was able to stop adding it. However, when they dropped the copper to 7mg/kg the circles came back. Now although I no longer feed Supa Rat I do use Dr Squiggles Essentials Plus, which you can add to the drinking water and does contain a very good range of essential minerals. Most of the other supplements come as a dry powder which needs adding to wet food. As I don't feed wet food to my adults these are not suitable for me. I also add some cat chow which has about 30mg/kg copper."

COPPER AND SHUNAMITE TYPE MIXES

Almost all commercial rat, rabbit and dog foods have copper sulphate added, primarily because the ingredients used do not contain sufficient usable copper to maintain full health. Levels of copper in commercial feeds vary, but rats are thought to need about 5mg of *usable* copper per kg of feed and to achieve this higher levels (usually between 10 and 15mg/kg) should be offered, as not all of the copper will be absorbed. This is partly because of antinutrients which are explained on page 48 and in Chapter 13.

When a rat or rabbit food is used as a base for other ingredients the copper levels can be diluted by the addition of low copper components. Whether you make up a mix for your rats from scratch, use a commercial base food or feed only a manufactured rat or rabbit food, you will need to consider the levels of copper in the overall diet and (if necessary) include some high copper foods, or rely on supplementation.

Mixes that are based on straight grains, even those with added dog kibble or shrimps, seeds and legumes, have the potential to be deficient in copper in relation to a rat's requirements. If feeding straights, a vegetarian or vegan homemade mix it is probably sensible to supplement copper to some degree.

Copper may be supplemented using a vitamin and mineral mix, such as Dr Squiggles Daily Essentials or SF50 (the recent replacement for SA37), or by using crushed copper tablets (available from Holland & Barrett and other health food stores). Feeding copper-rich foods such as liver, legumes, seeds, nuts and shellfish can also boost dietary intake. Liver should not be over fed due to the potential for vitamin A toxicity; around once or twice a week at most.

Copper is excreted efficiently by the rat, mostly via bile into the digestive system and faeces, and it can therefore be supplemented safely as toxicity is unlikely. Changing the diet to be copper rich is the more appropriate 'treatment', but copper supplements may help to relieve symptoms more quickly and are sometimes useful in the longer term.

THOUGHTS ON SELENIUM

Selenium is a trace mineral that is required in very small amounts to sustain health. It combines with proteins to form vital antioxidant enzymes, which help to protect the body against cellular damage from free radicals. These enzymes also have a role in regulating thyroid function and maintaining a healthy immune system. It is probable that rats with low selenium levels are more prone to certain illnesses and infections, some of which might be life threatening. It is also likely that higher selenium levels help to protect against cancer.

Selenium enters the food chain via soil, and the amount found in plants varies considerably depending on the level in the soil in which they were grown. Animals who feed on selenium rich plants also have good levels of selenium in their muscles. The most selenium rich soils are found in the USA.

The best source of dietary selenium is the brazil nut (though levels vary). Despite their very high fat content, a small piece of brazil nut makes a good regular treat for your rats, maybe once or twice a week. Selenium can easily be supplemented if required. It is contained in all of the Dr Squiggles Daily Essentials range.

REFERENCES

[1] Science 3 February 2006: Vol. 311 no. 5761, pp. 666 - 670
Rats Smell in Stereo
Raghav Rajan, James P. Clement, Upinder S. Bhalla
[2] Learning Memory 2006 13: 794-800
Temporary basolateral amygdala lesions disrupt acquisition of socially transmitted food preferences in rats
Yunyan Wang, Alfredo Fontanini and Donald B. Katz
[3] Journal of Gerontology. 1988 Jan;43(1):B5-12.
The influence of dietary protein source on longevity and age-related disease processes of Fischer rats.
Iwasaki K, Gleiser CA, Masoro EJ, McMahan CA, Seo EJ, Yu BP.
[4] International Journal of Food Sciences and Nutrition 1996, Vol. 47, No. 5, Pages 417-425
Influence of Dietary Fats Upon Systolic Blood Pressure in the Rat
Simon C. Langley-Evans1, Alan G. Clamp, Robert F. Grimble and Alan A. Jackson
[5] Handbook of laboratory animal science: Animal models, Volume 2
By G. L. Van Hoosier, Per Svendsen
[6] Behavioral and Neural Biology Volume 27, Issue 1, September 1979, Pages 120-124
The effects of high fat diet on reproduction in female rats
Francine Wehmer, Mary Bertino and Kai-Lin Catherine Jen
[7] Federation of American Societies for Experimental Biology Journal 2009
Deterioration of physical performance and cognitive function in rats with short-term high fat feeding
Murray et al.
[8] The New England Journal of Medicine Volume 354:1601-1613 April 13, 2006
Trans Fatty Acids and Cardiovascular Disease
Dariush Mozaffarian, M.D. et al
[9] The American Journal of Clinical Nutrition
Cereal dietary fiber consumption and diverticular disease: a lifespan study in rats
N Fisher, CS Berry, T Fearn, JA Gregory and J Hardy
[10] Biochemical and Biophysical Research Communications Vol 303, Issue 2, 4 April 2003, Pages 483-487
Decreased plasma and tissue levels of vitamin C in a rat model of aging: implications for antioxidative defence.
B. van der Looa et al

CHAPTER TWO - OVERVIEW

Rat food versus grain mixes
    Why not just feed rat food?
Cereal grains
Processing grains
Phosphorus in grains
Individual cereal grains
    Grains containing lower levels of phosphorus
    Grains containing higher levels of phosphorus
    Pseudo cereals
General points about cereals
    Groats
    Nutritional content
    Phytic acid and phosphorus
    Sprouting
    Buying grains online
Human grade cereals
    Reasons for adding human grade cereals to a mix
Cereals list

Chapter two
Understanding ingredients:
Part one - cereal grains

Rat food versus grain mixes

A rat's diet should generally consist primarily of unrefined and minimally processed plant material; mainly carbohydrate in the form of grains, seeds and vegetables. To this, a small amount of animal protein - or soya - would usually be added. A good selection of ingredients is important to provide the widest range of nutrients and to simulate the natural diet of a rat. Many commercial mixes are limited in terms of ingredients and suitability and rat owners often try to improve on what is available. This can be achieved by modifying a commercial rat or rabbit food, or by making up your own mix from scratch. This is not as difficult as it sounds and this book aims to help equip you to do just that.

Why not just feed 'rat food'?
There are a number of grain mixes and complete foods (nuggets) that are marketed for rats in the UK. However, these tend to suffer from one or more common problems, which mean that there are generally better ways to feed a rat.

Unsuitable ingredients - many of these mixes contain alfalfa and other hay or straw pellets, which are primarily fibre, and offer very little in the way of nutrients to rats. They are almost always rejected, but when eaten can actually decrease the amount of minerals absorbed from other foods taken at the same time. Oatfeed and wheatfeed are similar high fibre products which are aimed at larger ruminants (cows, sheep) and hind gut digesters, like rabbits who all need a high fibre diet. Manufacturers may use these cheap ingredients to fill out a mix in order to make it seem more economical than it is. Other unsuitable ingredients include, but are not limited to, sugar, sunflower seeds (allergenic to some rats) and peanuts (high protein and fat), where these make up more than a small proportion of the overall mix.

Poor quality ingredients - this is particularly problematic where low quality 'meat' is used, such as chicken derivatives. Issues relate not only to the suitability of the animal parts as a nutritional source, but also to the ethical considerations for the welfare of the animals that provide the meat. Where meat is imported, hormone and antibiotic residues can also be a problem. 'Vegetable derivatives' are sometimes used, which tend to be plant parts that are surplus to requirement in other industries, and will vary within a particular feed over time, depending on what is available. Poorer quality ingredients tend to have a lower nutrient content and are often harder for the rat to digest. Where they are high in fibre they will also reduce the absorption of essential minerals like iron and copper .

SKEW TO LESS PALATABLE INGREDIENTS - some mixes list primary ingredients that are not particularly palatable to the majority of rats, such as flaked peas, whole wheat grains and grass pellets. These ingredients, when present in quantity, are often overlooked and this can lead to waste and an imbalance of nutrients. Manufacturers may use these ingredients to fill out a mix and reduce costs, but all waste effectively increases the amount you are paying for the remaining feed. A home-made mix can sometimes be slightly more expensive than a cheap commercial mix, but it can be designed so that there is no waste at all.

COLOURINGS AND FLAVOURINGS - these may be added to make the mix look more attractive to humans, or to make dull ingredients more palatable. Flavourings often add sugar to the mix, which can depress immunity and cause obesity and tooth decay. Many artificial colorants are linked, at higher levels, to physiological and behavioural changes and possible tumours.[1,2,3]

ARTIFICIAL PRESERVATIVES - these are common ingredients in rodent nuggets or mixes containing animal protein. Where manufacturers don't add these to feed themselves, they do not always appear on the list of ingredients, but may still be included as the preservative for any 'bought-in' animal fat. If you are concerned to find a feed that is free from artificial preservatives, look for labelling that states "contains no (or free from) artificial (or EC permitted) preservatives" rather than those that claim only to have "no *added* artificial preservatives." Packaging may also refer to these preservatives as antioxidants. It is possible that some of these preservatives may have unwanted effects on health and these are discussed in Chapter 13.

NUTRITIONAL SUITABILITY - there are a few generic mixes that don't even match the basic requirements of a rat, being well above the recommended 4-5% fat and 10-14% protein levels. Some are also high in fibre, often through including ingredients that rats may reject. Some fibre is essential and of benefit in supporting a healthy gut, but fibre also reduces the absorption of many micronutrients and in excess can contribute to deficiencies.

INACCESSIBLE VITAMINS AND MINERALS - Vitamins A, C, D, E and copper are often supplemented in generic mixes, but in some cases are added to the pellets in the mix. If the rat rejects these, the supplements are wasted, potentially leading to a deficiency, especially where vitamin D is concerned.

UNIFORMITY - some commercial feed manufacturers approach the problem of providing a nutritious, balanced diet for rats, by presenting their food in a pellet form (nugget). This can be extremely monotonous for an animal that is an opportunistic omnivore, designed to thrive on variety, and can lead to reduced intake. Some people also report increase tumour occurrence in rats fed primarily on certain pellets, but this is anecdotal and there is no evidence based information available. More discussion of the importance of variety and pleasure in relation to rat diet can be found on page 16 and chapter in 11.

CEREAL GRAINS

The term cereal is used interchangeably with the word grain to mean grasses that are grown for their edible fruit seeds. Many of these seeds are encased in a dry, inedible husk - also called chaff or hull - but somewhat confusingly, hull will sometimes also be used to refer to the edible bran layer. A whole grain is a grain where the hull (husk) may, or may not be present, but the whole of the edible fruit seed remains intact. "Wholegrain" can also refer to a *processed* grain where none of the seed has been removed during processing.

The edible fruit seed of a cereal plant comprises three parts:
• Bran - outer protective seed coat. It contains the majority of the fibre and a large amount of the vitamin and minerals in a grain.
• Germ - an area of concentrated nutrients near the base of the kernel. It contains large amounts of vitamins and minerals.
• Endosperm - the primary energy source for the growing plant. It mainly consists of carbohydrate and protein.

Phytonutrients are found in both the bran and the germ. These are organic compounds that are found in plants and whilst they don't add to nutrition, are thought to promote health, protect against cell damage and support repair within the body. Further information can be found on page 169.

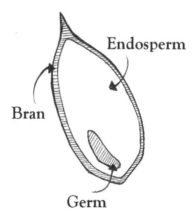

Figure 1: Parts of a cereal fruit seed (hull/husk removed)

The presentation of an unprocessed whole grain often includes the hull (husk), and while this is inedible it can provide enrichment as it must be stripped off before the grain is eaten, which expands the process of eating. This may slow down the intake of food orientated rats and help with weight management. When making up a mix many people choose to use some grains in their hull (husk), some whole grains and some processed grains, as all forms have their own particular benefits.

PROCESSING GRAINS

The processing of grains takes two main forms:
1. Processing of the whole grain - for example, micronized flakes.
2. Processing of the grain after stripping off the bran layer and sometimes the germ - for example, pearl barley or white rice.

Whole grains contain antinutrients which in the raw (unprocessed) state reduce the accessibility of some of the nutrients, particularly minerals. There is more detail on specific antinutrients on page 48 and in chapter 13. When a whole grain is processed it reduces the antinutrients, which in turn increases the amount of micronutrients that a rat can glean from eating the grain. This aspect of processing is an entirely positive thing, however, most processing also involves some form of cooking and this makes the energy in the grain more accessible, which can potentially lead to problems with weight gain. Cooking the grain may also reduce the amount of B group vitamins in the processed product, however these tend to be added back in to human grade cereals.

To put processing in context, if you feed a generic rat or rabbit food it will likely contain minimally processed whole grains in the form of micronized flakes, and some more heavily processed extrusions (cooked biscuits and pellets). Some feeds also contain a few whole grains like wheat, oats and maize. Processing at the level needed to make micronized flakes, even where the entire mix is involved, is perfectly acceptable for a rat's nutrition. Some wholegrain human grade cereals are processed to a similar degree, such as whole rolled oats (not instant porridge oats), pot (not pearl) barley, quinoa, brown rice or flaked wheat (not the breakfast cereal often called wheat flakes), and the same applies to them.

Processing and cooking affect the nutrient content of grains, and the availability of nutrients.[4] Some B group vitamins and vitamin C are reduced by heating by around 10 to 25 percent, but dry grains do not contain vitamin C, so only the B group are a concern in this instance. Protein itself is not reduced in amount by heat, though its structure changes and it can become more, or less, digestible depending on the protein and the cooking process. Starch is gelatinized at high temperatures and generally becomes easier to digest. Legumes and many whole grains contain a proportion (roughly 10%) of resistant starch, that is, starch that cannot be digested by a healthy individual. Resistant starch is also resistant to the effects of cooking, and remains even after moderate processing. It is thought that resistant starch decreases the calorie load of food and increases fat metabolism, both of which can help to maintain a healthy weight. It also increases fermentation in the large intestine (a result of bacterial activity), and can help to maintain colonic health.[5] Minerals are unchanged by heat, but the antinutrients that prevent their absorption are reduced, making the minerals present more available. The improved environment in the colon that is induced by a diet containing good amounts of resistant starch also results in better absorption of minerals from the caecum; the blind pouch at the point where the small intestine joins the colon.[6]

Some whole grains undergo more rigorous processing to make them more palatable to humans, such as puffed wheat, shredded wheat, rice cakes and whole wheat pasta. These processes could be likened to those involved in making the extrusions that feature heavily in most rodent mixes, and to the production of dog biscuits and kibble. The amount of energy needed to digest the more processed parts of a mix is less and the energy within them more accessible. Including a proportion of these cereals can be desirable for a number of reasons (see page 51) but in general terms a healthy mix for the average adult rat should major on the less processed grains.

White grains are those that have had the bran layer and germ stripped away, and as a result are primarily energy and protein. I tend to avoid them for general purposes in feeding rats, but they can become extremely useful in a few specific situations:

- Feeding the sick and elderly.
- Supporting rats with kidney disease.
- Trying to establish weight gain.
- At very low environmental temperatures.
- During periods of heavy activity or stress (for example, before a show).

Even so, they should only be a proportion of the whole diet, due to their lack of vitamins and minerals.

PHOSPHORUS IN GRAINS

Throughout this book the phosphorus content of rat food will crop up as a recurring theme. This is because elderly rats are extremely likely to have a degree of kidney disease, and once the disease process begins a high intake of phosphorus can increase the rate at which the disease progresses. Since the age of onset varies between rats, I prefer to make this a consideration in all adult diet, however it should always be remembered that phosphorus is *essential* to any rat's health and good levels are needed to support growth and reproduction. There is no benefit in feeding a low phosphorus diet to a rat who has perfectly functioning kidneys, but when feeding mixed age groups the phosphorus content of the diet should be a consideration. For this reason many people do pay attention to the phosphorus levels of the ingredients they use. Not all grains have equal phosphorus levels, and some processing will reduce the levels further. Heavily processed grains usually have greatly reduced phosphorus levels, especially where the bran and germ are removed. However, some whole grain cereals are relatively low in phosphorus due to the processing they undergo. Examples would be rice cakes and shredded or puffed wheat.

INDIVIDUAL CEREAL GRAINS

What follows is an expansion of the most common grains used in rat mixes and they are grouped here according to the phosphorus content of the whole grain. This information will help those who are trying to formulate a mix that is 'kidney friendly', which should major on the grains with lower phosphorus levels. This is not meant to suggest that such a mix should not include any of the high phosphorus grains, only that they should probably make up a small part of the whole. Where you are feeding rats who already have kidney disease, it is preferable to avoid the high phosphorus grains entirely.

It should be noted that sources often vary in giving the nutritional content of grains, and this is due to variance between different strains of each grain and also the conditions in which a plant was grown, including the country of origin. As an example, selenium levels in grains grown in the United States are generally much higher than those grown in the UK, due to the low levels of selenium in our soil. For this reason, the nutritional data provided (protein, fat and phosphorus levels) should be taken as a guide only. I have tried to find at least two sources for each grain and have then reported the average values.[7] When you buy human grade whole grains the packaging will list actual values for that particular product.

GRAINS CONTAINING LOWER LEVELS OF PHOSPHORUS

MAIZE
Maize (corn) is commonly used in rat mixes and can be found in many forms. Unprocessed kernels are sold as whole maize, or can be chopped into 'grits' which are often sold mixed with wheat. Micronized flaked maize is heated and squashed, while puffed maize can be oven baked or pressure puffed. Further processing produces ingredients such as corn meal and corn feed. Maize should always be of good quality as it is prone to mould contamination, with micronized flakes and human grade products making contamination unlikely. Rather confusingly, 'corn' is occasionally used as a generic term for grain, or to describe wheat.
Protein 9%, fat 5%, phosphorus 210mg/100g.

BARLEY
Barley is widely used in animal feeds, often in flaked form (hulled, heated and compressed). It can also be fed as a whole grain although the outer hull (husk), which is inedible and removed before eating, is all that is lost in the

hulling process - but micronization (heating and squashing into a flake) may make the grain more palatable. Pot barley and pearl barley may also be fed and although they have lost some nutrients to processing, this makes them highly suited to being fed in kidney protective diets.
Protein 10%, fat 1%, Phosphorus 275mg/100g.

MILLET

The millets are a group of grasses with small round seeds that come in a variety of colours. The coloured shell is a hull (husk) and is usually stripped by the rat. The grain itself is very nutritious, with good levels of protein, B group vitamins and minerals such as iron. Millet still in its hull (husk) can be found in bird feed stores, while hulled millet is now widely available in health food shops. 'Mixed millet' is used to describe a blend of various types of millet seed, and the various coloured varieties often have slightly different nutritional values.
Protein 11%, fat 4%, phosphorus 285mg/100g.

SORGHUM (DARI/MILO)

Sorghum is related to millet and has a similar nutritional quality and make up, but has a larger grain size. It is generally only found in the UK as animal feed, often available from bird feed stores. Millets and sorghum are often thought to be high in fat, but this is not actually true.
Protein 11%, fat 3%, phosphorus 285mg/100g.

RICE

Rice is seldom added to generic mixes despite it being a grain that is helpful in terms of supporting kidney health. Paddy rice refers to the whole and unprocessed rice grain still in its hull (husk), and it can be found in some bird feed stores. Hulled rice is the brown rice available in health food stores and supermarkets. This is a minimal process; the outer (inedible) hull is removed mechanically by a machine that mimics the action of two stones, while the rice bran is retained. Further processing (milling) removes the bran layer and polishes the rice into its white form. Rice can also be oven baked or pressure puffed (at very high temperatures), resulting in crisped rice (e.g. Rice Krispies), or puffed rice (e.g. rice cakes). White rice is used for crisped products, but puffed rice and rice cakes are made from brown rice.

Wild rice is a different strain and is suitable for rats, but is often more expensive.
Protein 8%, fat 2.8%, phosphorus 325mg/100g.

GRAINS CONTAINING HIGHER LEVELS OF PHOSPHORUS

RYE
Rye is a grain that is closely related to wheat and barley. It is rarely seen as a component of rat food, but can sometimes be found as whole grain, cracked grain or flakes in health food stores. It is difficult to separate rye bran from the grain and therefore, most rye products are whole grain and high in phosphorus. Some processed rye based foods, such as Ryvita are somewhat lower in phosphorus than the whole grain (around 300mg/100g for the plain varieties).
Protein 15%, fat 2.5%, phosphorus 375mg/100g.

WHEAT
Wheat is another common component of rat mixes, usually presented as micronized flakes, extruded biscuits or whole grains. Whole grains usually have the outer hull (husk) removed and they are small, hard seeds that some rats reject. Flaked wheat is the whole grain heated and squashed; a process that retains a lot of the nutrients, but makes the grain more readily digestible. Extrusions are highly processed and often made from wheat flour and a range of other ingredients. They are usually artificially coloured in order to appeal to human preferences for foods that are visually pleasant and interesting. Wheatfeed is a high fibre pellet (around 40% fibre), comprised primarily of wheat bran and endosperm. It represents fairly inaccessible nutrition to a rat, and if eaten will reduce the amount of minerals absorbed from the rest of the feed. Many whole grain wheat cereals suitable for human consumption can readily be fed to rats, and some white wheat products, where the bran has been removed (such as couscous and white pasta), are useful for elderly and sick rats.
Protein 11%, fat 2%, phosphorus 400mg/100g.

SPELT
Spelt is an ancient species of wheat that is now marketed in its own right. It

is a high protein grain (up to 17%) and is a little higher in phosphorus than wheat, but is a good source of copper. Spelt is sold primarily for human consumption in the UK and can be found as whole grain or flakes in some supermarkets and health food shops.
Protein 14-17%, fat 3%, phosphorus 400mg/100g.

KAMUT (KHORASAN WHEAT)
Kamut is a registered trade name for a particular strain of wheat. It has higher protein content (around 15%) than wheat and also contains higher levels of many minerals including selenium (Kamut is a product of the USA).
Protein 15-16%, fat 2%, phosphorus 400mg/100g

OATS
Oats are one of the few cereals often presented in commercial mixes within their hull (husk), which is inedible and will be rejected, but many rats enjoy the oat grain itself. Oats can also be found as groats - the grain with the hull removed, and as rolled oats - either in or out of the hull, and with or without the bran. Horse grade rolled oats are rolled inside the hull, while rolled oats for human consumption often have both the hull and the bran layer removed. Oatfeed is a high fibre pellet made from the hulls (Yes, the chaff that rats strip off whole oats and discard!) of oats. It has very little food value to a rat, and conversely is likely to reduce the absorption of minerals from the rest of the feed, if it is eaten at all. Porridge oats, especially the instant types are stripped of their bran layer prior to rolling, but health food stores often sell rolled oats that are wholegrain. Oats with the bran intact are very high in phosphorus, but instant porridge oats are significantly lower. Pinhead oatmeal is chopped oat grains and contains much of the oat bran, therefore it remains high in phosphorus.
Protein 17%, fat 7%, phosphorus 525mg/100g.

PSEUDO CEREALS

QUINOA
Quinoa is often considered a grain but in fact is more closely related to the beet family. In its natural state it has a bitter and unpalatable coating which

must be removed before eating. This can be removed by repeated rinsing or by soaking and rinsing, but the quinoa sold for human consumption in the UK is generally pre-rinsed. The prepared grains can then boiled in a similar way to rice, but can also be fed raw to rats. It has a good protein content (which varies up to 18%) and like soya, contains all of the essential amino acids, but to varying degrees. Quinoa offers high levels of iron and calcium, and has similar levels of phosphorus as millet, which contains 285mg/100g. It is an excellent grain for feeding to support growth and reproduction (see Chapter 6).
Protein 14-18%, fat 6% phosphorus 305mg/100g.

BUCKWHEAT
Buckwheat is actually a fruit seed (from the same family as rhubarb), not a grass seed and is therefore not a true grain. It is easy to source completely unprocessed, in the hull (husk), as it is frequently sold as bird seed. Hulled buckwheat is sold for human consumption. It contains good amounts of phosphorus, selenium, iron, copper and zinc.
Protein 11%, fat 2.5% phosphorus 325g/100g.

GENERAL POINTS ABOUT CEREALS

GROATS
Groats is a word used to describe the whole grain after any inedible hull (husk) has been removed. It actually describes the de-hulled form of any grain, but is primarily used in referring to oats and wheat.

NUTRITIONAL CONTENT
Grains vary in the amount of micronutrients they contain, but there are certain trends. All grains are primarily carbohydrate, and their low fat and moderate protein values make them the perfect base of any rat mix. A good mix should contain a number of different grains as this gives the maximum spread of amino acids and micronutrients. Grains are generally high in B group vitamins (except for B_{12}) and vitamin E, and most of the rat's requirements for these vitamins would be adequately met from a variety of whole grains. The same is true of manganese, zinc, potassium, phosphorus,

magnesium and iron. Selenium levels vary in grains depending on the soil levels of the area where the grain was grown, and a rat's requirement for selenium may be higher than is generally listed, so grains should not be relied upon as the only dietary source. Likewise, levels of copper and calcium in grains are only able to supply about a half and a fifteenth of the daily requirement of these minerals respectively.

Vitamin and mineral content is decreased greatly by any processing that removes the bran coating from around the seed. This is one reason why whole grains and minimally processed whole grains (like micronized flakes) need to make up a large part of the cereal fed to rats. The carbohydrate content of 'white' grains (those where the bran has been removed) is roughly the same, but is digested and absorbed (as glucose) more readily by the rat, than with whole grain. If highly processed carbohydrate is fed in excess it can lead to weight gain, not only because of the accessibility of the starch, but also because the rat will use less energy in processing the food. These same qualities make white carbohydrates perfect for elderly and sick rats. Heavily processed carbohydrates are generally lacking in vital nutrients that are present in the whole grain, such as vitamins and minerals, and care should be taken to ensure that these are supplied in other ways when using mainly processed grains. Some human grade cereals that are suitable for rats have added B vitamins and iron, which can be useful in helping to boost the nutritional content of a mix, or the diet overall.

PHYTIC ACID (PHYTATE) AND PHOSPHORUS

It will be noted on many occasions within this book that older rats will benefit from a low phosphorus diet and this is further explained in Chapters 7 and 8. However, phosphorus is an essential mineral that is found in every living cell, both in the nucleus and in the cell membrane, and is also used in energy production and growth. Without enough phosphorus an animal becomes very ill. It is only once the kidneys begin to degenerate that dietary phosphorus becomes a problem and accelerates decline. However, as the kidneys need to lose 70-75% of normal function before signs of illness show, it is wise to consider phosphorus intake for all adult rats who are over 18 months or so, and where mixed age groups include older animals.

In many grains phosphorus is held in the form of phytate which renders it less accessible because non-ruminant animals lack significant amounts of the enzymes needed to separate the phosphorus from the phytate. It is held within the insoluble fibre of the bran layer of the grain. Low phytic acid mutations of many cereal plants have now been developed, specifically to increase the availability of phosphorus and other minerals, but these are not yet widely available. Phytates also bind with minerals like magnesium, calcium, iron, copper and zinc in the gut, to reduce their absorption. There is research to suggest that the effect of phytates in rats fed primarily a whole grain, unprocessed diet is significant in reducing mineral absorption and decreasing growth.[8] Cooking, soaking (especially in water with some lemon juice or vinegar added) and sprouting, all help to neutralise phytates and break down the fibre, allowing some phosphorus (and other minerals) to be absorbed.

Rats have a variety of means of accessing some phosphorus (and other minerals) during the digestive process, even from high phytate strains of grain and these are discussed further on page 295. Therefore it is best to assume the bio-availability of the phosphorus in grain, and feed a majority of the low phosphorus and refined grains to those rats who are over about 18 months and more likely to have kidney wear and tear.

It should be noted that phytates also have a positive role in that they are antioxidants, may protect against some cancers and aid bone health with aging. More information is included in Chapter 13.

SPROUTING
As cereals are seeds they are all very easy to sprout, and sprouting generally occurs quickly; within about 3-4 days. Sprouting neutralizes phytic acid (see above) and also activates enzymes (phytase) within the grain, which makes the nutritional components of the grain more accessible to the rat during digestion. Grains that have been heated significantly during processing will not sprout, as the enzymes will have been destroyed by the heat. Details of

how to sprout grains and other seeds can be found on pages 184 to 187.

BUYING GRAINS ONLINE

http://www.ratrations.com - UK rat food site, selling a wide range of grains and grain mixes, in a range of quantities.

http://www.buywholefoodsonline.co.uk - UK human whole food shop (primarily organic), selling a range of grains, in a variety of quantities.

http://www.millbryhill.co.uk - UK animal feed store, selling large sacks of straight grains under *Small holder*, plus rolled oats in the *Equestrian* section.

http://www.ethicalsuperstore.com - UK organic and fair-trade superstore, which has a good range of grains and sells in bulk.

http://www.goodnessdirect.co.uk - UK health food shop, selling whole grains, with a wide selection of groats and minimally processed rolled grains.

http://www.grains2mill.co.uk - UK source of some lovely naked whole grains and grain mixes, ideal for sprouting. Also sell buckets of human grade, GM free whole maize (corn).

Review : ratRations online rat store.

"I have been shopping regularly at ratRations.com (previously Junglegold) for some time now, and have had nothing but excellent service. It is a small, rural, family run business and I have found them to be very willing to cater for my own particular nuances. If you need help with an order I would suggest phoning them, as you will find them extremely helpful and accommodating. They stock a massive range of food items, plus many other rat related products, and I am pleased to be able to buy my entire mix from the one online source and my local supermarket. As well as oodles of separate ingredients for mix-making, they also sell a range of pre-mixed feeds for use in a variety of circumstances. All of the products are good quality, with many of the food items being human grade from health food shop suppliers. There is also a good range of supplements to complement your homemade mix. Carriage is always an issue when ordering heavy feeds online, and understanding their pricing structure might help you when placing an order. Up to 10kg will cost between £4.75 and £6.95 depending on the size of the parcel, but then anything from 10-40kg is £8. Over 40kg it's an extra £4 per 20kg. This means that it pays to buy towards the maximum weight for each price break, so that postage per kg is reduced. Buying 39kg works out at only 21p per kg carriage. Buying 2kg would work out at £2.38 per kg! For

this reason it makes sense to try to order in groups with other local ratters, or people you have contact with via rat clubs, gatherings or the like." (AC)

HUMAN GRADE CEREALS

Many people add some human grade cereals to their mix, and indeed it is quite possible to create a good base mix entirely from human cereals. In this context 'cereals' does not just mean breakfast cereals, but can include all flaked and whole grains sold for human consumption, for example, flaked barley, de-hulled buckwheat, quinoa, pasta, rice, noodles, rice cakes, popping corn, bread and any other cereal food produced for human use.

Cereals have to be processed to a degree to be consumed by humans, and this processing improves the accessibility of nutrients for rats too. When mixed with unprocessed grains, this is generally a useful thing as a little processing has many benefits. Often the most nutritious cereals are somewhat processed whole grains, for example flaked grains, as the processing reduces antinutrients and makes micro-nutrients more readily available.

REASONS FOR ADDING HUMAN CEREALS TO A MIX:
• Variety of taste and texture.
• Adding accessible vitamins and minerals.
• Ease of purchase (supermarket/health food shop).
• Easier on the kidneys of aging rats to have some processed cereal.
• Helps to maintain weight during sickness, cold weather, where rats are not food orientated and in old age.
• Rarely contain added artificial colours and preservatives.
• Any form of processing tends to reduce levels of antinutrients.

When choosing human grade cereals, try to choose a good mix of grains and consider the degree of processing and the amount of sugar. To make this easier I am including this excellent list of breakfast cereals, categorised by sugar content, which was compiled by Alison Blyth and is reproduced with her kind permission. All nutrients are listed per 100g unless otherwise stated.

This list is by no means exhaustive and as products may change from time to time, it is sensible to get used to checking nutritional values for yourself. Packaging in the UK will give values per 100g, so calculating percentages isn't required, and grams per 100g equates to the percentage of a nutrient. For example, a cereal that has 9g of sugar per 100g is 9% sugar.

CEREALS LIST - GROUP 1
Cereals which are fine for regular use (either <5% sugar, or 5-10% sugar, but entirely from fruit)

WHEAT
Sainsburys Mini Wheats (0.7% sugars)
Protein: 11.8g; Carbs: 69.9g; of which sugars: 0.7g; Fat: 2.3g; of which saturates: 0.5g; Fibre 11.8g; Sodium: <0.1g.
Shredded Wheat (0.9% sugars)
Protein: 11.6g; Carbs: 67.8g; of which sugars: 0.9g; Fat: 2.5g; of which saturates: 0.5g; Fibre 11.8g; Sodium: trace.
Shredded Wheat Bitesize (1% sugars)
Protein: 11.8g; Carbs: 69.9g; of which sugars: 1g; Fat: 2.6g; of which saturates: 0.5g; Fibre 11.9g; Sodium: trace.
Quaker Puffed Wheat (2% sugars)
Protein 11.5g; Carbs 74g; of which sugars: 2g; Fat 2.5g; of which saturates 0.5g; Fibre 8g; Sodium 0.02g.
Tesco Value Wheat Biscuits (2.5% sugars)
Protein: 13.7g; Carbs: 69.5g; of which sugars: 2.5g; Fat: 2.5g; of which saturates: 0.4g; Fibre 7.5g; Sodium: 0.27g.
Weetabix (standard) (4.4% sugars)
Protein: 11.5g; Carbs: 68.4g; of which sugars: 4.4g; Fat: 2g; of which saturates: 0.6g; Fibre 10g; Sodium: 0.3g.
Tesco Healthy Living Wheat Biscuits (4.4% sugars)
As for standard Weetabix.
Weetabix Gold (4.4% sugars)
As for standard Weetabix.

Waitrose Wholewheat Biscuits (4.4% sugars)
As for standard Weetabix.
Weetabix Organic (4.9% sugars)
Protein: 10.9g; Carbs: 66.8g; of which sugars: 4.9g; Fat: 2.2g; of which saturates: 0.3g; Fibre 11g; Sodium: 0.34g.

CORN

Plain corn-cakes (0.8% sugars)
Protein: 13.1g; Carbs: 79g; of which sugars: 0.8g; Fat: 3.7g; of which saturates: 0g; Fibre 14.2g; Sodium: 0.01g.
Tesco Value Cornflakes (2.7% sugars)
Protein: 7.6g; Carbs: 85.1g; of which sugars: 2.7g; Fat: 0.7g; of which saturates: 0.1g; Fibre 3.3g; Sodium: 0.2g.
Tesco Organic Cornflakes (4% sugars)
Protein: 8g; Carbs: 80g; of which sugars: 4g; Fat: 0.8g; of which saturates: 0.2g; Fibre 5g; Sodium: 0.7g.
Whole Earth Organic Cornflakes (4% sugars)
As for Tesco Organic Cornflakes
Dove Farm Organic Cornflakes (4% sugars, from rice syrup)
Protein: 10.3g; Carbs: 81.7g; of which sugars: 4g; Fat: 1g; of which saturates: 0.2g; Fibre 0.3g; Sodium: 0.3g.

RICE

Kallo Puffed Brown Rice (values should be similar for any plain puffed rice) (1.1% sugars)
Protein: 8g; Carbs: 80g; of which sugars: 1.1g; Fat: 3g; of which saturates: 1g; Fibre 9g; Sodium: 0.2g.
Kallo No Added Salt Rice Cakes (2.2% sugars)
Protein: 8g; Carbs: 78.7g; of which sugars: 2.2g; Fat: 2.8g; of which saturates: 0.6g; Fibre 5.1g; Sodium: 0.01g.

OATS

Porridge Oats (these are Jordans, but values should be similar for any plain oats) (1.1% sugars)
Protein: 11g; Carbs: 60g; of which sugars: 1.1g; Fat: 8g; of which saturates:

1.5g; Fibre 9g; Sodium: trace.
Weetabix Oatibix (normal size NOT bitesize) (3.2% sugars)
Protein: 12.5g; Carbs: 63.7g; of which sugars: 3.2g; Fat: 8g; of which
saturates: 1.3g; Fibre 7.3g; Sodium, 0.15g.

OTHER
Flaked Barley, from Holland & Barrett (0.1% sugars)
Protein: 7.9g; Carbs: 83.6g; of which sugars: 0.1g; Fat: 1.7g; of which
saturates: trace; Fibre 6.5g; Sodium: 0.03g.
Flaked Rye, from Holland & Barrett (trace sugars)
Protein: 8.2g; Carbs: 75.9g; of which sugars: trace; Fat: 2g; of which
saturates: trace; Fibre 11.7g; Sodium: 0.01g.
Flaked Spelt, from Holland & Barrett (0.2% sugars)
Protein: 11g; Carbs: 73.3g; of which sugars: 0.2g; Fat: 3g; of which
saturates: 0.24g; Fibre 9g; Sodium: trace.
Jordans Multigrain Porridge (oats, wheat, barley and rice) (1% sugars)
Protein: 10.4g; Carbs: 60.9g; of which sugars: 1g; Fat: 5.5g; of which
saturates: 1g; Fibre 10g; Sodium: trace.
Food Doctor Porridge Mix (oats, barley, spelt, buckwheat & rye) (1.2% sugars)
Protein: 10.2g; Carbs: 65.8g; of which sugars: 1.2g; Fat: 6.5g; of which
saturates: 1.3g; Fibre 8.2g; Sodium: 0.02g.
Weight Watchers' Flakes with Apple (8.1% sugars, from fruit)
Protein: 10.4g; Carbs: 67.4g; of which sugars: 8.1g; Fat: 1.6g; of which
saturates: 0.4g; Fibre 14.4g; Sodium: 0.5g.

GROUP 2
Cereals which are ok in small amounts, or as an occasional treat (<20%
sugar from fruit, or low sugar, but higher fat from seeds/nuts)
Food Doctor Cereal Mix (1.5% sugars. 27.2% fat from seeds and nuts)
Protein: 16.6g; Carbs: 44.2g; of which sugars: 1.5g; Fat: 27.2g; of which
saturates: 4.3g; Fibre 7.7g; Sodium: 0.01g.
Mornflake Oatbran cereal (2.1% sugars, but 15.2% fibre)
Protein: 14.8g; Carbs: 49.7g; of which sugars: 2.1g; Fat: 9.7g; of which
saturates: 1.6g; Fibre 15.2g; Sodium: 0.05g.
Toasted Bran, from Holland & Barrett (7.9% sugars, from the bran, fibre

and protein are also quite high)
Protein: 16.6g; Carbs: 42.1g; of which sugars: 7.9g; Fat: 4.5g; of which
saturates: 0.9g; Fibre 22.8g; Sodium: 0.2g.

Food Doctor Muesli Base (11.6% sugars, from fruit. 14.2% fat from seeds)
Protein: 12.1g; Carbs: 55.5g; of which sugars: 11.6g; Fat: 14.2g; of which
saturates: 2.4g; Fibre 7.1g; Sodium: 0.01g.

Dorset Simply Delicious Muesli (12% sugars from fruit)
Protein: 10.8g; Carbs: 59.2g; of which sugars: 12g; Fat: 9.5g; of which
saturates: 1.7g; Fibre 7.4g; Sodium: <0.1g.

Pertwood Muesli Fruit and Seeds (14.2% sugars from fruit)
Protein: 11.4g; Carbs: 55.5g; of which sugars: 14.2g; Fat: 6.7g; of which
saturates: 1.1g; Fibre ?g; Sodium: trace.

Jordans Natural Muesli (15.3% sugars, from fruit)
Protein: 8.9g; Carbs: 60.7g; of which sugars: 15.3g; Fat: 4.7g; of which
saturates: 0.8g; Fibre 10.4g; Sodium: trace.

Alpen No Added Sugar (15.9% sugars from fruit)
Protein: 10.7g; Carbs: 64.3g; of which sugars: 15.9g; Fat: 5.9g; of which
saturates: 0.7g; Fibre 7.7g; Sodium: 0.17g.

Kelloggs Raisin Wheats (16% sugars from fruit)
Protein: 9g; Carbs: 69g; of which sugars: 16g; Fat: 2g; of which saturates:
0.4g; Fibre 9g; Sodium: trace.

Dorset Organic Fruit, Seeds and Nuts (18.9% sugars from fruit)
Protein: 10.8g; Carbs: 56.6g; of which sugars: 18.9g; Fat: 9.8g; of which
saturates: 3g; Fibre 8.4g; Sodium: <0.1g.

Jordans Porridge raisin and apple (18.6% sugars from fruit)
Protein: 9.1g; Carbs: 58.8g; of which sugars: g; Fat: 4.7g; of which saturates:
0.8g; Fibre 10.4g; Sodium: trace.

Jordans Muesli Organic (19.3% sugars)
Protein: 9.1g; Carbs: 58.5g; of which sugars: 19.3g; Fat: 8.6g; of which
saturates: 2.7g; Fibre 9.4g; Sodium: trace.

GROUP 3

Cereals which I wouldn't give rats at all (sugar levels are from added sugar,
and are over 5%, or are sugar from fruit and over 20%). Anything involving
the words frosted, chocolate, honey, maple syrup, caramel, or golden.

WHEAT

Weetaflakes (12.4% sugars)
Shreddies (15.5% sugars)
Honey Nut Shredded Wheat (17.5% sugars)
Cranberry Wheats (18.9% sugars)
Apricot Wheats (19% sugars)
Sainsburys Raisin Wheats (22.2% sugars)
Shredded Wheat Fruitful (25.1% sugars)
Weetabix Wheetos (23.5% sugars)

CORN

Kelloggs Cornflakes (8% sugars)
Tesco Cornflakes (8.9% sugars)
Sainsburys Cornflakes (8.9% sugars)
Kelloggs Crunchy Nut with berries (28% sugars)
Crunchy Nut Nutty (33% sugars)

RICE

Kelloggs Rice Krispies (10% sugars)
Sainsburys Rice Pops (9.7% sugars)

OATS

Quaker Oat Crisp (13% sugars)
Oatibix bitesize (14.2% sugars)
Oatibix bitesize with sultana and apple (19.3% sugars)
Jordans Porridge apricot and sultana (23.2% sugars)
Quaker Oat Granola (26% sugars)

BRAN FLAKES

Sainsbury's Bran (low sugar but 36% fibre)
Alpen Crunchy Bran (14.6% sugars)
Tesco Bran (16.2% sugars)
Sainsbury's Hi-fibre Bran (16.2% sugars)
Kelloggs All-Bran (17% sugars)
Tesco Value Branflakes (17.1% sugars)
Tesco Healthy Living Branflakes (17.1% sugars)

Sainsbury's Organic Branflakes (17.1% sugars)
Sainsbury's Branflakes (17.2% sugars)
Kelloggs Bran Flakes and All-Bran Bran Flakes (22% sugars)
Sainsbury's Sultana Bran (32.2% sugars)
Kelloggs Sultana Bran (33% sugars)
Tesco Healthy Living Sultana Bran (30.8% sugars)

OTHER/MULTIGRAIN
Sainsbury's Wheat Flakes with Oatbran (16.6% sugars)
Sainsbury's Oat and Bran Flakes (13.5% sugars)
Tesco Special Flakes (11.6% sugars)
Sainsbury's Healthy Balance Rice and Wheat (15.7% sugars)
Tesco Healthy Living Wheat Flakes with Oatbran (16.6% sugars)
Special K, normal (17% sugars)
Fitnesse (16.8% sugars)
Grapenuts (8.8% sugars)
Jordan's 3 in 1 Strawberry (19.6% sugars)
Sainsbury's Balance with Red Fruits (19.9% sugars)
Kelloggs Optivita varieties (20% sugars)
Sainsbury's Crunch Organic (20.1% sugars)
Jordans Superfoods Muesli (20.3% sugars)
Kelloggs Just Right (21% sugars)
Sainsbury's Hooplas (21.5% sugars)
Cheerios (21.6% sugars)
Alpen standard and original (21.8% sugars)
Special K Bliss (23% sugars)
Nestle Clusters (23.3% sugars)
Special K with berries (24% sugars)
All Jordan's Country Crisp varieties (24-35% sugars)
Crunchy Nut Clusters (25% sugars)
Kelloggs Fruit and Fibre (25% sugars)
Sainsbury's Fruit and Fibre (26.4% sugars)
Jordans Special Muesli (26.6% sugars)
Dorset Super High Fibre (27.5% sugars)
Sainsbury's Fruit and Nut Muesli (28.9% sugars)

Tesco Value Fruit and Fibre (30% sugars)
Dorest Cranberry, Cherry and Almond (31.4% sugars)
Cinnamon Grahams (34.2% sugars)
Kelloggs Crunchy Nut (35% sugars)
Honey Nut Cheerios (35.4% sugars)
Jordans Special Fruit Muesli (36.1% sugars)
Dorset Berries and Cherries (41% sugars)

REFERENCES

[1]Bollettino chimico farmaceutico 1997 Nov;136(10):615-27.
Physiological effects of some synthetic food colouring additives on rats.
Aboel-Zahab H, el-Khyat Z, Sidhom G, Awadallah R, Abdel-al W, Mahdy K.
[2]Reproductive Toxicology, Volume 26, Issue 2, October 2008, Pages 156-163
Effects of tartrazine on exploratory behavior in a three-generation toxicity study in mice
Toyohito Tanaka, Osamu Takahashi, Shinshi Oishi and Akio Ogata
[3]Handbook of Food Technology, 2002 edition, SS Deshpande
[4]Beyond vegetarianism - Looking at the Science on Raw vs. Cooked Foods
Jean-Louis Tu http://www.beyondveg.com
[5]Carcinogenesis 2007 28(2):240-245
Effect of dietary resistant starch and protein on colonic fermentation and intestinal tumourigenesis in rats
R. K. Le Leu, I. L. Brown1, Ying Hu, T. Morita, A. Esterman and G. P. Young
[6]Journal of Nutrition. 2001;131:1283-1289
Class 2 Resistant Starches Lower Plasma and Liver Lipids and Improve Mineral Retention in Rats
H. W. Lopez et al
[7]http://www.gograins.com.au/grainsnutrition/ie/ie4_2.html
[8]Nutrition Research, Volume 18, Issue 6, June 1998, Pages 1029-1037
Dietary phytate reduces magnesium bioavailability in growing rats
Josef Pallauf, Manfred Pietsch and Gerald Rimbach
Used throughout Chapter 2
World Review of Nutrition and Dietetics. 1999, vol 84, pp 19–73
Cereal Grains: Humanity's Double-Edged Sword
Loren Cordain

"When having a smackerel
of something with a friend,
don't eat so much that you
get stuck in the doorway
trying to get out."

Winnie the Pooh (AA Milne)

CHAPTER THREE - OVERVIEW

Pulses - edible legumes
 Discussion on individual legumes
 Antinutrients in beans
 Percentage nutrients in soaked legumes
 Buying legumes online
Meat and meat substitutes
 Labelling
 Ethical considerations
 Dog kibble - information and reviews
 Buying quality dog kibble online
 Alternative dry animal protein sources
 Buying dry animal protein sources online
 Vegetarian alternatives to dry animal protein
 Alternative wet animal protein sources
 Ethical considerations
 Buying wet animal protein online
Seeds and nuts
 Discussion of individual seeds
 Discussion of individual nuts
 Buying seeds and nuts online
Vegetables
 Discussion of individual dried vegetables
 Home drying vegetables
 Buying dried vegetables online
Fruit
 Discussion of individual dried fruits
 Buying dried fruit online
Herbs
 Buying dried herbs online

Chapter two
Understanding ingredients: Part two - legumes, meat, seeds, nuts, vegetables, fruit and herbs

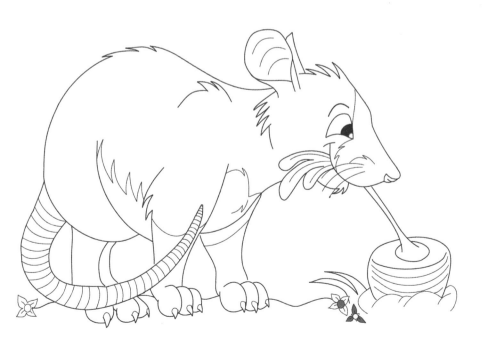

Pulses (edible legumes)

All percentage values of nutrients given are for the dry legume, and once soaked the percentage value drops significantly because of the water that is absorbed. The values for soaked and boiled legumes are listed towards the end of this section. For reference, levels of nutrients in micronized and soaked, then roasted legumes, are closer to the levels in the dry state.

Soya

Soya beans are high protein oilseeds and as such can be dried and then revived by soaking, (so dried beans can still be sprouted). Dry soya beans are approximately 40% protein, 20% fat, 35% carbohydrate and 5% ash (minerals). The protein in soya contains all of the essential amino acids, though limited amounts of methionine and cysteine, and is readily digested and absorbed. However, the soya bean contains fairly high levels of both phosphorus and phytates.

Soya is thought to have a number of health benefits and also some health issues, which are discussed further in Chapter 6. Soya can be purchased as a whole bean (which needs to be soaked and cooked or sprouted), micronized flakes (animal feed) or roasted soya nuts. The whole bean is also available as a frozen food that is prepared by boiling. Processed forms of soya include textured vegetable protein, which is made from soya flour that has been processed and dried into spongy pieces, milk, yoghurt, tofu and miso. Micronized soya flakes are used most frequently by feed manufacturers and individuals making up their own mixes. They are around 35% protein and 19% oil.

Ingredients lists of generic mixes may also include soya bean oil (solvent extracted oil that may be partially hydrogenated) and soya bean meal (made from toasting the rest of the bean matter once the oil has been extracted).

Peas

Peas are spherical legumes that come in a number of varieties and are a common component of rat and rabbit mixes. They are generally presented as micronized flakes, but can be purchased whole or split into two halves in their dry form for human consumption. They contain about 15% protein and only 1% fat, plus a range of B vitamins, vitamin C, iron, magnesium, zinc and phosphorus in good amounts. Peas can also be sprouted or fed raw; spilt legumes will not sprout.

CHICK PEAS

Chick peas come in two main varieties; a smaller dark green type and the commonly available large, pale variety. They are presented as the whole dried pea, which can be soaked and then roasted, sprouted or boiled. Raw dried chick peas should not be fed as they contain an enzyme inhibitor that reduces the digestion of protein in the intestine. Chick peas contain 23% protein, 5% fat, 64% carbohydrate and a variety of minerals and vitamins including copper.

LENTILS

There are many varieties of lentils, with the most readily available being red and green lentils. They can be bought whole or split and may be fed dry or cooked as they are not considered to contain high levels of anti-nutrients in their raw state. Lentils do not need to be soaked before cooking. I have found that whole green lentils are more readily eaten raw while all common varieties are well received when cooked. Lentils can be sprouted but you need to source whole lentils, as split pulses will not sprout. They contain 26% protein, 1% fat and 60% carbohydrate, plus excellent quantities of iron.

OTHER LEGUMES

There are many other varieties of beans which can be fed to rats once cooked, such as butter, haricot and black eye beans, and other varieties like French beans can be fed raw. Two varieties deserve a special mention in terms of their ability to grow into a very palatable bean sprout; the mung and azuki (adzuki) bean. These small beans sprout rapidly and are widely available as bean sprouts for human consumption, however the raw sprouts are high is phosphorus and potassium and so are probably best avoided for older rats.

ANTINUTRIENTS IN BEANS

It is generally well understood that some beans should not be eaten raw as they contain substances called antinutrients that have a negative effect when ingested. These effects can range from reduced absorption of other nutrients, to severe illness and death.

Like grains, many legumes contain phytic acid (see Chapters 2 and 13), but they also contain other anti-nutrients, most notably protease inhibitors and haemagglutinins.[1] Protease inhibitors are proteins that inhibit the action of the enzyme protease, the function of which is to allow protein to be digested in the gut. Haemagglutinins cause both red and white blood cells to clump together and are present in large amounts in kidney beans, but in lesser amounts in broad and lima beans. In a 1992 study, rats who were fed red kidney beans raw as 1% of their overall diet, died within 2 weeks[2]. Red kidney beans have the highest levels of anti-nutrients and must be soaked, boiled rapidly and then cooked to render them harmless.

While all legumes contain some anti-nutrients, these can be at low levels, which make some pulses (like peas and lentils) safe when eaten raw. To put this into perspective most nuts, grains and vegetables also contain some anti-nutrients, but many are eaten raw. Anti-nutrients are discussed further in Chapter 13.

As a general rule, most beans should be soaked and cooked before feeding, to make the nutrients more accessible. Canned beans are a convenient alternative, as they do not have to be soaked or cooked (but should be rinsed before feeding), however, they may have slightly lower levels of most nutrients. Chick peas, whole lentils, whole peas and the small beans (mung and adzuki) are safe simply soaked and sprouted and nutrients are highest in this form.

NUTRIENTS IN SOAKED AND COOKED LEGUMES

Canned varieties will be slightly lower.
Mung beans – protein 7%, fat 0.4%
Lentils – protein 6.8%, fat 0.4%

Soya - protein 13.5%, fat 7.7%
Split peas - protein 6.6%, fat 0.4%
Chick peas - protein 7.7%, fat 2.6%
Haricot beans - protein 8.2%, fat 0.7%
Red kidney bean - protein 7.9%, fat 0.5%

BUYING LEGUMES ONLINE

http://www.ratrations.com - UK rat specific feed store, with a range of pulses and legumes.
http://www.haiths.com - UK bird food site, look under *Cage and Aviary Birds* for a small selection of legumes.
http://www.millbryhill.co.uk - UK animal feed store, selling large sacks of peas and micronized soya under *Small Holder.*
http://merlinsmenu.co.uk - UK supplier of small volumes of soya flakes.
http://www.ethicalsuperstore.com - UK human organic and fair trade superstore, which has a wide range of legumes.

MEAT AND MEAT SUBSTITUTES

Meat and meat derivatives are found in various forms in most nuggets and mixes sold specifically for rats, and in the dog kibble (complete dog food) which is often added to rabbit mixes or straight grains to provide some animal protein. If you are concerned about the quality of the meat used by manufacturers, you will need to look carefully at the labelling to try to determine what a product actually contains.

LABEL READS: MEAT
In high quality meat based extrusions the meat will be identified according to which animal it came from and is clean flesh derived from slaughtered mammals. It can include muscle, tongue, diaphragm, oesophagus and heart, with associated fat and overlying skin, as well as blood vessels, nerves and sinew where they are a natural part of the flesh. Ideally the ingredients list would identify the source, for example, "lamb", but where the generic term "meat" is used it can be from any mammalian animal source. Under UK and EU legislation only species designated for human consumption

may be used in pet food, but this is not the case in many other countries.

LABEL READS: POULTRY

This is the highest quality presentation of edible bird species, and is clean flesh and skin that may also contain any of the parts, or the whole of the carcass, with the exception of feathers, feet, heads and intestines. Ideally the list of ingredients would identify the source, e.g. "chicken", but where the generic term "poultry" is used it can be from any species of bird bred for human food consumption.

LABEL READS: MEAT MEAL

Meal is rendered (chopped, cooked and then dried) mammal tissue and can vary considerably in quality. It does not include blood, hair, hoof, horn, hide trimmings, manure, stomach and rumen contents beyond small amounts that might be unavoidably included during normal processing. It may be the product of only one animal and will then be called, for example, "beef meal". Meat meal with high levels of ash will have high bone content, and is sometimes referred to as "meat bone meal". The proteins in meat bone meal are low quality and difficult to digest.

LABEL READS: POULTRY MEAL

Poultry meal is rendered clean flesh and skin that may also contain any of the parts or the whole carcass, with the exception of feathers, feet, heads and intestines. It may be the product of one species and will then be called (for example) "chicken meal".

LABEL READS: FISH MEAL

Fish meal is rendered clean fish (un-decomposed) either whole fish or fish cuttings (or a combination), with or without the extraction of part of the oil. If one species of fish only is used, it will be called (for example) "salmon meal".

LABEL READS: BONE MEAL

Bone meal is made from rendered bones and has a high mineral content; in this form the minerals have good bioavailability, meaning that they are easily absorbed by the body.[3]

LABEL READS: MEAT DERIVATIVES (BY-PRODUCTS)

These are poor quality, highly variable, animal derived rendered products. I was amazed to find out that in some countries they include *any* warm blooded land animal, and sources suggest that some rendering plants will accept dead zoo animals and even euthanized animals from large rescues. In the UK and EU, derivatives have to be from species that would also be eaten by humans, so this is not an issue that will occur in British products. Derivatives contain very little, or even no flesh, but may be comprised of any part of the carcass once the flesh is removed, although they must be substantially free of hooves, horn, bristle, hair and feathers, as well as digestive tract contents (the intestines are emptied prior to inclusion). Fish derivatives are of a similar low quality.

LABEL READS: DIGEST

Digest is a liquid that results from the 'digestion' of clean, undecomposed animal tissue, comprising both protein and fat. Enzymes are added to the animal tissue which break it down into a digestive soup of amino acids and fatty acids, preservatives are added and then the liquid is sprayed over the surface of complete dog/cat feeds. It is primarily used as a flavouring to increase palatability, and almost all kibble will be coated in digest.

ETHICAL CONSIDERATIONS FOR MEAT PRODUCTS

Many people will be concerned about the welfare of all animals that serve to produce food for themselves and their pets. Ethically sourced meat in pet food is somewhat harder to find than in human food, but foods that include organic meat are likely to have high welfare standards. The easiest way to achieve a mix that contains ethically sourced meat protein is to use a rabbit food or straight grain base and add your own high quality kibble such as *Burns Organic* or *Organipets Adult Organic*. Another possibility is to feed a mix that does not include meat, and include fresh animal products in the diet. Some people will prefer to have entirely vegetarian rats and this option is discussed further in Chapter 7.

DOG KIBBLE - REVIEWS

BURNS ADULT AND SENIOR - brown rice and chicken (other flavours suitable). A small to medium bite-sized expanded pellet. Suitable for adding in small quantities to a grain mix.
Ingredients: brown rice, chicken, oats, peas, chicken oil, sunflower oil, seaweed, vitamins A, D_3, E and minerals (including copper).
Analysis: protein 18.5%, oil 7.5%, fibre 2.2%, copper 15 mg/kg

Reviews: *"Good quality dog kibble with a smallish bite size, ideal for rats. It is well received and seems palatable. Burns try to maintain high standards in terms of animal welfare and they are approved by the British Union for the Abolition of Vivisection as there is no animal experimentation involved in the testing of their products."* (Alison C)

"Was one of the better kibble's I have used in my Shunamite diet mix. It was quite natural and the rats seemed to love it." (Rhi01)

BURNS ORGANIC
Ingredients: organic rice, organic oats, organic barley, organic fish, fish oil, organic sunflower oil, seaweed, vitamins and minerals.
Analysis: protein 18.5%, oil 7.5%, fibre 4%, ash 4.5%, copper 15mg/kg

SKINNER'S FIELD AND TRIAL - salmon and rice
Ingredients: whole rice (40%), salmon meal (17.5% dry weight), naked oats, peas, sunflower oil, linseed, beet pulp, vitamin A, D_3, E and minerals.
Analysis: protein 20%, oil 12%, fibre 3.5%, ash 5.5%, copper at 10mg/kg

Review: *"I used to use Skinner's Field and Trial dog kibble. It was really good, and adored by the ratties. Very good quality stuff for a good price. I don't add kibble anymore which is the only reason I don't buy it anymore."* (Stacey C)

WAINWRIGHT'S ADULT COMPLETE - salmon and potato
Ingredients: salmon protein (min. 23%), potato (min. 21%), sorghum, whole grain barley (min. 10%), Atlantic fish meal, whole linseed (min. 4%), sugar beet pulp (min. 5%), sunflower oil, dicalcium phosphate, alfalfa,

natural seaweed, sodium chloride, potassium chloride, yucca extract, methionine, marigold extract, rosemary extract, vitamins A, D_3 and E.
Analysis: protein 21%, oils and fats 10%, fibre 3.5%, ash 7.2%, copper 12mg/kg. Vitamin E and C as EC permitted antioxidant. No added colours, flavourings or preservatives.

Review: *"Very popular kibble with my rats, probably the favourite, and despite it being fairly fishy it didn't stink the house out when fed and didn't smell quite so strongly as other fishy mixes. I particularly liked the inclusion of linseed and seaweed. The kibble pieces seemed to stick powders like garlic powder to them better than most, possibly due to the slightly higher oil content. It's a good back up to adding in vitamins and minerals if your mix seems to be lacking a little."* (Jemma)

JAMES WELLBELOVED SENIOR/LIGHT - ocean white fish and rice (other flavours suitable)

Ingredients: rice, barley, ocean white fish meal, whole linseed, vegetable gravy, peas, olive oil, alfalfa, fish oil, natural seaweed, chicory pulp, sodium chloride, parsley, nettle, calcium carbonate, lysine, glucosamine, chicory extract, DL-methionine, chondroitin, yucca extract, threonine, JWB special ingredients. Min 17.5% fish, min 28% rice, min 15% barley, min 0.3% JW+.
Analysis: protein 18%, oil 8.5%, fibre 4.5%, ash 7%, omega-3 fatty acids 2%, omega-6 fatty acids 1.3%.

Review: *"Nice quality natural kibble. Made the mix smell fairly fishy but it was always popular with the rats, though they did prefer Burns and Wainwright's to it slightly. The pieces were also larger than some other kibbles I've used, and I prefer smaller pieces as it better spreads them out. A little dusty at times but relatively low fat and not to high levels of protein."* (Jemma)

AUTARKY NATURE LITE

Ingredients: maize, chicken meat meal, rice, whole linseed, beet pulp, carrot and green leaf vegetables (min 4%), chicken fat, mixed herbs and spices; wide range including dandelions (min 2%), prairie meal, yeast, natural antioxidants lecithin, mixed tocopherols (vitamin E), vitamin A, C, D_3, copper and citric acid.

Analysis: protein 17%, oil 7%, fibre 3.5%, copper 20 mg/kg

Review: *"100% natural herbal formula. Wheat and gluten free. No genetically modified ingredients. Free from artificial colourings, flavourings and preservatives. Suitable for adding in small quantities to a grain mix. Quality kibble with medium to large bite size. Good for adding copper to a mix. Quite large pieces which some rats don't like."* (Alison C)

FISH4DOGS FINEST SALMON COMPLETE (SMALL BITE)
Ingredients: salmon 30.5%, potato 30.5%, herring meal 21.4%, salmon oil 7.6%, beet fibre 6.4%, brewer's yeast 2.1%, minerals 0.8%, vitamins 0.7%.
Analysis: protein 26%, oil 12%, ash 9%, fibre 2.5%, copper 18 mg/kg

Review: *"With over 50% fish content plus salmon oil, this is an excellent kibble for adding protein to a dry mix to support reproduction and rapid growth. The piece size really is 'small bite' and even younger rats seem to be able to manage it. I use this routinely now from pregnancy through until the babies are about 8 weeks and it is well received."* (Alison C)

ORGANIPETS ORGANIC COMPLETE DOG FOOD - ADULT
Ingredients: organic fresh chicken (min 22%), organic whole rice (min 10%), chicken meal, prairie meal, organic oats, organic barley, organic peas, organic skimmed milk, maize protein, organic sunflower oil, chicken oil, whole linseed, seaweed meal, vegetable pomace, salmon oil, organic herbs (including oregano, rosemary, sage and thyme). With natural antioxidant Vitamin E (tocopherol-rich extracts of natural origin). This product is made with a minimum of 79% organically approved ingredients.
Analysis: protein 28%, oil 11%, ash 6%, fibre 2.5%, copper 20mg/kg

BUYING QUALITY DOG KIBBLE ONLINE:
http://www.burnspet.co.uk - Burns products.
http://www.organipets.co.uk - Various organic dog foods.
http://www.wellbeloved.com - James Wellbeloved products.
http://www.fish4dogs.com - Fish4Dogs products.
http://www.k9capers.com - Wide range of dog food.

ALTERNATIVE DRY ANIMAL PROTEIN SOURCES
Freeze dried fish, fish skins, fish flakes and fish biscuits.
Freeze dried insects such as crickets and earthworms.
Freeze dried shrimps.

A CLOSER LOOK AT RIVER SHRIMPS
Protein 60%, fat 11%, fibre 4%, moisture 8%, ash 10%.
Shrimps seem to be an ideal source of animal protein for rats, having good levels of vitamin B_{12}, copper, iron and selenium; nutrients that can be lacking elsewhere in the diet. The river shrimps sold by Nature's Grub and ratRations are farmed specifically for food in China and gamma irradiated to ensure that they are free from parasites.

I tend to favour dried shrimps over dried insects, not only because of the nutrient content detailed above, but also because dried insects tend to have a much higher percentage of fat.

JAMES WELLBELOVED PURE INDULGENTS
Cat treats with fish and parsley.
Ingredients: Fish, parsley. Min 98% fish.
Analysis: protein 85%, oil 4%, ash 7%, fibre 0.2%

FISH4DOGS TIDDLERS SEA BISCUITS
Ingredients: 95% cod, 5% rice flour
Analysis: protein 58%, oil 2%, omega 3 0.3%, ash 20%, fibre 1%

Review: *"I use a large pair of scissors to cut these little biscuits into 6 smaller pieces (this isn't hard to do), and then I add them to my over all mix, especially when I am feeding to support reproduction and rapid growth. My rats are very enthusiastic about them and whilst they do smell fishy they are not overpowering."* (Alison C)

FISH4DOGS TIDDLERS SEA JERKY
Ingredients: 100% fish skins
Analysis: protein 85%, oil 2.6%, omega 3 0.35%, ash 12%, fibre 0.6%

Review: *"As with the Sea Biscuits, I tend to cut these into smaller pieces and add to the dry food, especially for mums and babies. They are more brittle than the biscuits but still cut easily with a large pair of scissors. They seem to go down well with the rats and I like the fact that they have a bit of omega 3 fish oil in them, every little helps to boost their vitamin D."* (Alison C)

BUYING 'DRY' ANIMAL PROTEIN ONLINE

http://www.ratrations.com - Good selection of dried water creatures and insects.

http://shop.naturesgrub.co.uk - Good selection of dried water creatures and insects.

http://www.fish4dogs.com - Tiddlers fish skins and biscuits.

VEGETARIAN ALTERNATIVES TO DRY ANIMAL PROTEIN
HAPPIDOG NUGGETS

Ingredients: wheat, maize, soya, wheatfeed, prairie meal, Sugar beet pulp, sunflower oil, rice, pasta, dicalcium phosphate, yeast, linseed, salt, vitamin supplement, fructo-oligosaccharides (FOS), rosemary, parsley, natural antioxidants, yucca extracts.

Analysis: protein 20%, oil 8%, fibre 4%, ash 8%, moisture 9%, vitamin A, D_3 and E, copper 14mg/kg

Review: *"Contain no artificial colours, are vegetarian and are not tested on animals, so are good for people looking for ethical ingredients. We've been feeding them as part of our mix, in place of adding a meat based dog kibble, for about 3 years with no problems and the rats always scoff them down. Can be bought in 2.5kg bags for around £6, available online."* (Gemma Driscoll)

BENEVO VEGETARIAN DOG FOOD

Ingredients: full fat soya, maize, rice, refined sunflower oil, peas, sugar beet, brewers yeast, vegetable pomace, fructoolgiosaccharides (FOS), minerals, vitamins.

Analysis: protein 21%, oil 10%, fibre 3.5%, copper 16mg/kg

MICRONIZED SOYA FLAKES

Micronized soya flakes are produced by cooking the beans using infrared technology (similar to microwaves but at a higher energy level) and then rolling them into flakes. This process reduces antinutrients and improves digestibility. 35% protein and 19% oil.

SMALL HOLDER RANGE - PIG STARTER/GROWER PELLETS
Vegetarian Society approved. See details and review on page 109.

ALTERNATIVE WET ANIMAL PROTEIN SOURCES
- Good quality wet cat food (Applaws - some organic varieties, HiLife, Natures:menu).
- Good quality wet dog food (Burns Penlan Farm range, Naturediet, Applaws - some organic varieties, Natures:menu, Fish4Dogs salmon mousse).
- All unprocessed meat, fish, and eggs produced for human consumption, suitably cooked. Organic human protein foods are more easily sourced.

FISH SELECT - APPLAWS ADULT CAT FOOD TINS
Ingredients: sea fish caught using dolphin friendly methods.
Tuna: 75% tuna, 6% rice, 19% cooking water.
Tuna and Prawn: 52% tuna, 23% prawn, 1% rice, 24% cooking water.
Tuna and Seaweed: 48% tuna, 1% rice, 0.02% seaweed, vegetable gelling agent.
Analysis: moisture 82%, protein 13%, oils and fats 0.3%, fibre 1%, ash 2%

Review: *"It's made from 'real' ingredients, actual meat and vegetables rather than derivatives and dodgy chemicals, so it's much better quality than many commercial wet foods. When you open the can it smells very tasty and you can see flakes of meat and the odd pea or mini-shrimp-thing rather than the usual jellied mulch you'd get in a pet food tin. The rats absolutely adore it, especially mixed with couscous and a sprinkle of seaweed powder."* (Jird)

CHICKEN SELECT - APPLAWS ADULT CAT FOOD TINS
Ingredients: chicken used is organic.
Chicken: 75% chicken, 1% rice, 24% cooking water.
Chicken and Cheese: 70% chicken, 5% cheese, 1% rice, 24% cooking water.

Chicken and Pumpkin: 50% chicken, 24% pumpkin, 1% rice, and 25% cooking water.
Analysis: moisture 82%, protein 13%, oils and fats 0.3%, fibre 1%, ash 2%.

FINEST SALMON MOUSSE - FISH4DOGS
Ingredients: 99% salmon and 1% seaweed extract
Analysis: protein 14%, oil 10%, ash 2%, fibre 0.5%, omega 3 2.7%, omega 6 0.22%

Review: *"This is basically just an easy way of feeding cooked fish and I tend to use these pouches when raising litters, or in a more diluted mix for our rats' weekly fresh meal. I have found that rats tend to prefer fish when it is mixed into a carbohydrate food and I tend to combine a sachet into a base of cooked grain, and then add some chopped vegetables if desired. Very well received in this manner."* (Alison C)

CHICKEN WITH VEGETABLES AND RICE - NATUREDIET
One of many varieties.
Ingredients: chicken, minimum 60% , vegetables, minimum 5%, brown rice, minimum 5%. omega 3 (provided by flax, fish oil & meat) minimum 0.25%, omega 6 (provided by flax, fish oil & meat) minimum 0.75%, natural ground bone, kelp, herbs (rosemary and rubbed sage)
Analysis; protein 10% , oil 8%, fibre 1%, ash 2%, moisture 75%, vitamins A, D_3 and E

SENIOR/LITE - NATUREDIET
Ingredients: rabbit and turkey (min. 60%), brown rice, vegetables, natural ground bone, kelp, herbs (rosemary and rubbed sage), omega 3 and 6 (provided by flax, fish oil and meat), vitamins and minerals.
Analysis: moisture 75%, protein 8%, oils and fats 7%, fibre 1.5%, ash 2%, vitamin A, D_3 and E.

Review: *"Looks unappealing due to the fact everything is pretty much mushed together, smells good and it was a big hit with the rats. It seems easier to mix in powders, easier to get a consistent mess. Tub is a little big for 4 rats, though it freezes well so good for kidney friendly mix."* (Jemma)

EGG, BROWN RICE AND VEGETABLES - BURNS

Penlan Farm Range.

Ingredients: free range egg (min 20%), organic brown rice (min 20%), vegetables (min 20%), vitamins and minerals.

Analysis: protein 5.7%, oil 3.3%, fibre 1.1%, moisture 69.4%, ash 0.7%, vitamin A, D_3, E and copper (8mg/kg).

Review: *"Probably the best product I am aware of in terms of ethical considerations and rat-tailored nutrition, for feeding to all adult rats, including those with deteriorating kidneys. The ingredients are sourced from Burns' own farm project and whilst the vegetable content may vary, the actual vegetables used in any batch are listed on the packaging (my current batch has carrot and swede). The product is a firm, pleasant smelling wet food, perfect for adding kidney diet supplements to, and has been well received by the rat taste testers here!"* (Alison C)

CHICKEN, BROWN RICE AND VEGETABLES - BURNS

Penlan Farm Range.

Ingredients: organic chicken (min 20%), organic brown rice (min 20%), seasonal vegetables (min 20%), vitamins and minerals.

Analysis: protein 4.8%, oil 2.6%, fibre 2.3%, moisture 78.6%, ash 1.5%, vitamin A, D_3, E and copper (8mg/kg).

LAMB, BROWN RICE AND VEGETABLES - BURNS

Penlan Farm Range.

Ingredients: lamb hearts (min 20%), organic brown rice (min 20%), seasonal vegetables (min 20%), vitamins and minerals.

Analysis: protein 4.95%, oil 3.3%, fibre 0.7%, moisture 78.2%, ash 1.5%, vitamin A, D_3, E and copper (8mg/kg).

CHICKEN WITH VEGETABLES AND RICE - NATURES:MENU

One of many varieties.

Ingredients: chicken minimum 61%, peas minimum 4%, carrots minimum 4%, rice minimum 6%, minerals, various sugars.

Analysis: protein 10%, oil 7%, fibre 1%, ash 2.5%, moisture 75%, vitamin A, D_3, and E.

LAMB WITH VEGETABLES AND RICE - NATURES:MENU
Senior variety.
Ingredients: lamb, peas, carrots, rice.
Analysis: protein 8%, oil 7%, fibre 2.5%, ash 1%, moisture 75%, vitamin A, D_3 and E.

Review: *"Nice consistency, smells appealing, the rats liked it but also liked to bury the meat pieces in their litter which was messy. They preferred the peas to the meat; strange creatures. The rats preferred this one to the adult lite."* (Jemma)

CHICKEN, RABBIT, VEGETABLES AND RICE - NATURES: MENU
Lite variety.
Ingredients: chicken, rabbit, peas, carrots, rice.
Nutrition: moisture 75%, protein 8%, oils and fats 7%, fibre 2.5%, ash 1%, vitamin A, D_3 and E (tocopherol).

Review: *"Nice consistency, smells appealing, the rats liked it but also liked to bury the meat pieces in their litter which was messy, preferred the peas to the meat again."* (Jemma)

CHICKEN AND LAMB - NATURES: MENU
Puppy variety.
Ingredients: chicken, lamb, rice.
Analysis: moisture 75%, protein 11%, oils and fats 7%, fibre 2.5%, ash 1%, vitamin A, D_3 and E (tocopherol).

Review: *"Again a nice appetizing mix, not particularly high in protein for a puppy food but a nice occasional treat for younger rats."* (Jemma)

CHICKEN AND TURKEY - HiLIFE
Cat pouch (one of many varieties).
Ingredients: turkey and chicken (in variable proportions, minimum 60%), vitamin & mineral supplements, tapioca.
Analysis: protein 11%, oils and fats 2%, fibre 0.5%, ash 2%, moisture 83%, vitamin A, D_3 and E (alphatocopherol), copper (cupric sulphate).

CHICKEN BREAST WITH VEGETABLES — HILIFE
Dog pouch (one of many varieties).
Ingredients: chicken breast (minimum 50%), vegetables (carrots minimum 4%, peas minimum 4%), sunflower oil, vitamin & mineral supplements, tapioca.
Analysis: protein 13.5%, oils and fats 2%, fibre 0.5%, ash 1.5%, moisture 81.5%, vitamin A, D_3 and E (alphatocopherol), copper (cupric sulphate).

GENERAL COMMENTS
Most of these fresh foods have a moisture content of around 75%, so to make a comparison between these and a dry product, you need to multiply the percentage nutrients by 4 to get roughly equivalent levels. For example, if the protein is 11%, this equates to around 44% if the product was a dry kibble. Some products, like Fish4Dogs mousse and Naturediet, are high in fat and should be limited for this reason. However, the added oils in Naturediet (fish and flax) and the natural salmon oil in the Fish4Dogs product are beneficial oils.

ETHICAL CONSIDERATIONS
Burns Penlan Farm Range source their meat from their own organic, free range farm.
Applaws do not use any battery farmed chicken or eggs and the tuna used is a non-endangered species, caught using dolphin friendly and sustainable methods.
Naturediet source all of their meat from the UK
Natures:menu source their meat from the UK, Ireland or Europe
HiLife source all of their chicken from Thailand

BUYING WET ANIMAL PROTEIN ONLINE
http://www.ratwarehouse.com - Applaws, Natures:menu, Naturediet.
http://www.burnspet.co.uk - Burns.
http://www.naturediet.co.uk - Naturediet.
http://www.fish4dogs.com - Fish4Dogs.
http://www.k9capers.com - HiLife, Applaws, Natures:menu.

SEEDS AND NUTS

Seeds and nuts are generally nutrient rich, though should be restricted because of their high fat content. However, fats are essential for growth and well-being and the oils in seeds often have beneficial health properties.

HEMP
Hemp seed is a large round seed that is about 80% fatty acids (omega 6 and omega 3) and 20% protein. It is one of the few plant protein sources to contain all essential amino acids, with lysine being present in the smallest quantity. The seed oil is an excellent source of essential fatty acids, may help reduce inflammatory skin problems, and is excellent for improving coat condition. Hemp seeds can be sprouted, although some (particularly those sourced from the USA) are irradiated to render them infertile because of their relationship to cannabis. However, the strains of hemp that are used for industrial cultivation contain only a tiny proportion of the psycho-active drug found in cannabis.

LINSEED
Also called flax, linseed is a small brown or golden seed, which is high in omega 3 and lignans, which are considered to have health benefits such as slowing tumour growth and protecting the heart from disease. Flax oil may also help with conditions such as diabetes (stabilising blood sugar), and kidney failure (slowing progression).

PUMPKIN
Pumpkin seeds are large, flat and green, though they are sometimes sold within their white seed coat. They are a good source of protein, omega 3 and omega 6 fatty acids. Pumpkin seeds are particularly rich in iron, as well as supplying a number of other minerals in smaller amounts.

MELON
Melon seeds are frequently available and discarded as part of a human diet and can easily be converted into a free rat treat. They are comparatively low in fat and contain a number of minerals in fair amounts including copper,

selenium and potassium. To prepare, rinse the seeds thoroughly and then lay them out in a single layer on some kitchen roll on a sunny window ledge, where they will take 2 or 3 days to dry out. Alternatively, slowly roast them in a cool oven.

MILK THISTLE

This seed contains silymarin, which is a complex mixture of polyphenols, flavonoids and other potentially beneficial plant chemicals. Extract from the seed has been shown to have positive effects in reducing liver damage caused by toxins, reducing the growth of cancer cells and reducing insulin resistance in type 2 diabetes.

SUNFLOWER

I have included these because they sometimes appear in generic rat mixes but may be best avoided for some rats. Like other seeds they are rich in essential fatty acids and minerals, but individual rats may develop skin reactions (scabs and sores) if they eat sunflower seeds, and perhaps there are better options that do not have the same allergenic properties for some rats.

NUTS

Nuts are, by loose definition, large oily kernels (the fruit or seed of a plant) held within a hard shell, and they often contain healthy oils. Some - like walnut and almonds - may help to prevent heart disease. They are also an excellent source of Vitamin E, antioxidants and minerals such as copper and selenium. Nuts make an excellent nutritious treat for rats, though they are generally very high in fat and therefore should be limited. A nut still in its shell can provide a rat with literally hours of fun and interest, as it works to get the kernel from inside.

The only nut that is low in both fat and protein (0.6g and 3.4g respectively) is the sweet chestnut and these can be fed freely. They are a good source of B vitamins, vitamin C and carbohydrate. Sweet chestnuts should be fed cooked as they contain a lot of tannic acid, and can cause diarrhoea when fed raw. There is a method for roasting fresh chestnuts on page 290. Of the other varieties of nut, one of the most useful must be walnuts as they are a good source omega 3 fatty acids (known to have a protective effect on the cardio vascular system), vitamin E, selenium (antioxidant) and iron.

Hazelnuts, pine nuts, cashews, Brazil nuts and walnuts have protein levels around 10-15%, while almonds are 21% and peanuts (actually a legume) 25%. All contain high levels of fat - between 45 and 70% - with Brazils and pine nuts being the highest, however, Brazil nuts are the best food source of selenium and in that respect are great for feeding in small pieces to support reproduction and rapid growth.

COCONUT

The coconut can be fed in all manner of ways and because of its high fat content can be useful in increasing calorie intake for a sick rat. Coconut water (from the centre of a fresh, immature coconut) is a highly nutritious drink, containing fructose, protein, antioxidants, vitamins, minerals and fibre. Coconut milk is made from the flesh creamed with water or milk and is calorific due to its high fat content, however, despite being saturated the fat in coconut flesh may have some associated health benefits, including immune system support. The flesh can also be given, but in moderation because of its high fat content (around 33%), and is available fresh or dried. Drying the flesh removes water and therefore increases nutrient levels even further, pushing the fat content up to 64%.

BUYING SEEDS AND NUTS ONLINE

http://www.ratrations.com - Wide selection of seeds and nuts.
http://www.spiceworld.uk.com - Good choice of human grade seeds.
http://www.ethicalsuperstore.com - Lots of organic and fair trade, human grade nuts.

VEGETABLES

A number of dried vegetables are available to add to dry mixes and some generic mixes include dried vegetables, most commonly carrots. Vegetables add variety, and are a low fat, nutrient rich addition to any mix.

CARROT
The carrot is a wonderful vegetable that is full of beta-carotene; a precursor of vitamin A. It is also rich in antioxidants and contains minerals such as calcium and iron. Dried carrots are readily available either on their own or in vegetable mixes and seem to be very palatable to rats.

MUSHROOM
Mushrooms are a good source of copper and selenium, but they are not always greeted enthusiastically by rats. They are readily available dried - or you might try drying your own.

PARSNIP
Parsnips are a great source of a number of vitamins, particularly vitamin K, C and folate. They are hard to source on their own, but are frequently included in packets of mixed roots.

LEEKS
Leeks are rich in vitamin C, K and A and also contain good levels of iron and manganese. They are often included in dried vegetable mixes.

SWEDE
A root vegetable that is high in vitamin C, potassium, manganese, calcium and magnesium. Swede is often included in dry mixed vegetables or mixed root packs.

TOMATOES
A good source of vitamins A, C and K. Tomatoes are sometimes included in mixed vegetable packs and can also be found as an individual dried vegetable.

BEETROOT
These purple root vegetables contain good amounts of folate (vitamin B_9) and are available in a shredded, dried form, which seems to be well liked by rats. Beetroot juice is a strong colorant and can tint urine pink.

RED BELL PEPPER

Red peppers have great levels of vitamins A, C and E and also contain a wide range of minerals. They can be easily sourced alone or as part of a mixed vegetable pack.

GARLIC

The medicinal properties of garlic have long been recognised and are well understood. Fresh garlic will give the greatest benefits, but good quality dried garlic is easy to use in a mix, and palatable. Garlic is a powerful stimulant of the immune system, and has a general anti-microbial effect against viruses, fungi, protozoa, bacteria and other parasites. It has a positive effect on cardiovascular health, and has anti-cancer properties. Garlic is also an excellent source of selenium, which is an antioxidant.

Many rat owners use garlic powder every day just mixed into their grain mix (it tends to stick to the extruded biscuity bits). This may have some health benefits, probably keeping parasites at bay and boosting immune system health, however, it also has the effect of making the whole of the diet smell and taste of garlic which may reduce the sensory benefits of providing a wide and varied mix. An excellent alternative is shredded horse garlic (such as that made by Global Herbs) where whole cloves are crushed and dried quickly and include roots and skin, resulting in a nutritionally superior product. The garlic in this form, still has good levels of the plant chemicals that are needed for a beneficial effect.

Fresh garlic is even more beneficial, and can be fed daily. Feeding fresh garlic has been proven to reduce the formation of mammary cancer cells in rats - but it must be fed in one of two ways to have this effect, either raw, or chopped and left to stand for 10 minutes before cooking (e.g. microwaving for a minute). If the cloves are cooked whole, or chopped garlic is cooked without the standing period, the enzymes involved with cancer prevention are destroyed. The effects of raw garlic were found to be huge - with a decrease of 64% in the rate of cancer cell growth. The 'chopped and left to stand for 10 minutes before microwaving' garlic reduced cancer cell formation by 41%, with oven cooking reducing effectiveness down to 21%.

However, it should be noted that these were cancerous growths and not the usual lipomas and fibroadenomas that female rats are so prone to.

HOME DRYING VEGETABLES

Many vegetables can be successfully dried in a conventional oven and when choosing vegetables for drying look for those that are fresh, of excellent quality and fully ripe. All vegetables should be cleaned thoroughly and cut into small pieces or thin slices. Drying time will be between about 6 and 24 hours, depending on the size of the pieces and type of the vegetable. The oven should be set on the lowest setting possible, and the door may need to be propped open a little in order to allow the moist air to circulate. When the food is nearly dry it will scorch easily – at this point turn the heat off and prop the door open to finish drying. Fully dried vegetables should feel dry and brittle, but warm vegetables will still feel soft and pliable, so to test dryness, remove a piece from the oven and allow to cool. If you have a warm boiler cupboard (or similar) you may be able to use this instead of the oven, but drying will take several days.

Successful drying depends on having:
- enough heat to dry the food without cooking it.
- dry air to absorb moisture from the food.
- good air circulation to replenish the dry air.

BUYING DRIED VEGETABLES ONLINE

http://www.ratrations.com - UK rat specific feed store, with an excellent range of individual and mixed dried vegetables.
http://www.spiceworld.uk.com - UK store offering a limited selection of human grade dried vegetables.
http://www.bunnybazaar.com - UK rabbit store with a selection of dried vegetables.

FRUIT

Some commercial mixes contain dried fruit, with banana being the most common, and dried fruit can be used as an ingredient for a homemade mix. I would recommend adding no more than treat proportions, primarily for interest, antioxidants, vitamins and minerals. It is best to choose fruits with no added sugar, and if possible free from preservatives as many dried fruits are preserved with sulphates and these may be linked to health issues such as allergies and respiratory irritation. Dried cranberries are high in vitamin C and antioxidants, currants are a useful source of copper and dried apples are a great source of soluble fibre and antioxidants.

BUYING DRIED FRUIT ONLINE

http://www.ratrations.com - UK rat specific store with a good range of dried fruit.

http://www.bunnybazaar.com - UK rabbit store with a good range of dried fruit.

http://www.ethicalsuperstore.com - UK organic and fair-trade superstore which has a wide range of organic dried fruit under *Groceries & Everyday; Store Cupboard.*

A comprehensive list of vegetables and fruit and their suitability in terms of feeding to rats is included as Appendix 2, page 314.

HERBS

There are many kinds of dried rabbit herbs available and rats seem to enjoy most of these. Dandelion is an excellent source of calcium and phosphorus, in a ratio that is perfect for bone health and growth, and is probably the second best green source of these minerals, after kale. The garden or meadow herbal mixes are also very well received. Many herbs are thought to have medicinal properties - though usually a tincture of the herb is needed to concentrate the active compounds, in order to get any measurable effect. However, it is wise to mention any herbs you are adding to the diet when consulting a vet. Favourite herbs here are mint, lemon balm, basil and dandelion. Considering herbs individually, or the medicinal properties of their concentrates, is a vast topic in its own right and outside of the scope of this book

Herbs are fairly easy to dry at home using similar techniques to vegetables detailed above, but shorter drying times.

BUYING DRIED HERBS ONLINE

http://www.ratrations.com - UK rat specific site, with a good range of dried herbs.

http://www.spiceworld.uk.com - UK human grade herbs.

http://www.bunnybazaar.com - UK rabbit store with a range of dried rabbit herbs.

REFERENCES

[1] http://ressources.ciheam.org/om/pdf/c22/97605920.pdf

[2] Journal of the Royal Society of Health. 1991 Jun;111(3):119. The effect of the consumption of red kidney beans on the growth of rats and the implications for human populations.

[3]Journal of Food Composition and Analysis. Volume 17, Issues 3-4, June-August 2004, Pages 321-329
In vitro bioavailability of calcium from chicken bone extract powder and its fortified products
Sirirat Sittikulwitit et al

Chapter four - overview

Commercial mixes - information and reviews
      Rabbit food
      Rat food
      Other feeds sometimes chosen by rat owners

Chapter four
Commercially prepared
mixes and reviews

COMMERCIAL MIXES
INFORMATION AND REVIEWS

There are many and varied ways of feeding your rats an adequate diet and for many people using a commercial mix as a base food, or mixing two or three together to increase variety, are convenient and appropriate methods. With this in mind, I have included the following information in order to help readers to make informed choices about which products will best suit their own rats and their circumstances. Each commercial mix is detailed in terms of the ingredients, nutritional analysis and particular strengths and weaknesses. The ingredients and nutritional content, where quoted, have either been taken from packaging, or are as provided on request from the manufacturer. Every effort has been made to ensure that they are an accurate representation of the product, but as recipes are liable to change over time, please check the packaging prior to making a purchase.

Wherever possible a review is also included and these comments represent the views of the individuals concerned. They are not necessarily the views of the author, nor can they be guaranteed to be an accurate representation of the product.

It should also be noted that the inclusion of a grain mix does not constitute a recommendation by the author. Many commercially prepared grain mixes can be improved simply by them mixing with another product. Ingredients vary from mix to mix and variety can be increased by this simple measure. Likewise, the limitations of one preparation can be compensated by the strengths of another, so if you chose this method look for two very different products such as Harrison's Banana Rabbit Brunch and Link Premium Rat Food.

RABBIT FOOD

ALPHA HERBAL DELUXE RABBIT
Ingredients: cooked flaked peas, extruded wheat discs, cooked flaked maize, rolled oats, cooked flaked beans, whole wheat, cooked flaked barley, locust

beans, soya oil, dried grass, dried herbs, minerals and vitamins. Contains EC permitted colours.

Analysis: protein 12.4%, fat 3.5%, fibre 5%, copper 9.5mg/kg

Pros: a wide variety of ingredients, which are all suitable for rats. Low fat.
Cons: highly coloured with artificial colours. Processed wheat biscuits make up a substantial proportion of the mix. Vitamins are added to the biscuits so if a rat doesn't like these it will miss out on essential micro nutrients. Peas are the primary ingredient and are often least favourite. Copper level on the low side.

Review: *"Originally I used Alpha Herbal Deluxe (AHD) rabbit food as a base for my homemade mix, and it was generally very well received by my rats. All parts of the mix were readily eaten, except for the split peas, which were ignored. My rats were very healthy with an excellent coat condition on this base mix, which I used for at about 10 months. However, the company has recently changed the formula, and it seems to include more artificial colours. This is a big shame as I consider the old style AHD to be an excellent base mix for rats, but I wouldn't use the new style AHD because of the additives."* (Andy Joiner)

HARRISON'S BANANA RABBIT BRUNCH

Ingredients: banana chips, micronized peas, micronized maize, micronized barley, extruded wheat disks with added vitamin mix (A, D and E), flaked carrots, micronized beans, oats, banana essence (flavouring only; does not add sugars), contains EC permitted colours.

Analysis: protein 14%, oil 2%, fibre 5.5%, copper 5mg/kg

Apart from the fructose in the banana chips, there is a small amount of honey used in their processing.

Pros: good variety of ingredients and contains none that rats will generally reject. Skewed towards maize and barley making it a feed with potential for part of a kidney friendly mix. Not highly coloured.
Cons: bananas may make it less suitable for older rats because of their potassium content, though this is not likely to be a problem once kidney disease is established. As the kidneys fail, urine output increases and salts (including potassium) are lost with the urine, so low potassium is more

likely to be a problem than too much. Vitamins are added to the biscuits, so where a rat rejects these it will miss out on essential micro nutrients. Low copper level. Not widely available.

Reviews: *"I use Harrisons Banana Brunch as the base for my mix. The ratties all love it, it isn't coloured and has lots of yummie looking bits in it. I was actually looking at it in the shop I buy it from today thinking how yummie it looked; it was 1pm and I hadn't eaten lunch! I have used other bases as variety for my ratties but they do seem to love the Banana Brunch."* (Max_n_Monty)

"The rats loved this food as a base mix for their Shunamite diet. However, it can be difficult to get in local shops, and is usually only found online, which means you have to pay for postage and packaging charges. For larger rat families, this could be economical, however, small rat families may find it is too expensive to pay the postal charges for a small amount of food. However, if you do have a supplier local to you, then the benefits of this mix are fantastic and there is no wastage at all." (NewRat)

MR JOHNSON'S SUPREME RABBIT
Ingredients: flaked peas, rabbit nut (wheatfeed, lucerne, sunflower meal, treated straw, oatfeed, limestone, molasses, salt, soya oil, monocalcium, phosphate, vitamins A, D and E, minerals), flaked barley, extruded biscuits (wheat, barley, wheatfeed, permitted colours), flaked maize, locust beans, whole barley, contains EC permitted colours.
Analysis: protein 15%, oil 3%, fibre 10%, ash 5.5%, copper 20mg/kg

Pros: good range of ingredients if the rats eat the whole mix. Copper level good. Not too highly coloured.
Cons: much of the nutrition is in the rabbit nuts which may not be eaten, and may not be well digested because of their fibre content. Wheatfeed, oatfeed, straw and lucerne are all high fibre, pelleted feeds aimed either at ruminant animals (cows, sheep) or those who rely on hind gut digestion strategies (like rabbits). Some pellets will be rejected entirely and others may not be well digested. Peas are the primary ingredient and are often least favourite.

Review: *"My rats love the Mr Johnsons Supreme - nothing is wasted, but I can only get it in teeny bags from Spar, so not big enough to feed all of the mouths in my house! It smells nice, and looks appealing - although it is quite heavy on peas."* (Lillyland)

MR JOHNSON'S JASPER RABBIT
Ingredients: flaked peas, rabbit nut (wheatfeed, lucerne, sunflower meal, treated straw, oatfeed, limestone, molasses, salt, soya oil, monocalcium, phosphate, vitamins A, D and E, minerals), flaked barley, extruded biscuits (wheat, barley, wheatfeed, permitted colours), whole barley, flaked maize, locust beans, chopped alfalfa, dried carrot rings, contains EC permitted colours.
Analysis: protein 15%, oil 3%, fibre 11%, ash 5.5%, copper 20mg/kg

Pros: good range of ingredients if the rat eats the whole mix. Copper level good. Not too highly coloured.
Cons: much of the nutrition is in the rabbit nuts which are often rejected, and may not be well digested because of their fibre content. Wheatfeed, oatfeed, straw and lucerne are all high fibre, pelleted feeds aimed either at ruminant animals (cows, sheep) or those who rely on hind gut digestion strategies (like rabbits). Some pellets will be rejected entirely and others may not be well digested. Peas are the main ingredient and are often least favourite. Alfalfa provides no accessible nutrition to rats.

Review: *"I've used Mr Johnson's Jasper rabbit once, for a few days when I had to wait for another feed to come in after ordering it. The rats didn't mind it and they would eat it all, but I found it to be mainly flaked peas and the rats' poo went quite soft when I fed it. It returned to normal once their food did!"* (shibby69)

MR. JOHNSON'S SUPREME RABBIT MIX WITH FRUIT
Ingredients: cooked flaked peas, cooked flaked barley, cooked flaked maize, wheat biscuits, oats, barley, banana slices, carrot slices, pineapple chunks, vitamin and mineral pellet (vitamin A, D and E and copper), contains EC permitted colours.

Analysis: protein: 14%, oil: 3%, fibre: 10%, copper 15 mg/kg, sugar 5.5% (5.5g per 100g)

Pros: nice variety of ingredients and the fruit and carrots are very palatable. Adequate copper level. Not highly coloured.
Cons: vitamins and minerals rely on all rats liking the pellets. Peas are main ingredient and are often least favourite. Sugar content fairly high for a base mix or complete feed.

MR JOHNSON'S CLOVER COUNTRY CRUNCH

Ingredients: oats, micronized peas, micronized barley, micronized maize, micronized beans, barley, alfalfa (lucerne), wheatfeed, oatfeed, sunflower extract, locust bean, wheat, calcium carbonate, soya oil, molasses, sodium, chloride, mono-calcium phosphate. Added mint and rosemary. Vitamin and minerals. Flavour.
Analysis: protein 13.5%, oil 3.5%, fibre 10%, copper (as cupric sulphate) 15 mg/kg

Pros: good range of ingredients and contains some herbage. Not too highly coloured.
Cons: high proportion of pellets which many rats will reject, could lead to a lot of waste. Wheatfeed, oatfeed and lucerne are all high fibre, pelleted feeds aimed either at ruminant animals (cows, sheep) or those who rely on hind gut digestion strategies (like rabbits). Some pellets will be rejected entirely and others may not be well digested. Good copper level. Oats are primary ingredient, which makes it unsuitable for older rats unless mixed with other ingredients.

Review: *"I feed Clover Country Crunch to which I also add pasta twists or pasta bows, dried fruit, cereal (bran flakes or Weetabix - any low sugar brands). The rats go crackers for this mix, and they don't seem to favour particular bits, which I feel is good as the rats must enjoy it all. I am also happy that there is no waste/leftovers in the bowls as you get with some other brands. It is good value and appears to be good quality plump shiny grains and not at all dusty."* (Hayley)

MR JOHNSON'S BELVEDERE TROPICAL FRUITY

Ingredients: rabbit nut (wheatfeed, lucerne, sunflower meal, treated straw, oatfeed, limestone, molasses, salt, soya oil, monocalcium phosphate, vitamins and minerals, flavour), micronized peas, micronized maize, micronized beans, extruded biscuits (wheat, barley, wheatfeed, permitted colourants), fibre pellet, (wheat, lucerne, oatfeed, wheatfeed, limestone, soya oil), dried raisins, dried banana slices, soya oil, flavourings.
Analysis: protein 15%, oil 5.5%, fibre 10%, ash 5.5%, copper 20mg/kg

Pros: good copper level. Good range of ingredients.
Cons: the rabbit nuts and fibre pellets may be rejected by most rats, leading to waste and lack of micronutrients. Since the vitamins and minerals are added to the rabbit nut it is likely most rats would be deficient over time. Wheatfeed, oatfeed, straw and lucerne are all high fibre feeds aimed either at ruminant animals (cows, sheep) or those who rely on hind gut digestion strategies (like rabbits). Lack of grains makes it better used in addition to a high grain feed, if at all.

Review: *"This food has large pieces of fruit which the rats love, but the waste is high with all the pellets being left. It smells yummy though."* (Scoobylyn)

BURGESS SUPA RABBIT DELUXE

Ingredients: toasted pea flakes, grass pellets, whole oats, toasted maize flakes, extruded biscuits, toasted wheat flakes, whole wheat, soya, oil and herbs, dicalcium, phosphate, calcium carbonate, contains EC permitted colours.
Analysis: protein 13.5%, oil 4%, ash 4%, fibre 9%, vitamins A, D3 and E, copper (cupric sulphate) 30 mg/kg

Pros: fair range of ingredients. Really good level of copper: vitamins and minerals sprayed over whole mix. Not too highly coloured, though their are some lurid green wheat biscuits!
Cons: a number of the ingredients are not particularly palatable to rats; contains lots of grass pellets, which are often rejected or provide little

nutrition at best. Quite heavy on wheat products (extruded biscuits, whole wheat and wheat flakes).

Review: *"I really like the smell of this food and the rats seem really keen on eating it. There are no banana flakes to pick out which is great for my bucks. Available in 3kg bags making it last for a very long time as a base for my dry mix. The green biscuits and pellets are often left untouched, but it seems to help with my bucks coats in terms of shine, and they don't seem to gain weight excessively."* (Amy M)

BURGESS SUPA NATURAL
Ingredients: flaked peas, extruded biscuit, whole oats, flaked maize, flaked beans, flaked wheat, whole wheat, flaked barley, dried grass, molasses, contains EC permitted colours.
Analysis: protein 12.5%, oil 2%, fibre 9%, Ash 4%, vitamins A, D3 and E, copper (as cupric sulphate) 15mg/kg

Pros: fairly good range of ingredients, most of which are palatable to rats. Adequate copper level. Vitamins and minerals sprayed over whole mix and not added to a pellet which could be rejected.
Cons: coloured, processed wheat biscuits make up a substantial proportion of the mix. Peas are the primary ingredient and are often least favourite. Quite heavy on wheat products (extruded biscuits, whole wheat and wheat flakes). Dried grass will often be rejected. Molasses may increase the sugar content of the feed.

Reviews: *"Before I moved to straights I used Burgess Supa Natural, and it was okay but not great. It doesn't have any of those wasteful little grass pellet things in it, but it does contain a lot of red and green coloured pellets (might be extruded wheat?) that my boys absolutely loathed. They did eat everything else though. Also, I found it to be quite dusty and spent far more time than is normal or healthy sieving dust out of my rats' dry mix."* (Jird)

"Burgess Supa Natural makes up half of the base for the boys mix. I find it has a good amount of variety but also that a lot of the bag is just filled up with seeds. There's very often lots of little seeds left at the bottom of the bowl. However, one of the things I like best is that it doesn't contain alfalfa, whereas if it did it would have

even more left in the bowl. I find that a lot of commercial rabbit mixes do contain alfalfa so this is a plus for me." (wizzyjo)

BURGESS SUPA FRUITI
Ingredients: toasted flaked peas, toasted flaked wheat, oats, extruded biscuits, whole wheat, grass pellets, flaked maize, dried carrot, dried banana, dicalcium, phosphate, calcium carbonate, contains EC permitted colours.
Analysis: protein 13.5%, oil 3%, fibre 7%, ash 4%, vitamins A, D3 and E, copper (as cupric sulphate) 15 mg/kg.

Pros: fairly good range of ingredients, most of which are palatable to rats. Adequate copper level. Vitamins and minerals sprayed over whole mix. Not too highly coloured. Banana and carrot are generally well received and are minor ingredients.
Cons: peas are the primary ingredient and are often least favourite. Quite heavy on wheat products (extruded biscuits, whole wheat and wheat flakes), grass pellets will often be rejected.

Reviews: *"The rats loved the whole banana chips and it smelt very nice. It was one of their favourite mixes and was always scoffed quite quickly although it did have some coloured biscuits the rats weren't fussed on. A positive thing is that it is easily available from stores."* (Rhi01)

"I love this food as it smells lovely and the rats seem to like it. The only part that gets left is the grass pellets which are too small to pick out by hand. The banana flakes are big enough to be picked out by hand which is great for feeding the older bucks." (Chixie)

"Great to add variety to the mix, the only bits left are the alfalfa pellets and carrot bits. Wish they did bigger bags, as my bunnies love it too, but it is expensive." (Shlugh)

"The rats enjoy this mix alongside Pets At Home Rabbit Muesli as the base mix for their Shunamite diet. It's a great alternative to other base mixes and is easy to source at Pets At Home. I wouldn't recommend it for larger rat families due to the fact that

you can only buy it in 1kg bags and it may not be economical for them. The rats tend to leave the pellets in the food, which does mean wastage." (NewRat)

CHUDLEY'S RABBIT ROYALE

Ingredients: grass, wheat, oats, oatfeed, barley, peas maize, alfalfa, wheat feed, dehulled soya bean, herbs (marigold flowers, mint and nettle), carrot, glucose, straw, soya oil and fruit.
Analysis: protein 12%, oil 2.5%, fibre 14%, ash 6%, copper 30 mg/kg

Pros: nice mix of ingredients, with some herbs, vegetable and fruit. Great copper level. Not coloured. Smells great!
Cons: Lots of pellets and grass so high in fibre - vitamins and minerals may be added to pellets (this isn't clear), so could potentially be lost to any rat that rejects them. Wheatfeed, oatfeed, grass and alfalfa are all high fibre, pelleted feeds aimed either at ruminant animals (cows, sheep) or those who rely on hind gut digestion strategies (like rabbits). Some pellets will be rejected entirely and others may not be well digested. Added glucose (sugar levels not listed).

WAGG BUNNY BRUNCH

Ingredients: contains peas, wheat, wheat feed, oatfeed, oats, flaked maize, lucerne, whole maize, sunflower meal, vegetable oil, apple, grape, grass, syrup, minerals, locust bean meal, linseed, yeast.
Analysis: protein 13%, oil 4%, fibre 10%, ash 5%, copper 16mg/kg

Pros: fairly good variety of ingredients. Copper levels good.
Cons: a lot of ingredients in pellet form, which are likely to be rejected by the majority of rats. Vitamins and minerals may be added to pellets (this isn't clear), so could potentially be lost to any rat that rejects them. Includes some unsuitable ingredients like grass and lucerne - sunflower meal may cause skin irritation for some rats. Wheatfeed and oatfeed are high fibre pellets aimed either at ruminant animals (cows, sheep) or those who rely on hind gut digestion strategies (like rabbits).

SNEYD'S WONDER RABBIT NATURAL FRUIT

Ingredients: flaked peas, flaked maize, flaked wheat, oats, extruded wheat, locust beans, dried grass, molasses, banana slices, pineapple chunks, vitamins A, D and E.
Analysis: protein 13.5%, fat 2.5%, fibre 10%, ash 5%, copper level was not on packaging, nor supplied by company on request.

Pros: fairly good range of ingredients and mainly palatable ingredients. Fruit adds interest and nutrients. Not highly coloured
Cons: peas are the main ingredient and are often least favourite. Dried grass will probably be rejected. Fruit and molasses will increase the overall sugar content.

Review: *"This is sold in 15kg bags but some stockists also sell it loose so smaller quantities can be purchased. It smells fantastic and the rats love it. Of course the banana slices go first, but they do only make up a small percentage of the feed (and even smaller once mixed in with the rest of the ingredients I put into our dry mix), so it is suitable for all age groups. They do seem to eat everything, and are in excellent condition."* (Kate Rattray)

LINK FRUTTI SUPREME RABBIT

Ingredients: flaked beans, flaked peas, flaked maize, lucerne, locust beans, banana, extruded fruity wheat nibbles, papaya, tropical fruits, raisins, oats, yucca extract, vitamins, minerals, fruit flavour.
Analysis: protein 14%, oil 3%, fibre 8%, copper 7 mg/kg

Pros: plenty of unusual and palatable ingredients making an effectively low grain base food. Ideal to mix with another high grain feed or human grade grains and cereals. Not too highly coloured – the fruity wheat nibbles are bright red, but they are not a major proportion of the mix.
Cons: likely to be fairly high in sugar from fruits and lacks a variety of grains. The lucerne (alfalfa) will likely be rejected by most rats. Low copper.

Review: *"I was having trouble finding some of the recommended feeds and came across Link Frutti Supreme Rabbit, which is very much liked it seems by all my ratties! There are virtually no leftovers. I add muesli, dried pasta twists, cornfakes and puffed wheat. Actually the puffed wheat seems least liked."* (Kel)

PETS AT HOME RABBIT MUSELI

Ingredients: wheat, toasted pea flakes, oats, wheatfeed, toasted maize flakes, oatfeed, grass, sunflower extract, whole maize, apple and grape in extruded nuggets, vegetable oil, lucerne, vitamins and minerals, syrup, carob meal, linseed. With antioxidant: EC additive.
Analysis: protein 13.5%, oils and fats 4%, fibre 10%, copper 10mg/kg

Pros: good range of ingredients, though some will be lost in rejected pellets. Inclusion of linseed.
Cons: wheatfeed, oatfeed, grass and lucerne are all high fibre, pelleted feeds aimed either at ruminant animals (cows, sheep) or those who rely on hind gut digestion strategies (like rabbits). Some pellets will be rejected entirely and others may not be well digested. Also contains artificial preservatives, fairly low copper levels and some added sugar.

Review: *"The rats love this and they get it alongside Burgess Supa Fruiti as their base mix for their Shunamite diet. It's a great alternative to other base mixes but is easily accessible at Pets At Home superstore, and is cheap to buy for smaller rat families."*(NewRat)

JOLLYES FRUITTI GUINEA PIG FOOD

Ingredients: flaked wheat, lucerne, flaked peas, carrot, whole and flaked maize, flaked beans, vitamin C pellets, tropical fruits, bananas, fruity wheat nibbles, carrot oil, yucca extract, vitamins and minerals.
Analysis: protein 16.7%, oil 4%, fibre 9.5%, copper content unavailable.

Pros: good range of ingredients including some interesting ones, all of which are palatable to rats except for the lucerne (alfalfa) pellets. Almost uncoloured (has a very few bright pink and green biscuits, which are presumably the vitamin C pellets).
Cons: contains a lot of dried fruit including apple, banana, dates, pineapple and what looks like papaya, so the sugar content is likely to be fairly. Alfalfa

pellets will most likely be wasted. Copper unknown.

A good mix to add to another rabbit or rat food, that has a variety of grains and does not contain fruit.

Review: *"I bought this, as it seemed to be the most promising feed Jollyes had in store when I went searching for rabbit food, to complete this section of the book. Out of all the samples I brought home, this was one of the feeds I would be most likely to choose to feed to my own rats, if I didn't use straights. It would be ideal to mix into another grain based feed, like PAH rat muesli. Apart from the alfalfa pellets it all looks very appetising, and I was happy to mix what I bought into my own food, something I can't say for all of the feeds I brought home! The wheat is actual little wheat flakes (the human cereal kind, not micronized flakes), and there's a lot of different fruits in there. Happily, there are hardly any brightly coloured biscuits. Well received by the rats except for the alfalfa pellets, which I picked out and used in their litter tray!"* (Alison C)

RAT FOOD

PETS AT HOME RAT MUESLI
Ovo-vegetarian recipe

Ingredients: extrusions, sugar beet pellets, egg, fructo-oligosaccharides (FOS), toasted barley flakes, toasted oat flakes, whole oats and wheat, toasted bean flakes, whole maize and toasted maize flakes, carob pods.

Analysis: moisture 12%, protein 14%, oils and fats 4%, fibre 5%, ash 4%

Pros: good variety of ingredients and egg protein source which is beneficial for kidney health. The FOS is an artificial sweetener which has the benefit of increasing bacterial fermentation in the colon, which can improve the availability and absorption of calcium, fatty acids and B vitamins (from coprophagy).

Cons: processed extrusions and pellets are primary ingredients, and the wheat extrusions contain artificial colours. Sugar beet pellets often contain both sugar and molasses and are high in fibre so nutrients may not be easily extracted.

Review: *"This food is one of the better generic mixes I've used. There are a few coloured biscuits in it which were always left by the rats and quite a lot of the seeds. However, on the whole the rats seem to like it, it leaves their fur shiny and they don't seem to gain excessive amounts of weights unlike some other generic mixes."* (Rhiannon Simms)

PETS AT HOME RAT NUGGETS

Ingredients: wheat, maize, wheat bran, chicken meal, soya, unmolassed beet pulp, poultry fat, mono-calcium phosphate, calcium carbonate, Profeed® min 0.3%; fructo-oligosaccharides (FOS), Vitamins A, D3, E
Analysis: protein 16%, fat 4.5%, fibre 3.5%, copper 24mg/kg.

Pros: great copper level. The FOS is an artificial sweetener which has the benefit of increasing bacterial fermentation in the colon, and this improves the availability and absorption of calcium, fatty acids and B vitamins (from coprophagy).
Cons: limited ingredients – two grains, one legume and chicken. The beet pulp is a high fibre filler. Uniform taste, smell and texture of pelleted food is poorly suited to rats; best used mixed into other feeds, if at all.

Reviews: *"I use this as part of my base food as it's easy to get hold of, and the rats seem to like it. I haven't seen it available in bags larger than 1kg though."* (Jenny)

"Comes in a 4kg bag too. I had a bag come with my girls that I am using in their new mix, and they eat the nuggets readily. My previous boys had this as their main diet, with home grown vegetables (I didn't know any better) and both lived to 29 and 30 months without a single trip to the vet until the end." (Shlugh)

SUPREME REGGIE RAT
Vegetarian recipe
Ingredients: wheat, maize, flaked maize, flaked peas, oats, soya, alfalfa, soya oil, locust bean, banana, vitamins and minerals, sodium chloride, coloured with EC additives, stabilisers, sodium sulphate.
Analysis: protein 14.5%, oil 3%, fibre 4%, ash 5%, copper 10mg

Pros: fair range of ingredients. Low fat. Soya as main protein source.

Cons: alfalfa is presented in a pellet and as such is often rejected by rats. Contains large amount of highly coloured extruded wheat biscuits. Fairly low copper level. Added salt!

Review: *"I am feeding some Reggie Rat at the moment and they seem to love it, minus the small seeds and larger brown pellets! I do feed additional treats and yummy vitamins along with it though just in case. Also, it's very dusty in the packet - sometimes I have to sieve it out a bit as the larger pieces are always at the top and you can be left with tiny dusty parts towards the end of the bag."* (rskemp)

SUPREME SCIENCE SELECTIVE RAT
Vegetarian recipe
Ingredients: wheat, soya, barley, oats, soya oil, apple (2.5%), blackcurrant (2.5%), limestone flour, methionine, lysine, salt, vitamins and minerals. Preserved with EC additives.
Analysis: protein 14%, fat 4%, fibre 4%, ash 5%, vitamins A, D3, E, calcium, phosphorus and copper 10mg/kg.
Methionine and lysine are essential amino acids that have been added as levels in soya are low. Interestingly methionine may actually be best kept restricted as there is some evidence that restriction extends lifespan in mouse studies.[1]

Pros: soya protein source which makes these suitable for people looking for a vegetarian feed, also may help to delay onset of kidney issues. Low fat.
Cons: limited ingredients. Copper level fairly low. Preservative may be BHT or Ethoxyquin, labelling unclear. The uniform taste, smell and texture of pelleted food is poorly suited to rats; best used mixed into other feeds, if at all.

Reviews: *"Seemed very artificial and the rats thoroughly ignored it in the mix."* (Rhiannon)

"These make up half my base food and the boys generally like them. Before I fed a version of the Shunamite type diet, this was all the boys were fed on and they had beautiful soft shiny coats and seemed very healthy so I try to keep them in my mix because of this. I find they prefer the Science Selective over the coloured pieces in the

Supa Natural, but I do give a mix of both just to stop them from becoming bored by it." (wizzyjo)

"These nuggets don't look particularly appetising, and my rats don't seem too bothered about it (although they do eat it). I use this as a small part of my base mix, as apparently the phosphorus levels are quite high, and I would expect that the sugar content is also relatively high; the packet doesn't actually tell you sugar levels which is concerning!" (Jenny)

BURGESS SUPARAT RAT ROYALE (NUGGETS)

Ingredients: wheat, maize, peas, beet pulp, soya, chicken meal, poultry fat, monocalcium phosphate, salt, fructo-oligosaccharides (FOS), methionine.
Analysis: protein 16%, oil 6%, fibre 3.5%, ash 4%, copper 12mg/kg
Methionine is an essential amino acid, which is low in soya. Interestingly it may actually be best kept restricted as there is some evidence that restriction extends lifespan in mouse studies.[1]

Pros: the FOS is an artificial sweetener which has the benefit of increasing bacterial fermentation in the colon, which can improve the availability and absorption of calcium, fatty acids and B vitamins (from coprophagy). Fair copper levels.
Cons: fat already over the RDA without including many omega 3 fatty acids and if you wanted to add seeds or fish oils the overall fat would be quite high. Limited range of ingredients. Beet pulp is a filler ingredient. Uniform taste, smell and texture of pelleted food is poorly suited to rats; best used mixed into other feeds, if at all.

LINK PREMIUM RAT

Ingredients: flaked beans, whole maize, extruded chicken meat bones, flaked maize, flaked peas, locust beans, extruded wheat sticks, grass pellets, banana, assorted tropical fruit, raisins, monkey nuts, carrot, vegetables, sunflower seeds.
Analysis: protein 14%, oil 4%, fibre 6%

Pros: nice range of ingredients, including vegetables.

Cons: low grain mix, but would make a nice addition to a high grain feed. Grass pellets are likely to be rejected. Monkey nuts and sunflower seeds can contribute to skin problems, but they are both minor ingredients here so this is unlikely to be an issue. Copper level for this feed was not readily available.

JR FARM RAT FEAST
Ingredients: maize, flaked maize, wheat, extruded cereals, oats, meat pellets, wheat flakes, locust beans, spelt, flaked peas, cracked wheat, sunflower seeds, carrot, oat clusters, vitamised oats, shrimp (1%). Added vitamins A D3 and E.
Analysis: protein 12.6 %, fat 8.1 %, fibre 4%, ash 4.5 %

Pros: good range of ingredients, including some really interesting additions like seeds, carrots and shrimps.
Cons: some listed ingredients are vague such as "extruded cereals" and "meat pellets" which makes it harder to assess the quality of the product. Again, it is not entirely clear, but the vitamins may only be added to the "vitamised oats" in which case the mix could be lacking in some nutrients (particularly vitamin D) if this ingredient is rejected by a rat. Fat content is well over the recommended requirement. Copper level for this feed was not available.

Review: "*I tried JR Farm Rat Feast the other day and the rats loved it. Very little was wasted and they took no time at all to scoff their bowl! It also smells lovely.*" (Lor x)

JR FARM RAT FOOD
Ingredients: rodent pellets, grain extrusions, vitamin pellets, wheat, meat extrusions, corn, oat, corn flakes, pea flakes, broad bean flakes.
Analysis: protein 15.1%, oil 6%, fibre 7%, ash 5.5%.

Pros: fair range of ingredients.
Cons: some listed ingredients are vague such as "grain extrusions" and "rodent pellets" which makes it harder to assess the quality of the product.

Vitamins added to a pellet, which will mean these are unavailable to any rat who rejects them. Protein on the high side for older rats and fat already over the RDA without including many omega 3 fatty acids – if you wanted to add seeds or fish oils the overall fat would be quite high. Artificially coloured extrusions are second biggest component. Copper level for this feed was not available.

VITAKRAFT EMOTION RAT BEAUTY
Vegetarian recipe
Ingredients: oat hulls, corn flakes, wheat, pea flakes, soy flakes, wheat flakes, oat flour, oat, soy grits, alfalfa meal, peanut kernels, date, carob, wheat bran, sunflower meal, corn flour, pumpkin seeds, wheat flour, molasses, red beet pulp, skimmed milk powder, cane molasses, malt sprouts, apple juice concentrate, calcium phosphate, carrot flour, calcium carbonate, vegetable oil, turmeric, wheat germ meal, aloe vera powder, artificial colouring, vitamins and minerals including iron, selenium, zinc.
Analysis: protein 13%, fat 6%, fibre 8%, vitamin A, B group, C and D. Copper not listed.

Pros: good range of grains and ingredients, although some of those listed are the ingredients for extrusions and pellets. Some attempt made at using natural colours. Range of added vitamins and minerals.
Cons: may be low in copper. Some unsuitable ingredients like alfalfa. Some pellets which may be rejected and it is unclear whether the vitamins and minerals are added to the pellets or the whole mix.

RUPERT RAT
Ingredients: wheat biscuits, chicken, cooked flaked maize, cooked flaked soya, cooked flaked peas, wheat, locust beans, cooked flaked barley, rolled oats, vitamin and mineral pellet, Vitamin A, D, E and Copper.
Analysis: protein 16%, oil 5%, fibre 5.5%, ash 5%, copper 15 mg/kg

Pros: nice range of grains and legumes. Good copper level.

Cons: highly coloured as wheat extrusions are the primary ingredient. The vitamins and minerals added in pellet form, which means any rat who rejects this ingredient will miss out on the micronutrients .

Review: *"I mainly use the Reggie Rat but as I get towards the bottom of the bag it seems that only the "boring" bits are left. I think the boring bits sink, so the best bits remain at the top and we use them all up first. So I use the Rupert Rat to mix in with the Reggie to boost up all those yummy squashed pea type flakes and the flaked maize. Rupert seems to have a lot of these type of bits in the mix and mine go for these bits first. Someone told me that Reggie is well balanced nutritionally (I don't know if that is so); I guess that's why I use that mostly and use the Rupert to keep their grub interesting."* (Blitzy)

XTRA VITAL RAT
Ingredients: cereals, vegetables, derivatives of vegetable origin (including fructo-oligosaccharide - FOS), meat and animal derivatives, oils and fats, minerals, echinacea.
Analysis: protein 14.7%, fat 5.1%, fibre 6%, copper 14 mg/kg

Pros: good copper levels. Meat is better quality than some rendered meat sources, but 'animal derivatives' is a lower quality protein source. The FOS is an artificial sweetener which has the benefit of increasing bacterial fermentation in the colon, which can improve the availability and the absorption of calcium, fatty acids and B vitamins (from coprophagy).
Cons: difficult to assess mix of ingredients as descriptions are vague. Some highly coloured extrusions and some grass type pellets included. The latter are likely to be rejected by most rats, so some waste.

Review: *"We feed Xtra Vital and they love it. The only pieces they leave are the grass like pellets. Our mums have good size litters and the kittens grow to very good sizes. Adult rats do not get overweight on it; they stay a fairly nice firm rat."* (Jess)

XTRA VITAL CARE+ RAT
Ingredients: cereals, derivatives of vegetable origin (inc yucca, echinacea and fructo-oligosaccharide - FOS), vegetable protein extracts, seeds, minerals, meat and animal derivatives, yeasts, algae (spirulina).

Analysis: protein 22.5%, fat 5%, fibre 4.5%, ash 5.1%, copper 23.3 mg/kg

Pros: excellent copper levels. Meat is better quality than some rendered meat sources, but 'animal derivatives' is lower quality protein source. The FOS is an artificial sweetener which has the benefit of increasing bacterial fermentation in the colon, which can improve the absorption of calcium and fatty acids and availability of B vitamins (from coprophagy). Algae may give some health benefits.

Cons: difficult to assess the mix of ingredients as descriptions are vague. Despite all the extrusions having the same recipe some are highly coloured, presumably to make it look more interesting to owners! The uniform taste, smell and texture of pelleted food is poorly suited to rats. Best used mixed into other feeds, if at all. Protein level is way above the amount needed for maintenance, and is more suited to levels needed to support reproduction.

WILKINSON'S RAT MIX

Ingredients: extruded wheat, torrified wheat, whole oats, grass pellets, poultry meat extrusions, whole maize, flaked maize, flaked peas, flaked beans, flaked soya beans, pellets, soya oil, vitamins A, D3, E and copper, EC permitted colorants.

Analysis: protein 15%, oil 4.5%, fibre 7%, copper 10 mg/kg

Pros: good range of ingredients, 'poultry meat' refers to higher end quality of flesh from any edible bird species.

Cons: contains two types of pellets which may be rejected by the majority of rats and it isn't clear whether the vitamins and minerals are added to the pellets. If so deficiencies would be possible. Some colorants. Copper at a fairly low level.

Review: *"The girls have had the Wilco Rat Mix before. It's quite cheap and they didn't mind it. I found it was like Reggie Rat but without the garish colours, however, there were always quite a lot of small seeds and bits left in the food dish (including those dark little tubes - I think they are grass) so this offset the cheapness of it (but the birds benefited)."* (Joanne)

ARGO RAT & MOUSE CUBES

Ingredients: cereal grains, oil seed products, fish products, vitamins A, D3, E, selenium, copper.
Analysis: protein 18%, oil 2.5%, fibre 3.25%, copper 7 mg/kg

Pros: low fat.
Cons: very vague ingredients list, therefore the overall quality is difficult to assess. The copper level is low and protein high for maintenance, but low for reproduction. Best used added to a varied mix for reproduction and growth (if at all). Uniform taste, smell and texture of pelleted food is poorly suited to rats; best used mixed into other feeds, if at all.

Review: *"I have been feeding mine on lab blocks made by Argo, for about 4 months. The rats actually love them, and for me they are very cheap (I get through 20kg a month easily). I have fit rats, some a weeny bit wider than they should be but you couldn't call any of them obese, despite being 18% protein. Coats are incredibly glossy and smooth."* (Sue)

OTHER FEEDS

DODSON AND HORRELL PASTURE MIX (horse feed)

Ingredients: oatfeed, barley, wheat, cereal straw (treated), cane molasses, maize, wheatfeed, peas, vegetable oil, dehulled soya bean meal, herbs, limestone, dicalcium phosphate, salt, carrots, linseed, full fat soya, minerals, fruits. Vitamin A, D and E.
Analysis: protein 9.5%, oil 4%, fibre 15%, copper 30mg/kg

Pros: cheap, fairly good range of ingredients. Addition of linseed oil and soya. Low protein and fat. Great copper level.
Cons: only available in large sacks. Oatfeed (which is primarily processed oat husks), cereal straw and wheatfeed (primarily bran), may be rejected by rats and if eaten, will offer little in terms of nutrition but may reduce the absorption of minerals from the diet. Molasses increases sugar content. Calcium level in this feed provides only one third of a rat's maintenance requirements and one sixth of that needed to support reproduction.

Review: *"This feed seems to work best as a basic adult feed all year round for house rats but doesn't appear to provide enough calories during the winter for rats kept outside in sheds. Not all rats will eat the pellets."* (Ann Storey)

DODSON AND HORRELL BUILD UP MIX (Horse feed)
Ingredients: barley, oatfeed, full fat soya meal, wheat, glucose syrup, grass chaff, cane molasses, unmolassed sugar beet, dehulled soya bean meal, wheatfeed, limestone flour, maize, soya oil, peas, extracted sunflower, full fat linseed, dried carrots, salt, dicalcium phosphate, vitamin/mineral premix, blackcurrant extract, curcumin, yeast, calcined magnesite, l-lysine.
Analysis: protein 13%, oil 5.5%, fibre 12%, copper 40mg/kg

Pros: Fairly good range of ingredients, with some really useful additions like the soya, linseed and curcumin. Great copper level.
Cons: various added sugars. Oatfeed (which is primarily processed oat husks), grass chaff and wheatfeed (primarily bran), may be rejected by rats and if eaten, will offer little in terms of nutrition but may reduce the absorption of minerals from the diet. Calcium level in this feed provides one third of a rat's maintenance requirements and one sixth of that needed to support reproduction.

Reviews: *"Build Up mix is quite high in calories but is a very useful feed during the winter months for rats kept in sheds. Its also useful to build up rats who have had a period of insufficient feeding, or for growing or pregnant rats."* (Ann Storey)

"The Build Up Mix by D and H is great too, I use that all the time now, and my rats seem to stay at a quite nice weight if I watch their portions." (Laura)

DODSON AND HORRELL PIG GROWER PENCILS
Representative of a range of pig pellets available.
Ingredients: wheat, wheatfeed, dehulled soya, beans, full fat soya, molasses, limestone, dicalcium phosphate, salt, supplement, lysine and methionine.
Analysis: protein 16%, oil 3%, fibre 4%

Pros: cheap, complete food so nothing is wasted. Soya based feed. Low fat.

Cons: limited ingredients. Molasses increases sugar content. Rats are not well suited to the uniformity of taste, smell and texture of complete pellets.

SMALL HOLDER RANGE - PIG STARTER PELLETS

Ingredients: >40% wheat, 10-25% wheat feed, 10-25% soya, <10% expelled soya, barley, expelled linseed, oat fibre, calcium carbonate, di-calcium phosphate, sodium chloride, vitamins and minerals.

Analysis: protein 19%, oil 6.3 %, ash 5%, copper 30mg/kg

Non GM ingredients and approved by the Vegetarian Society.

Pros: soya is primary protein source. Excellent copper content.

Cons: limited ingredients. Rats are not well suited to the uniformity of taste, smell and texture of complete pellets. High in protein for adult maintenance diet, but excellent to add to a general mix to supply protein and copper.

"With pig food the pencils/nuts/pellets/rolls tend to be the same thing basically but different sizes; the rolls are often huge, kind of like a cork, but very dense. Those designed for the birthing/weaning period also tend to be quite high in protein, and some contain fishmeal/oils and so on and the rats seem to like the fishy ones. Marriage's (organic feeds) do a cracking fish one, that I used to use." (Laura)

REFERENCES

[1]Aging Cell, Volume 4, Issue 3, Pages 119 – 125 Published Online: 13 Apr 2005
Methionine-deficient diet extends mouse lifespan, slows immune and lens aging, alters glucose, T4, IGF-I and insulin levels, and increases hepatocyte MIF levels and stress resistance
Richard A. Miller et al.

CHAPTER FIVE - OVERVIEW

Making up a dry mix
The Shunamite diet - a history
    Suebee's mix
    Alison Blyth's current diet
    Jemma Fettes' current diet
The principles of a Shunamite type mix
    Base food alternatives
    Mixing straight grains to make a base food
The current Shunamite diet - what I feed my own rats
Buying ingredients online
Examples of other mixes

Chapter five
The Shunamite diet and other mixes

MAKING UP A DRY MIX

Making up your own mix offers you control over the type and quality of the ingredients used, and can enable you to provide an interesting and varied dry diet, whilst also catering for your own rats' particular needs. Obviously this approach can lead to nutritional problems if the mix does not contain the necessary nutrients that are required by rats (and in sufficient quantity), therefore, it is not enough to simply throw some ingredients together. The information on individual nutrients found in Chapter 1, and on common deficiencies in Chapter 7, should help you in this regard.

Ingredients used in home-made mixes are as diverse as the rat lovers who swear by them, and combinations vary from the simple to the intricate. The simplest might be mixing two feeds together (often a dog food and a rabbit food, or a rat and a rabbit food) or adding human grade cereals to a commercially prepared rat food.

THE SHUNAMITE DIET - A HISTORY

Early in 2001 I began experimenting with my own rat food, always keen to improve on what was available commercially, in response to my own growing understanding of the needs of my rats. One of my first inspirations was a mix called Suebee's Diet, which had been concocted by an American rat keeper and was popular in the States at the time. I have included Suebee's Diet here because it represents my 'roots' as far as the journey into rat nutrition goes.

SUEBEE'S MIX (SUZANNE MEREDITH, USA)

Suebee's overview
"So many of the commercial rat diets out there are full of ingredients that are either inappropriate for rats, or simply aren't liked by rats. This leads to a lot of waste, and a lot of fat, unhealthy rats. For example, most mixes contain tiny seeds and alfalfa pellets that do not get eaten. Rats have a hard time digesting alfalfa, so they rarely eat it. Peanuts and other nuts, while enjoyed by rats and fine as treats, contain too

much fat and protein to be a staple part of a rat diet. In an effort to keep my rats healthy and happy, I have been working on my own homemade diet. As I learn more and more about rat nutrition, the menu changes, so this is always work in progress."

Staple diet

"I have also had a hard time getting my rats to consistently eat lab blocks, so after reading a lot of dry dog food labels, I decided to feed my rats a staple diet of Nutro's Natural Choice Lite dog food. At 14%, it has lower protein than most of the lab blocks readily available, and contains no dried corn; just lamb and rice. It also contains no preservatives, which is becoming a big issue with me. I know it is also available in Australia and the UK.

I supplement the Nutro with a homemade grain mix, detailed below. I fill the bowl each evening, at "feeding time," giving them about half Nutro and half grain mix. I have two small bowls, one for the mix and one for the Nutro. It can be mixed; I just don't have a large enough bowl for my four males right now."

Grain mix

"This is a homemade mix that I have formulated using items from my local supermarket. As often as I can, I buy from the bulk bins or the store brands. The only item I tend to splurge on is the Total cereal, because it is very nutritious, and recommended by both the Rat Fan Club and my vet.

- *½ to 1 lb dry rolled oats*
- *1 lb puffed wheat cereal*
- *1 lb puffed rice cereal*
- *1 small box Total Cereal* (AC - Total is a flaked cereal with fruit and many added vitamins and minerals that is not available in the UK. If you can't get Total you can use a small animal multivitamin and mineral powder).
- *¼ to ½ lb roasted, unsalted soya nuts. These are somewhat high in protein, but contain valuable cancer-preventing agents, so they are a good addition to the mix. If you can't find them, you can work soya into their diet in other ways, such as soya milk, tofu, and soya yoghurt.*
- *½ lb dried fruits*
- *½ lb dry pasta*
- *¼ lb sunflower seeds*
- *¼ lb muesli*

Mix everything together in a huge bowl (or divide ingredients in half and make two batches if you don't have a bowl big enough for everything -- I actually end up doing three batches!). Store in an airtight container in a cool, dry place. This makes quite a lot of mix, and will last you quite a while if you only have a few rats -- I usually don't have more than four rats, and it lasts me two months."

I liked the idea of making my own mix, but some of the ingredients that Suzanne used were not available in the UK, and I started working on my own version using foods I could readily get hold of. That work continues today and somewhere along the way people started referring to what I was feeding as the Shunamite diet. For a while this became a fixed idea in people's heads - a formula - which was something it was never intended to be. To me, diet is a living, evolving thing that has a momentum all of its own. Knowledge is not static, and no diet is suitable for all people, feeding all rats, in all situations. For these reasons I have tried to encourage people to see what I feed my own rats as *the* Shunamite diet (which changes over time) and to refer to other mixes made up according to similar principles as Shunamite-type mixes. *Ideally, the Shunamite diet should really be seen as a set of principles or an ideology, rather than a prescription.* The principles remain solid, while the ingredients of a Shunamite-type diet can be many and varied.

Over the past few years I have been influenced again by the work done by Alison Blyth and Jemma Fettes. Alison feeds a diet created entirely from scratch, using grains purchased in health food shops and supermarkets, and has compiled the extensive cereals list which you will find in Chapter 2, and Jemma has done a lot of work investigating the use of unrefined grains, seeds and legumes as a basis for a rat mix, trying to think about the rat's natural diet and how we can mimic it. I am including a copy of their current diet for information purposes, but like me, they both reserve the right to change it over time!

ALISON BLYTH'S CURRENT DIET
"I basically feed a mix of equal parts of different human grade whole and flaked grains - it can be any combination of wheat, spelt, rye, barley, buckwheat, quinoa, oats, rice and anything else I can find. I try and have at least 4 different ones in

there and preferably more. I used to put plain puffed grains in as well, but my current rats don't seem to like them much.

There's no magic formula - just a minimum of 4 or 5 plain grains, then extras like whole-wheat pasta and seeds.

I feed this in parallel with healthy fresh food - mainly fruit and vegetables, with meat or fish added a couple of times a week, and cooked carbohydrate as a treat. I've found Tesco value muesli is quite a good base - it's got 3 or 4 grains in (oats, wheat and barley, I think), a few nuts and raisins, and no added sugar etc, and it's really cheap, so I'm currently using that with other grains bought separately and added.

For oldies, I cut back on the dry mix, and feed a grain mash in parallel - so cooked rice, pearl barley, whatever I've got really - sometimes I add a splash of olive oil for taste. I haven't found this necessary for old healthy ones (Cuthbert for example is now 34 months, on a normal diet, and apparently can't be bothered with getting old), but for anyone looking a bit doddery, it seems a good way of keeping up their interest in eating. I've had several rats who were kept pootling happily about, fuelled by a cooked grain mash for months after they gave up interest in eating their dry mix."

JEMMA FETTES' CURRENT DRY MIX

"The following forms the main portion of my rats' food, alongside daily fresh vegetables and occasional other fresh foods. Please note the exact make up of each of the sections varies depending on the rats' age, sex and current condition. The percentages given are by weight and are typical, but sometimes they change as a rats needs change. The figure after each ingredient is the amount by weight (grams) per kg feed.

Minimally processed grains – 60% of mix by weight

Flaked barley	*(150)*	*Great as rats age, also good to soak*
Paddy rice	*(100)*	*Low in protein so increase with age, can be a bit small for ailing rats*
Brown rice	*(75)*	*Low in protein so increase with age, can be a bit small for ailing rats*
Bruised oats	*(75)*	*Less as rats age, especially bucks*
Flaked corn	*(50)*	*Great as rats age, also good to soak*
Flaked peas	*(50)*	*Great as rats age, also good to soak*
Whole maize	*(25)*	*Low in protein so increase with age*

Quinoa   (25)   Can be a bit small for ailing rats
Millet sprays   (25)   A nice staple for all ages
Buckwheat   (25)   A nice staple for all ages

Processed grains – 10% of mix by weight
These cereals add vitamins and minerals and are easier to digest and have fewer antinutrients. If a rat is obese I would cut this section down to a minimum and replace with more minimally processed grains, and I would add a vitamin supplement to top the diet up.

Rice flakes   (25)
Puffed rice   (25)
Shredded Wheat   (25)   Reduce as rats age due to higher phosphorous levels
Cornflakes   (25)

Vegetables and herbs – 10% of mix by weight
Note, this works out quite a bit more by volume than weight as it is quite a light weight mix.

Dried vegetables   (50)   Generally dried leak, potatoes, carrots, parsnip and
                            beetroot
Dried leaves   (20)   One of dandelion, plantain, red clover, bramble
                            leaves etc
Rabbit herb mix   (25)   Many available, vary from mix to mix
White nettle leaf/
Coneflower   (5)   Possible immune boosting properties

Pulses – 5% of mix by weight
These are normally soaked and dry roasted before adding to the mix to make the nutrients more readily available.

Dried whole peas   (15)
Chickpeas   (20)   Reduce as rats, especially bucks, age as they are
                            high in phosphorous
Lentils   (15)

Main protein sources – 10% of mix by weight
The protein sources used do vary a lot, generally kibble will always be there but the others may alternate.

Dog kibble, senior	(55)	Generally fish based, increases the copper level and good for sticking powders to.
EMP/Egg food	(5)	Good for the young and ailing, good for soakable mixes.
Dried fish	(20)	Can be good for adding low fat protein when dieting, check types. Typically tuna flakes, cubes, whole dried fish, fish skin jerky etc.
Dried shrimps/ Water bugs	(20)	Typically river shrimp, garramus shrimp and tubifex. Shrimp particularly good for copper. High in protein and moderate fat so reduce as rats age or grow too fat.
Dried insects	(20)	Typically mealworms, earthworms, crickets, blood worms. High in protein and fat so reduce as the rats age or grow too fat.
Processed soya	(20)	Typically soya chunks, flakes and roasted soya beans.

Fruit, seeds and nuts - 5% of mix by weight
This part of the diet adds the treat like elements but they are also important for the overall protein, fat and copper content for the mix.

Dried banana	(5)	Reduce as rats, especially bucks, age as they are high in phosphorous
Locust bean pieces	(5)	
Currants	(10)	High in copper
Mixed berries	(5)	Typically goji, hawthorn, juniper, mountain ash rowan berries and rose hips
Linseed	(7.5)	Particularly useful for rats with kidney disease
Hemp seed	(7.5)	Great coat conditioner
Seeds and nuts (ideally in coats/shells)	(10)	Typically pumpkin seeds, pine nuts and wild grass seeds, can use sunflower seeds and monkey nuts for youngsters

Additives and extras
There are no solid rules on this section. Generally the mix is made up with a least some garlic and seaweed added (either powdered or in dried small pieces). A general vitamin supplement (such as Vionate or Senior Aid) may be added depending on how the rats are and the overall balance of the mix. Powders are incorporated into the mix with the occasional spray of water (then stirred in), not enough to get the food wet but enough to dampen the surface. Once or twice a week each rat gets the equivalent of 1ml of oil stirred into their dry mix (typically linseed, fish or evening primrose oils), to help with overall condition. As the rats age, linseed (flax) oil becomes

particularly important to help protect the kidneys. Every mix will also have a few unique ingredients added in small quantity primarily for variety, typically broken up egg noodles, pasta pieces, broken up rice crackers, popped popcorn, water crackers or anything else that catches my eye."

THE PRINCIPLES OF THE SHUNAMITE TYPE MIX

1. Take a suitable base food.
2. Add carefully chosen human cereals (may include pasta).
3. Add a source of protein.
4. Add seeds, vegetables and herbs for variation, additional micronutrients and interest.

CHOOSING A BASE MIX (At least 60% of your mix by volume)
All diets tend to have staple foods which form a regular and substantial part of the whole. I call these base foods. Generally (for rats) base foods should be grain based and include a good proportion of minimally processed grains. My preferred choice of base food is (currently) a mixture of straight grains, which are purchased individually and then combined. I feel this gives maximum flexibility for creating a mix that is ideally adapted to the needs of the rat, and also removes the negative aspects of generic mixes. However, there are plenty of other suitable commercial alternatives many of which are reviewed in Chapter 4.

HUMAN CEREALS (15 - 20% of your mix by volume)
These are extremely useful for adding variety, reducing phosphate levels, reducing anti-nutrients (which occur naturally in unprocessed grains and prevent the nutrients from being fully utilised), and adding vitamins and minerals (many human cereals are fortified). A list of cereals, along with their suitability in terms of feeding rats, can be found on page 51. As well as human breakfast cereals, many supermarkets and health food stores have other useful human grade cereals such as straight grains, rolled grains, hulled grains (such as brown rice and buckwheat) and pasta.

SEEDS, VEGETABLES AND HERBS (10-15% of your mix by volume)
These add interest, good oils, vitamins and minerals to a mix. Hemp seeds
are very popular but many other seeds can be used as well, and some seeds
may have specific properties and benefits. Pumpkin seeds are preferable to
sunflower, which can cause allergies and skin reactions in some rats. Dried
carrots, peppers, leeks and other vegetables are generally well received.
Herbs marketed for rabbits, such as dandelion, plantain, meadow mixes
and herb mixes are excellent and I try to put some of these into my mix.
Kelp and garlic are also useful additions which may also have beneficial
qualities.

PROTEIN SOURCE (Around 10% of your mix by volume)
This can be anything from soya flakes, chick peas, peas and other legumes,
to a quality dry dog food (like Burns) or freeze dried fish and insects. The
amount you need to add will vary depending on the amount of total
protein in the ingredients you are offering. For instance you would need to
add more (weight for weight) legumes or dog kibble to deliver the same
amount of protein as dried river shrimps, but shrimps are very light, so a
greater volume would is required.

TREAT INGREDIENTS
Nuts, dried fruit and other treats can be added to a mix in very small
amounts. Some people prefer to hand feed these individually to rats.

BASE FOOD ALTERNATIVES
Many commercial mixes are suitable for base foods, or you can create your
own base food from straight grains, either from a good health food shop or
supermarket as per Alison Blyth's mix above, or from an animal feed store.
The various commercially available feeds are reviewed in Chapter 4 and you
may feel that you wish to mix more that one of these together to create your
base, in order to increase variety.

MIXING STRAIGHT GRAINS TO MAKE A BASE FOOD
Straight grains include micronized barley flakes, rolled oats, oat groats,
whole oats, paddy rice, wild rice, brown rice, whole wheat, wheat groats,

micronized wheat flakes, rye flakes, whole corn, corn grits, flaked corn (maize), buckwheat, millet, sorghum (milo/dari), quinoa and spelt. For more information on these grains and where to source them, please refer back to Chapter 2.

EXAMPLE OF A BASE FOOD MADE FROM STRAIGHT GRAINS
3 cups micronized barley flakes
1 cup rolled oats
1 cup paddy rice (in hull as sold for birds)
1 cup brown rice
1 cup wheat groats (groats are grains without the inedible chaff/husk)
1 cup whole corn,
1 cup micronized corn flakes
1 cup buckwheat (in hull as sold for birds)
2 cups mixed millet

Many other combinations are possible, but the skew towards barley, rice and corn, rather than wheat, oats and rye in the mix above is intentional and designed to promote long term kidney health as rats age. Buckwheat is not wheat, or even a true grain; it is more akin to a fruit seed, and millet is an excellent grain source and not high in fat as is often assumed. Whether you are looking for a source of pre-prepared straight mixes or the individual grains, ratRations will almost certainly have what you are looking for. Other sites such as Goodness Direct offer a good range of human grade grains.

THE CURRENT SHUNAMITE DIET
WHAT I FEED MY OWN RATS

The mix I feed varies a little each time I make it up depending on which ingredients I have available at any given time, but I always add the majority of the ingredients listed below. The mix is designed to be kidney friendly in terms of long term kidney health. I feed this mix to all residents here except when supporting reproduction (until the babies are 8 weeks old) and also in old age. Pregnant does and those with young families get this mix without soya, but with extra dry animal protein added in the form of extra shrimps, fish biscuits, fish skin jerky and dog kibble. Elderly rats have the following mix without the shrimps and oats, but with a little extra soya.

4 scoops micronized barley flakes
½ scoop pearl barley
1 scoop flaked peas
½ scoop split peas or ½ scoop soaked and roasted chick peas
1 scoop micronized soya flakes
2 scoops flaked maize
2 scoops paddy rice
½ scoop brown rice
6 broken wholegrain rice cakes
1 scoop oat groats
½ scoop whole oats
½ scoop no added sugar muesli
2 scoops mixed millet
1½ scoops buckwheat
1 scoop white milo (dari)
1 scoop Shredded Wheat Bitesize or Puffed Wheat
1 scoop Weetabix Minis
½ scoop whole wheat mini pasta shapes
6 broken sesame seed Ryvita
¾ scoop hemp seeds
½ scoop linseed
¼ scoop pumpkin seeds
¼ scoop milk thistle seeds
½ scoop flaked carrots
¼ scoop red pepper
¼ scoop dried tomato
½ scoop dried mixed vegetables
1 packets rabbit herbs (various)
¼ scoop flaked kelp
1 scoop dried river shrimps
A few chopped cranberries
A few chopped Brazil nuts

A little dried beetroot
A little dried apple

BUYING INGREDIENTS ONLINE

http://www.ratrations.com - UK rat specific shop, selling all components of my current mix except for human grade cereals and fish biscuits.
http://www.goodnessdirect.co.uk - UK human whole food store, who sell a wide variety of grains, cereals, legumes, nuts, fruit and seeds.
http://www.millbryhill.co.uk - UK feedstore selling large sacks of grains and legumes.
http://www.bunnybazaar.com - UK rabbit store with a huge selection of dried herbage, and some fruit and vegetables.
http://shop.naturesgrub.co.uk - UK shop selling a good range of freeze dried insects, small fish and water creatures.
http://www.burnspet.co.uk - Burns products.
http://www.fish4dogs.com - Fish4Dogs products.

EXAMPLES OF OTHER DRY MIXES

DINKY'S DRY MIX

"This is roughly what I feed my boys. I mostly order online and I get organics and non-added sugars cereals – they are just exactly as it says on the packet. The sites I use include Goodness Direct and Country Products.

1 scoop of each of the following:
Rye flakes
Jumbo oats
Wheat flakes
Barley grain/flakes

Half a scoop of each of the following:
Bran sticks
Millet puffs (sometimes I use 1 scoop of these)
Rice grain/flakes - brown
Pasta (I vary shapes, colours and grains)

A handful of:
Seeds - pumpkin and linseed at the moment
Fruit - raisins at the moment

That's their staple diet, dry mix. Of course they get fresh fruit and veggies every day, some nice proteins on the weekend such as eggs and so forth. They get Dr Squiggles Daily Essentials when I clean them out (twice a week) also. In terms of experiences; the boys seem to be happy with the diet, they eat most things, they are a healthy weight and so forth as far as I can tell and their immune system seems to be quite good too.

The ordering online can be a little annoying as sometimes they are out of stock, you have to wait for orders and also P&P usually amounts to as much as the actual products but it is worth keeping the rats happy and healthy in my opinion."

Mr Claw's dry mix - tested by Hall and Oates

1/3 each of: Alpha Herbal Deluxe rabbit food, Burgess Suparat Royale, Beaphar Xtra Vital rat food.

Mix of: bran flakes, rolled oats and oat bran, jumbo oats, plain cornflakes, plain puffed rice, plain puffed wheat, broken up Ryvita (dark rye and multigrain ones).

Small quantity of: soup mix - barley, split peas, lentils, etc (dried beans removed - an arduous task!), dried wholemeal pasta, dried noodles, mix of pumpkin, sunflower, hemp and flax seeds, mix of raisins, sultanas and dried banana.

Supplements: (pinch of each given twice weekly) garlic powder and Scandinavian seaweed (from The Rat Warehouse).

The rats also have treats of mealworms, Shreddies, Cheerios and yoghurt drops, plus fresh food.

Kater's mix

Ingredients: (not necessarily in order) Sneyd's Wonder Rabbit Natural Fruit, Burns Chicken and Brown Rice kibble, flaked peas, flaked carrots, puffed quinoa, whole oats, buckwheat flakes, cornflakes, millet/rice/oatbran flakes, wholegrain puffed rice, wheat grain, dried whole earthworms, wild meadow seed, prestige parrot dinner, dried coconut chips, Naturals Crunchy Tubers mix, Burgess Excel Dried Country Garden Herbs, tuna bites, garlic powder, seaweed powder.

The protein rich things like seeds and worms are just in in very small quantities for a bit of variety. A lot of the ingredients are organic too. They so eat better than us!

CYCLING FEEDS

The mixes above are just a tiny selection of the scores of unique recipes that people choose for their rats, but they are representative of the kind of mix that is possible using human grade cereals, or rat and rabbit foods as a base. There is however, another way of achieving variety that is practised by a few breeders, and that is to cycle feeds on a weekly basis. This involved choosing 4 or 5 suitable feeds and feeding each for a week or so, before swapping onto the next in rotation. The advantage of this is that it creates variety and maximises micronutrients without having to mix feeds together. I know many people (including myself), thoroughly enjoy the process of making up a dry mix for our rats, but not everyone is the same, and cycling feeds gives another option for those who prefer to feed commercial mixes, but still wish to increase variety, interest and nutrition.

If you wish to cycle feeds then try to choose a number of different types of food, with varied strengths and ingredients. Don't leave too long between cycles; a week is about right, as fairly rapid cycling prevents the weaknesses (particularly deficiencies) of any one feed from having an effect. Remember to include at least some feeds that have soya, egg, meat or fish protein sources.

"'Well,' said Pooh, 'what I like best' -- and then he had to stop and think. Because although Eating Honey was a very good thing to do, there was a moment just before you began to eat it which was better than when you were, but he didn't know what it was called"

Winnie the Pooh (AA Milne)

CHAPTER SIX - OVERVIEW

Before conception
    Diet and fertility
Pregnancy
Lactation and rapid growth
    The developmental stage
    Weeks 1-3
    The rapid growth phase
    Early influences on growth, weight and lifespan
    The maturation phase
    Tail development as a measure of nutrition
    Failure to thrive and litter runts
Supplements and useful extras
    Using Feast, EMP and CeDe
    Buying supplements online
The soya debate
    Soya and reproduction
    Soya and tumour development
    Soya and longevity
    Soya and heart disease
    Soya and bone health
    Soya and thyroid function

Chapter six
Feeding for reproduction and growth

BEFORE CONCEPTION

Breeding animals should always be at the peak of fitness and condition before mating occurs, and this requires thought to be given to the diet, particularly in the run up to conception. A good quality diet which includes a full range of vitamins and minerals is essential; a variety of grains, seeds, pulses, some animal protein and fresh vegetables will help to achieve this. However, if you are in any doubt about possible shortfalls in the diet you are feeding, now is the time to supply a comprehensive vitamin and mineral supplement. It should be noted that this will only help ensure adequate levels of micro-nutrients and it is still essential that the diet provides good levels of protein, carbohydrate and suitable fats.

DIET AND FERTILITY

A number of dietary deficiencies can affect fertility in both male and female rats and some can also affect the female's ability to sustain a pregnancy. These include deficiency of vitamin D, vitamin B_{12}, vitamin E, vitamin C, zinc, iron, copper and l-arginine (an amino acid). Reproductive capacity is also affected by being very underweight or obese, or having too much fat or too little protein in the diet.

There has been an ongoing debate over recent years about the effects of soya on the reproductive abilities of humans, but in terms of fertility the effects of a high proportion of soya in the diet is only likely to affect those who are already sub-fertile. Small amounts of soya in the overall diet should have no effect on rats of normal fertility. The soya debate is complex and is expanded later in this chapter.

PREGNANCY

Pregnancy is a period of life that makes unique nutritional demands on a female rat's body. Almost every nutrient is required in increasingly greater quantities to support healthy, developing offspring. However, it is also a time requiring balance as over nutrition (at least in terms of calories) can have a negative impact just as surely as under nutrition. Indeed both chronic under nutrition and obesity can reduce the rate of conception, the amount of milk produced and the growth rate of babies, as can a diet that is high in fat.[1]

A pregnant doe will gradually increase the amount of food that she eats in order to compensate for the requirements of pregnancy. Assuming that you are already feeding a high quality mix there is no need to change the diet greatly at this time. The main exceptions to this are to increase protein up to about 20% and ensure that she has curly kale, dandelion, broccoli or other green leafy (mineral rich) vegetable most days. However, if your mix is potentially low in any essential nutrient it is wise to take steps to ensure that you make changes at this time. Many healthy mixes will be running at maintenance levels or below for nutrients like protein, copper, selenium, calcium, phosphorus, vitamin D and vitamin B_{12}, but the demands of reproduction can exceed those of maintenance by as much as a factor of 3.[2]

Because the mix I feed is intentionally fairly low in protein I do have to modify it slightly for pregnant does. I can do this easily in one of three ways; adding a quality low fat dog kibble (which also improves copper and vitamin D content), increasing another dry protein source (such as freeze dried shrimps) or increasing the amount of fresh animal protein I feed. In practice I tend to add kibble and other dry protein sources to my mix, and also use a good multivitamin and mineral supplement (such as Dr Squiggles Daily Essentials) a few times a week. Giving a little cooked lamb's liver once a week during pregnancy can also serve to boost many micro nutrients. Freeze dried liver in the form of dog treats is also available, which can be added to your mix.

It is relatively easy to increase the nutritive quality of a rat's diet without greatly increasing the calorie content. This is important because when does become overweight they tend to have more birthing issues, as do those who grow unusually large babies in the uterus. Both issues are more likely if the calorie load of a pregnant doe's feed is greatly increased. It is sufficient to allow the doe to consume more calories by simply eating more food as the pregnancy progresses. Realistically, a pregnant doe should put on a little body fat beyond the weight of babies, placentas and fluid. This is needed during lactation to supply reserves of energy when demand is at its highest. From laboratory studies the expected weight of the placenta, fluid/sac and kitten at the time of birth are approximately 0.6g, 0.7g and 5g respectively[3], giving a combined weight of around 6.3g per kitten carried. In view of the relative size of our pet rats it is likely that this figure is slightly increased in the domestic environment, and the only example I have seen of a breeder weighing kittens at birth showed the kittens at 6g rather than 5g. Of course the problem is that we never know in advance how many kittens a doe is carrying, so the best measure of excessive weight gain will still rely on observation.

The amount of food eaten by a female rat in 24 hours will vary from rat to rat and with the type of feed used. It is also dependant on environmental factors and activity levels. As a rough guide, most pre-pregnant does will be eating around 15 to 20 grams of dry food per day, though large does may consume more. Pregnant rats will be eating about 25% more by the end of their pregnancy than they eat for maintenance taking this up to between 19 and 25 grams. Most people don't weigh out their rats' food so it's easy to just provide about a quarter more food by volume than you usually do as the pregnancy progresses. Cagemates may gain a little weight but they won't be driven to eat in the same way that the pregnant doe is, and scattering the food at this time (rather than using a food bowl) will help them maintain a normal weight. You will also be free to restrict the remaining cagemates' diet to achieve a small weight loss if needed, once the pregnant doe moves into her nursery cage.

LACTATION AND RAPID GROWTH

Everything thing that I write here refers to females left to raise full (and often large) litters. Clearly the same feeding requirements cannot apply (or at least not to the same degree), where litters are reduced in size by culling or disease. Equally, if a doe naturally has a very small litter the nutritional needs of the family will be greatly reduced. It is extremely important to adapt information to suit your own unique situation. During lactation a doe should have food available at all times, but even with ad lib feeding she will at times drop into a negative energy balance and rely on stored fat during the period of feeding her young.[2]

A newly delivered doe will generally eat all of her babies' placentas as part of the process of cleaning up after the birth. This will mean that unless the litter is tiny she will feel satiated and may eat very little else in the 24 hours following birthing. This is normal and nothing to worry about.

Lactation is by far the most nutritionally demanding activity that a rat will ever engage in, and a doe's requirements for protein, calories, phosphorus, calcium, magnesium, vitamin D, zinc and selenium (amongst other micronutrients), are increased up to three fold. The amount of food eaten is also at its highest; two to three times more than needed for maintenance. The process of lactation is driven by a feedback mechanism that works on the principle of supply and demand. Therefore, milk production gradually increases with time until it reaches a peak, usually when the babies are between 3 and 4 weeks of age, and then gradually decreases until they are fully weaned. The volume of food available to mum should be adjusted to reflect this.

Interestingly, there is some evidence that reducing protein intake for the female over the lactation period may protect her offspring against kidney disease in later life.[4] Thus, a low protein diet for the mother may have the opposite effect during pregnancy and lactation; increasing kidney problems later in life when fed during pregnancy, and protecting against them when fed during lactation. On the basis of this information it might be most beneficial (at least in terms of life-long health and longevity), to feed around 20% protein during pregnancy, drop to around 12% for the first 3 weeks and then increase to about 20-25% for growth, reducing to maintenance levels of around 12-14% at 8 to 10 weeks. However, people feed rats for many reasons, and such a pattern would undoubtedly result in slower growth and possibly even a smaller end size. It is apparent that rats whose mothers get less protein when they are lactating will go on to eat smaller quantities of food throughout their lives (even when fed ad lib), and tend to have lower body weights. While this is advantageous in terms of kidney health, it may not be the best route if you are seeking to breed towards improvement in terms of conformation and robustness, with a view to future breeding and exhibition (where this is a consideration). It is also unclear what toll this method would take on the nursing doe in terms of her own health and lifespan, therefore, such considerations are probably best remaining academic, though moderation in terms of not *overdoing* feeding in the first three weeks of lactation is definitely wise.

After delivery the development of the babies follows three well documented stages.
1. Developmental stage (0 to 3 weeks)
2. Rapid growth phase (3 to 10 weeks)
3. Maturation phase 10 weeks onwards, ending around 10 to 12 months.
The growth rate over these three stages can be represented by a sigmoidal curve, where growth is slower to begin with, increases steeply then slows down again.

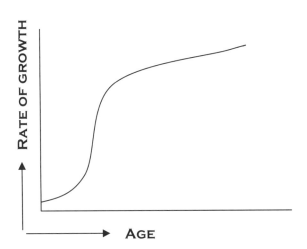

THE DEVELOPMENTAL STAGE
During the developmental stage the main food for the babies is the mother rat's milk, and although from 2-3 weeks of age the babies will begin to eat

solid food, the main considerations for feeding at this time are the needs of the doe. Indeed, there is no food that you can provide that will meet the babies' needs better than rat milk at this stage. The *average* composition of rat milk is:
- protein 12%;
- fat 15%;
- carbohydrate 3%;
- ash 1.5%.

WEEKS 1 TO 3

Lactation increases the appetite and food consumption of the doe by up to three times on maintenance amounts. A good proportion of this should be provided by a quality grain mix that includes seeds and legumes, plus some additional protein sources (such as dog kibble and dried shrimps). Fresh food can be used to add nutrients and should generally be protein rich and not just high in calories. However, many rats do prefer protein foods mixed in with some kind of carbohydrate base. Combinations that we have found particularly successful include:
- Brown rice and egg.
- Couscous and Dr Squiggles Insectivorous Feast.
- Chick peas and mackerel in tomato sauce.
- Liver cake (recipe page 285).
- Butter beans and tuna.
- Whole grain bread and Lactol (puppy milk).

Chicken wings/drumsticks and scrambled egg are generally well received on their own.

Daily mixed fresh vegetables, including some dark green leafy varieties should also be provided. Green leafy vegetables provide a readily accessible and balanced form of calcium and phosphorus to a rat - essential for milk production. In terms of calcium, kale has 205mg/100g, dandelion 187mg/100g, spring greens 145mg/100g, pak choi 105mg/100g and broccoli 88mg/100g.

I also add the following supplements to the diet on a regular basis:
- Calcivet (at least every other day)
- Dr Squiggles Daily Essentials or Tiny Animal Essentials (most days)
- Dr Squiggles BioPlus (most days)
- Salmon oil (most days)
- Seaweed powder (most days)

Complan is useful, particularly when supporting does with large litters, as it contains a good range of vitamins and minerals as well as protein, fat and carbohydrate. It is easy to mix into a variety of wet foods. It does, however, contain 40% sugar so don't overdo it! Further information on supplements that are useful in supporting reproduction can be found on page 139.

EXTRA PROTEIN SOURCES (DRY)
Burns dog kibble
James Wellbeloved dog kibble
Fish4Dogs Sea Jerky Tiddlers and Sea Biscuits Tiddlers
Fish4Dogs Finest Salmon small bite complete dog kibble
Dried river shrimps
Dried fish
Dried locusts
Freeze dried liver
Freeze dried insects

BUYING PROTEIN SOURCES ONLINE
http://www.burnspet.co.uk - Burns products.
http://www.wellbeloved.com - James Wellbeloved products.
http://www.fish4dogs.com - Fish4Dogs products.
http://www.ratrations.com - Freeze dried animal protein sources.
http://shop.naturesgrub.co.uk - Freeze dried animal protein sources.

THE RAPID GROWTH PHASE
During the beginning of this phase (from about 3 to 5 weeks) the doe is still feeding the babies, though they will be eating an ever increasing amount of solid food. Baby rats are generally fully weaned between about 4.5 and 6

weeks.

As the name suggests, growth for the babies over this period is fast and requires a lot of nutrients, particularly protein and micronutrients. Muscle increases over this time period by around 30% and bones grow significantly too.[5] The nutrition needed to maintain this growth is similar to that needed by the mother rat to support lactation at this point so the whole family need a good quantity of protein rich foods, with extra vitamins and minerals, notably calcium, phosphorus, Vitamin D, selenium and iron.[6]

At the beginning of this stage I generally work on about 50% of the diet being the dry grain-based mix and 50% being fresh foods, including daily protein foods and green leafy vegetables. By about 8 weeks old, I begin to reduce the fresh element of the diet until, by the end of the rapid growth phase at 10 weeks, the babies are more or less onto adult rations. Usually by 8 weeks, our babies have joined their life-long, mixed-age groups, so I tend to feed kidney friendly fresh food for the last couple of weeks. Eggy rice and Naturediet make up the bulk of the extra protein given here for those final weeks before they move onto adult diet.

EARLY INFLUENCES - GROWTH, WEIGHT AND LIFESPAN

One of the large influences on obesity in rats is overfeeding in kitten-hood and on through to early adulthood. Rats as a species seem to be well adapted to being underfed and poorly adapted to over-feeding. The only stage of life when under-nutrition (particularly a low protein diet; around 10%) is known to shorten a rat's life is during the prenatal and postnatal period up to about 8 weeks. This is because a lack of protein during the rapid growth phase can produce lifelong disturbances in metabolism[7], and low protein maternal diets, especially during pregnancy can increase the likelihood of kidney disease in adulthood.[8] Experimental diets that restrict calories over the rapid growth phase have resulted in shorter lifespan, while the same diets extend lifespan if fed from the beginning of the maturation phase onwards. This subject is expanded in Chapter 7.

When breeders began to raise full litters as a matter of course, we quickly realised that we had to increase the quality and quantity of food given to our larger litters, if we wanted to produce robust, healthy babies. The last few years have been a steep learning curve and I think it is now agreed that feeding at this stage can be overdone, as well as underdone. Many of us have, for periods, overfed our babies, who have then grown into chubby teenagers and overweight adults. This is because early overfeeding can permanently alter aspects of fat metabolism, resulting in fatter adult rats.[9]

During pregnancy and for the first few weeks of life it is essential for the well-being of both mother and babies, that the nutrition provided keeps up with the nutrition required. Failing to do this may result in weakened, fine boned kittens, with thin, square tails, and underweight mothers who have raided their own bodies to supply the demands of their offspring. However, overfeeding will result in plump babies, with a predisposition to obesity. Like most other things in life, this is a skill that needs to be learned and perfected. It is perhaps most important to realise that requirements at this time are for extra protein, calories and micronutrients, but not for extra fat. Therefore, low fat protein options are ideal for providing the majority of the extra protein needed. Carbohydrates and protein should provide most of the extra calories required.

Volumes of food needed for growth (per fully weaned baby) are roughly the same as volumes that are needed per adult for maintenance, but nutrient requirements are higher. This means that the food given must be nutrient dense in order to meet the rapidly growing kitten's needs. Wherever fresh (wet) food replaces dry food, volumes need to be increased since much of the content of fresh food is water.

A vegetarian diet will readily support reproduction and rapid growth so long as adequate egg and milk protein is given.

FRESH FOODS FOR THE RAPID GROWTH PERIOD
- Kale, spring greens or young dandelion leaves.
- Broccoli.
- Carrot.

- Chicken - whole wings and drumsticks provide the higher protein flesh and the benefits of mineral rich bones to chew on.
- Egg - scrambled or boiled and chopped; mixed (before cooking) into porridge; mixed into cooked rice and then microwaved; soaked into wholemeal bread and cooked in a touch of olive oil.
- Fish - raw, cooked or tinned (lowest salt) mixed into a little cooked carbohydrate.
- Fish4Dogs salmon mousse.
- Lactol - bottled, over wholemeal bread or in porridge.
- Complan - mixed into other food such as EMP.
- Insectivorous Feast or EMP made up with Lactol into a mash, mixed into scrambled egg or couscous.
- Naturediet moist puppy food.
- Applaws or Natures:menu cat food.
- Legumes (chick peas, butter beans, peas) - soaked and cooked, tinned or sprouted.
- Banana.
- Avocado pear.
- Coconut milk.
- Mash made with Vitalin Original dog food.

Complan, coconut milk and other high fat (or calorie) options are only needed if the doe is really struggling to maintain normal weight.

THE MATURATION PHASE

During this phase, which lasts from 10 weeks to approximately 10 months rats continue to grow, but at a slower rate. The rate of growth is not consistent, and there are a number of growth spurts when changes over a period of weeks are very noticeable. From the perspective of feeding, this phase should be treated as maintenance, and a good quality dry mix plus fresh vegetables will be make up the diet for the majority of rats. A vegan or vegetarian diet will also support growth at this stage. Slow growth into adulthood is more beneficial to long term health than always feeding to maximum growth capacity. Underfeeding on the quantities that would be taken if fed 'ad-lib' (by around 20%) can achieve this and help to maximise longevity.

TAIL DEVELOPMENT AS A MEASURE OF NUTRITION

It is not fully understood exactly how tail development reflects nutritional status but I am convinced that it does. Even the meaty tails of large stud bucks sometimes become wasted and square in the decline of illness and old age. Underfed kittens seem to have square tails, while well fed kittens going through a steep growth spurt sometimes get a squarish edge to their tails, that soon reverts to full roundness as they slow down into adulthood. I am convinced that tails can be a good overall indicator of the nutritional status of a rat throughout its life and can be 'read' by the experienced breeder. Slight under nutrition during a growth spurt will result in a small degree of squaring around the base of the tail. This will soon round out when the growth slows again.

FAILURE TO THRIVE AND LITTER RUNTS

Sometimes one or more babies in a litter are either born small or fail to grow at the same rate at their siblings. Occasionally a larger proportion (or all) of a litter may be born runty, dead, dying or die within days of birth. The most usual cause for this is infection of the reproductive tract of the doe, and a number of microorganisms can cause this including Parvovirus, Mycoplasma or Pasteurella.[10]

True runts are those who are born very small in comparison to their siblings, usually because for some reason their nutrition in the womb was suboptimal. The most likely reason for this is placental insufficiency, where the placenta is small or unhealthy and does not adequately meet the foetus' nutritional needs. These babies have nothing physically wrong with them, they are simply malnourished. If they receive adequate nutrition after birth, they will rapidly catch up until they are of a similar size to the rest of the litter. However, it is possible that they will have been affected by their early malnutrition leading to an overall reduction in life expectancy.[7,8]

It is probably best not to try to supplement these babies by hand-feeding milk substitutes. There is no milk replacement that is anywhere near as good for rats as rat milk, and what the runt needs is to feed freely from his or her own mother. Where competition makes this difficult due to the number of babies in the litter, the best means of supporting the runt is to remove the largest babies for short periods; no more than an hour or so. You may need to do this where the litter size is over 12, as rats have 12 nipples, but do check that all are enlarged and functional, as occasionally not all of the nipples will be lactating. Make sure that you only remove the bigger babies after they have fed (take the litter down to 8-10 kittens left in the nest), and keep the others warm, for example, covered loosely in a fleecy material in a shoe box, kept in a comfortably warm room. Do not overheat them as this is far more likely to cause problems than them getting a little cool. You can do this two or three times a day as required. However, many runts hold their own - even in big litters - and such interventions are not necessary.

Rarely, kittens are born with a congenital abnormality that causes them to fail to thrive (grow at a normal rate), though the abnormality is not always obvious. Some of these issues will be incompatible with life and these kittens will generally fail to grow normally and die within the first few weeks. Sometimes the problem is less severe and can result in long term stunted growth and a frail constitution.

SUPPLEMENTS AND USEFUL EXTRAS

There are a number of supplements that are useful for supporting growing families. Some of these are:
- **DR SQUIGGLES CALCIVET** - a readily absorbed saturated liquid calcium and magnesium supplement, with vitamin D. Indispensible in supporting lactation, as it would be extremely difficult to supply calcium needs from diet alone at this time. When Calcivet (and other similar products) are used daily, the normal physiological system of moving calcium in and out of bones to supply demand becomes disrupted. This can cause a poverty of available calcium when the supplement is stopped. Use up to 5 times a week to support reproduction.

- **Seaweed powder** - excellent source of iodine, which benefits fertility, muscle, bone and tooth formation, coat and skin condition.
- **Dr Squiggles Daily Essentials or Tiny Animals Essentials** - general multivitamin/mineral supplements which are fairly comprehensive but do not contain calcium. Daily Essentials is added to drinking water and Tiny Animals Essentials is a powder which is sprinkled over 'wet' food. Both seem entirely palatable to rats.
- **Lactol** - puppy/kitten milk replacement. Make it up to the kitten specification for young rats, and dilute further if you want a lower concentration of calories and nutrients. Ingredients: whey powder, vitamin A, vitamin B_1, vitamin B_2, nicotinic acid, pantothenic acid, choline, lysine, methionine, selenium.
- **Salmon oil** - great source of essential fatty acids. Will also contain some vitamin D and vitamin A.
- **Brazil nuts** - included here as a supplement to support growth and reproduction because they are an outstanding source of selenium, and requirements for this micro-mineral are greatly increased at this time. A few chopped nuts added to each kg of feed will greatly help to supply the does selenium needs.
- **Dr Squiggles Insectiverous Feast** - a crumb based egg food, marketed for conditioning birds. Ingredients: niger seed, freeze dried vegetables, egg protein, cereal derivatives, vitamins A, D3, E, B1 (thiamine), B2 (riboflavin), B6 (pyridoxine), B12, biotin, choline bitartrate, folic acid, niacin, pantothenic acid. Minerals including selenium, iron, cobalt, manganese, copper, magnesium, zinc, sulphur and iodine. Comprehensive range of limiting amino acids including methionine and lysine, kelp extract, daphnia, insect larvae, waterflies, gammarus (shrimp) and conches. It is 23% protein.
- **EMP/CeDe** - these are somewhat narrower variations on the egg food theme and are generally egg biscuit crumb and seed mixes, often with a range of added vitamins and minerals.

Using Feast, EMP and CeDe

Supplied as a dry crumb and seed mix (though Feast is pre-moistened), these products are generally wet down before feeding to rats. Depending on the fat and protein requirements of the rats, they can be made in different ways. To maximize calorific and protein content when feeding to nursing does and young kittens, make up to a soft crumbly mix or sloppy porridge with Lactol. For older kittens, use cows, goats, soya, or rice milk. Great for adding to rattie baking, though moisten before you do so.

SUGGESTED ADDITIONS TO FEAST, EMP AND CEDE
- Grated fruit or vegetables (apple, carrot, pear).
- Peas and/or sweetcorn.
- Tinned fish including bones, which will boost calcium intake.
- Beat through a raw egg and then microwave to make a 'cake'.

BUYING SUPPLEMENTS ONLINE
http://www.ratwarehouse.com - A variety of rattie supplements along with helpful advice about what is best for your particular situation.
http://www.birdcareco.com - Dr Squiggles products, full range and larger sizes.
http://www.ratrations.com - A range of useful supplements and egg based biscuits mixtures.

THE SOYA DEBATE

Since the negative aspects of feeding a soya rich diet are primarily related to reproduction, I have decided to include a discussion of the pros and cons of feeding soya in this chapter. Soya is an oilseed, which is around 40% protein and 20% fat. The protein is readily digested and absorbed, and contains all of the essential amino acids, although methionine and cysteine are only present in small amounts. Soya also contains a number of antinutrients (discussed in Chapter 13) and the isoflavones (genistein and daidzein), which are converted by bacteria in the digestive system into a mild oestrogen. These phytoestrogens have antioxidant properties (that is, they help prevent cellular damage and boost immunity).

For many years the debate has continued about the benefits and drawbacks of feeding soya, and to be honest the more research is published, the more complicated the issues seem to become. I have no real wisdom about whether it is better to feed soya to rats or not. Personally, I think overall some soya in a mixed diet may be beneficial, especially in terms of kidney health and tumour prevention, but I feel everyone needs to make up their own mind so I will aim just to present some of the research findings.

SOYA AND REPRODUCTION
If you feed a mix with soya flakes in it you may wish to withhold these for a few weeks before conception and throughout pregnancy and lactation. There is evidence to suggest that feeding rats a diet which contain high doses of soya extracted phytoestrogens (50 to 1,000 times human intake level for body weight) affects their growth and the development of their reproductive organs.[11] Note that this is not feeding roasted or micronized soya beans as a small part of the diet, but rather an extract made from the concentrated plant hormones. There is, however, evidence to suggest that *high* dietary soya intake is associated with lowered sperm production in humans, but not with changes in sperm motility, or physical makeup. [12]

Feeding genistein during pregnancy and lactation has been shown to have a positive effect on the male rats' immune system and a negative effect on their reproductive system. Both effects are seen to a degree at both low and high doses, though the effect on the immune system was greater at the higher dose. The changes in the immune system explain the positive effects of genistein in reducing the occurrence of cancer, but more research is needed to know whether the ability to fight infection and auto-immune disease is also improved. In males, testosterone levels are reduced, testicular size may be decreased, maturity delayed and mating behaviour decreased. [13]

SOYA AND TUMOUR GROWTH
It seems to be accepted that the antioxidant in soya - genistein - provides some protection against some cancers (mammary, prostate and uterine), and can also slow tumour growth by reducing the rate of the abnormal growth of the blood vessels that feed them. [14] However, conflicting studies show that some hormonally driven tumours seem to be stimulated by dietary soya, and humans are advised not to have high soya diets (e.g. large

quantities of soya at every meal or isoflavone supplements) when they are diagnosed with cancer as these *may* exacerbate some tumours, particularly some mammary cancers. To add to the confusion, there are studies which show that phytoestrogens help to reduce high levels of oestrogen within the body and thus reduce risk of tumours that are driven by oestrogen. It is an ongoing debate and one that requires more definitive research. Pancreatic tumours can be induced in rats by giving a high volume of raw soya flour, but tumours only developed at these high doses.

SOYA AND LONGEVITY

It has been shown that soya has a protective effect against the development of kidney disease in rats, when used as the main source of dietary protein over some animal sources. Cases of end stage (terminal) kidney disease fell from 41% at time of spontaneous death on a casein (milk protein) based diet, to just 7% when soya was the protein element of the diet. The average (median) age at death of the casein diet was 730 days in comparison to 844 days on the soya, a difference of nearly 4 months.[15]

This seems to be a well accepted aspect of soya consumption and The American Association of Kidney Patients actually recommends soya protein as being useful in helping to control the rate of deterioration of chronic kidney disease.[16] Since almost all aging rats have a degree of kidney failure this is an important consideration for longevity. The effects are more striking in male rats because they tend to be more prone to the disease at an earlier age.

SOYA AND HEART DISEASE

Many research studies have shown an association between soya intake and a reduction in cholesterol, however the mechanism for why this occurs is not clearly understood. It is thought to be linked to the isoflavones. Since rats are not particularly prone to heart disease (except for heart failure that is secondary to chronic respiratory illness), this should really be considered to be a minor benefit.

SOYA AND BONE HEALTH

Lower doses of genistein, similar to those found in a mixed diet that includes some soya have been shown to reduce decalcification of bones in a similar way to oestrogen. However, at higher doses (supplementation levels) this effect might be reversed.[17]

SOYA AND THYROID FUNCTION

Soya isoflavones have been shown to reduce thyroid function in some individuals, whilst some soya products have been linked to increased thyroid function. The effects are not thought to be of particular importance unless thyroid stimulating medication is being given, when soya may interfere with its efficacy. High dietary iodine intake (seaweed provides this) has been shown to protect against any negative effect on the thyroid gland.

REFERENCES

[1]The Journal of Nutrition Vol. 128 No. 2 February 1998, pp. 390S-393S
Effects of Under- and Over-nutrition on Lactation in Laboratory Rats
Kathleen Maher Rasmussen
[2]Nutrient Requirements of Laboratory Animals, Fourth Revised Edition, 1995
[3]Biology of Reproduction, http://www.biolreprod.org
Placental and Fetal Growth and Development in Late Rat Gestation Is Dependent on Adrenomedullin
Andrea G. Witlin et al.
[4]BMC Nephrology 2006 Volume 7
Suckling a protein-restricted rat dam leads to diminished albuminuria in her male offspring in adult life: a longitudinal study
Clive J Petry
[5]Journal of Histochemistry and Cytochemistry, Vol. 50, 1097-1111, August 2002
New Fiber Formation in the Interstitial Spaces of Rat Skeletal Muscle During Postnatal Growth
Tetsuro Tamaki et al
[6]Journal of Nutrition 110: 1573-1580, 1980
Effect of Vitamin D Deficiency on Fertility and Reproductive Capacity in the Female Rat
Bernard P. Halloran and Hector F. Deluca
[7]International Journal Biological Science. 2008; 4(6): 422–432.

Post-Weaning Protein Malnutrition in the Rat Produces Short and Long Term Metabolic Impairment, in Contrast to Earlier and Later Periods
María del Carmen Miñana-Solis, Caolina Escobar
[8]British Journal of Nutrition. 2000 Jan; 83(1):79-85.
Evidence of progressive deterioration of renal function in rats exposed to a maternal low-protein diet in utero.
Nwagwu MO, Cook A, Langley-Evans SC.
[9]Paediatric Research November 2000 - Volume 48 - Issue 5
Perinatal Feedings Adversely Affect Lipogenic Activities but Not Glucose Handling in Adult Rats
Balonan, Lino C.; Sheng, Hwai-ping
[10]http://www.nfrs.org/parvo.htm

Soya references

[11]Biomedical and Environmental Sciences 21, 197-204 (2008)
Developmental and Reproductive Toxicity of Soybean Isoflavones to Immature SD Rats
Lei Guan, Yu Huang, Zhen-Yu Chen
[12]Human reproduction, July 2008
Soy food and isoflavone intake in relation to semen quality parameters among men from an infertility clinic
Jorge E. Chavarro et al
[13]Molecular Medicine 8(11): 742–749, 2002
Early Exposure to Genistein Exerts Long-Lasting Effects on the Endocrine and Immune Systems in Rats
Sabra L. Klein, Amy B. Wisniewski et al
[14]Proceedings of the Soc. of Exp. Biology and Medicine. 1995 Jan;208(1):124-30.
Antioxidant and antipromotional effects of the soybean isoflavone genistein.
Wei H, Bowen R, Cai Q, Barnes S, Wang Y.
[15]Journal of Gerontology. 1988 Jan;43(1):B5-12.
The influence of dietary protein source on longevity and age-related disease processes of Fischer rats.
Iwasaki K, Gleiser CA, Masoro EJ, McMahan CA, Seo EJ, Yu BP.
[16]http://www.aakp.org/aakp-library/Soy-Option
[17]Proceedings of the Society of Experimental Biology and Medicine. 1998 Mar; 217 (3): 345-50
Biphasic effects of genistein on bone tissue in the ovariectomized, lactating rat model.
Anderson, J J, Ambrose, W W, Garner, S C

CHAPTER SEVEN - OVERVIEW

Feeding to maximise health
    Basic rations - feeding to sustain life
Deficiencies in rat diet
    Essential amino acids
    Essential fatty acids
    Vitamin B_{12}
    Vitamin D
    Calcium
    Copper
    Selenium
Beyond basic rations - feeding for health
    Phytochemicals explained
    How do phytochemicals promote health?
Boosting the immune system
    Superfoods for rats
    Immune system boosting diet
Calories and lifespan
    Feeding for longevity
Other influences on lifespan
Feeding elderly rats
    Supplements that may help older rats
    Buying supplements online
Feeding a soft diet
    Making grains and seeds easier to eat
    Sprouting whole grains, seeds and legumes
    Suggestions for soft food diets
    Example diet plan

Chapter seven
Feeding for longevity, well-being and in old age

FEEDING TO MAXIMISE HEALTH

Many aspects of diet can have an influence over health and physical well being, and certain illnesses have also been linked to particular dietary trends. The most important aspect of any rat diet is that it is varied enough to be able to provide all of the necessary nutrients for life and health. Diets that are lacking in essential amino acids, essential fatty acids, vitamins and minerals are unable to support immune system (and general) health. As well as these essential nutrients, there are many edible plants that contain phytochemicals, such as carotenoids, flavonoids and phytates all of which, though not thought to be essential to life, have properties that may protect against aging and disease.

BASIC RATIONS
FEEDING TO SUSTAIN LIFE

Health is not just the absence of obvious disease, but also the presence of robust defences against disease, and a state of physical and mental well-being. Many diets contain sufficient nutrients to sustain life, but may still contain deficiencies that leave a rat in sub-optimal health.

When weighing up the pros and cons of any rat diet, it is important to note that the diet may be sufficient to sustain life at a basic level, while still being deficient in essential nutrients; this will eventually lead to malnutrition. A malnourished rat won't necessarily appear underweight, but growth may be affected and condition will be lacking. Deficiencies may also lead to specific signs such as pale ears, toes and gums (anaemia), patchy coat colour or susceptibility to infection.

A diet may also provide adequate nutrition, without necessarily promoting positive health benefits and peak condition. A rat fed on this kind of diet will be well nourished, but may lack condition and may be more prone to health issues such as infection, mammary tumours and kidney disease.

It is also vital to realise that it is not only commercial mixes that may be lacking. Indeed, home made straight grain diets are actually more likely to be deficient *unless* they are well planned, varied and supplemented, as all commercial mixes have at least some micronutrients added separately in the form of vitamins and minerals. Straight grains alone are not enough to provide a rat with optimal nutrition, and such a diet would be likely to lack a variety of key nutrients.

DEFICIENCIES IN RAT DIETS

Because of the nature of a rat's grain based diet there are some deficiencies that are more likely to occur than others and we will consider each of these in turn. Certain feeding trends like an all straight grain mix, soft food diet, vegetarian or vegan diet may make certain deficiencies more likely and I will try to refer to these where appropriate.

ESSENTIAL AMINO ACIDS (PROTEIN)

These will generally only become deficient when demand increases and outstrips supply. This can happen when a maintenance diet is used to support reproduction or rapid growth, and can also be a risk with some vegetarian and (particularly) vegan diets, especially at times of greater demand for nutrients, such as, during illness, reproduction or rapid growth. Symptoms of protein deficiency include reduced growth, poor appetite, lack of coat quality, infertility, muscle wasting, susceptibility to infection and mild anaemia.

Amino acids are required for maintenance, reproduction and growth, as every cell in a rat's body needs them both to develop and to carry out a myriad of essential functions. Some amino acids cannot be made within the body and *must* be consumed in the diet; these are called essential amino acids. Animal sources contain all of these in good amounts, while plant sources (even those that contain at least some of all of the essential amino acids) tend to be deficient in at least one of them. The essential amino acid that occurs at the lowest level in a particular plant is called the limiting amino acid, and it is only through combining plant sources with different amino acids, that the complete set are provided in meaningful amounts.

Imagine each essential amino acid as a different coloured Lego brick. To make a particular protein there will be a unique pattern of different colours joined together in a specific way, to create the final pattern (protein). If one colour is missing the final pattern cannot be made. Not all proteins use all amino acids, or in the same amounts, but it is easy to see how deficiencies can occur if the diet is low in a number of essential amino acids. While a vegetarian or vegan diet containing some soya is likely to be *sufficient for maintenance*, it may struggle to supply the increased demands of pregnancy, lactation and rapid growth. This should not be a problem for people who feed their rats a vegetarian diet that includes egg and/or milk protein, as given regularly these should easily make up the deficit. However, vegan rats are unlikely to fare so well and this seems to be borne out by research.[1] The available laboratory research is not without its flaws - such as the lack of varied fresh vegetables and supplements provided - so the rats may not have grown as well for reasons other than just protein deficiency.

ESSENTIAL FATTY ACIDS

Fats are awkward nutrients as you can eat a lot of them and still be left with imbalance, and without the benefits of 'good' fats. Essential fatty acids are those that can't be made within the body and they fall into two groups; omega-3 and omega-6. Both are needed in the diet because the body cannot convert one to the other. They are sometimes called polyunsaturated fats and are primarily the fatty acids alpha-linolenic acid (omega-3) and linoleic acid (omega-6), though some researchers suggest that there are other fatty acids that may be essential under specific conditions. Many rat diets rely heavily on omega-6 fatty acids and may be deficient in omega-3.

Saturated fats - primarily animal fats and those that remain solid at room temperature - are not essential and are often considered to have a negative impact on health, being linked (in humans at least) to heart disease, strokes and some cancers. The evidence for this is by no means solid and some diets that are high in saturated fat and very low in carbohydrate, have been shown to actually reduce cholesterol levels and blood pressure. It is likely that future research will continue to investigate and clarify the facts about saturated fat.[2] None the less, research involving rats has at the very least shown an increase in tumours and blood pressure in rats who have higher levels of saturated and/or polyunsaturated fat in their diet.[3,4] This increase in tumour development is seen as a result of overall fat consumption, and diets that contain either a combination of saturated and unsaturated fats, or high levels of polyunsaturated fats alone seem to have the greatest negative impact. Coconut fat is saturated, but may actually be beneficial, primarily due to the presence of lauric acid (a fatty acid thought to help support immune system health), but the evidence remains inconclusive.

A high intake of *any* fat will increase the risk of obesity and any associated diseases, and mammary tumours are generally more common in overweight rats or those on a higher fat diet.[5] This is because mammary tumours are driven by a high prolactin to oestrogen ratio, and ongoing high fat intake raises prolactin levels, resulting in an increased prolactin to oestrogen ratio.

Rats actually need very little fat (around 5% of the overall diet), and there is not thought to be an increased requirement to support reproduction or growth. Diets that are deficient in overall fat are rare, but deficiencies in essential fatty acids (primarily omega-3) may be seen where primarily meat (not fish) sources of fat are used. These deficiencies can result in slow and disrupted growth, skin lesions and poor coat condition. All symptoms will quickly respond to foods rich in essential fatty acids.

These include:
- Omega-3 - flax seed/oil, oily fish flesh/salmon oil, hemp seed, walnut, soya, fish liver oil.
- Omega-6 - nuts, soya, sesame seed, hemp seed, pumpkin seed, egg, meat.

However, rats are far more likely to suffer the negative effects of too much fat, than too little.

VITAMIN B$_{12}$

Vitamin B$_{12}$ is necessary for all of the metabolic processes that occur in body cells. It works closely with (and can be replaced to some extent by) folate (folic acid). At levels just below maintenance, signs of deficiency start to occur and would present as a generalised malaise, with reduced energy levels. Serious deficiency results in pernicious anaemia, a type of anaemia displaying neurological signs and intestinal problems. Not all signs will be present in every case.

I have included this vitamin because the main dietary sources are animal products, and it is therefore often raised as an issue for vegetarian or vegan rats. However, vitamin B_{12} is synthesized in useful amounts by bacteria found in the intestines, regardless of the quantity that is consumed in food. A significant amount of the synthesized B_{12} is passed out in the faeces, and because rats practice coprophagy (eating their faeces) they are very unlikely to ever become deficient.[6] However, rats who have litter trays that are changed frequently may be at risk of deficiency, as might any rat as they get older (as absorption from the gut is decreased). Because of the possibility of age-related deficiency, and the concurrent increase in the requirement for B group vitamins as rats age (as these may help delay a number of disease processes), many people supplement B group vitamins for elderly rats. Products such as Senior Aid are designed to support elderly animals and include a number of B group vitamins, including B_{12}.

Adding legumes, fortified human cereals, and leafy vegetables to a rat's diet supplies folate/folic acid, and this can also replace Vitamin B_{12} in many (but not all) body processes. Yeast extract (Marmite) contains both folic acid and Vitamin B_{12} and could be usefully added to rat scones or fresh food after being liquefied in a little warm water. Daily Essentials and Nutrical contain vitamin B_{12}.

VITAMIN D
Dietary sources of vitamin D are limited, namely eggs, oily fish and liver, plus a number of fortified foods which occasionally include some breakfast cereals. This vitamin is added to all commercially prepared rat and rabbit mixes.

There is no vitamin D in straight grains, seeds or vegetables and it is likely that rats fed on straight grain based, vegetarian and vegan mixes will need supplementation. A rat's requirement for vitamin D is equivalent to 1,000

IU/kg feed. Assuming an individual's intake to be between 20 and 30 grams per day this equates to 20 to 30 IU (0.5 to 0.75 micrograms) daily. Salmon flesh oil and cod liver oil are rich sources of vitamin D, but both naturally contain high levels of vitamin A as well.

In terms of international units the ratio of vitamin A to vitamin D required by rats is approximately 2.5:1, while for humans it is approximately 10:1, meaning that rats require proportionately less vitamin A in their diet. Presumably this is because humans manufacture a significant amount of vitamin D from exposure to sunlight, while our rats do not.

In salmon oil the ratio is about 6:1 and in cod liver oil and most human supplements, around 10:1. Because of this vitamin A toxicity is a possibility when using supplements, (problems begin to occur in humans at around twice the recommended dietary allowance of vitamin A), and it might be preferable to look for products that contain only vitamin D, to bring the ratio into a more favourable balance for our rats. The affects of vitamin A toxicity include loss of body weight, weakened bones and toxicity of the liver and kidneys, causing damage and disturbed function.[7]

SOURCES OF VITAMIN D
To provide the average rat with its daily requirement for vitamin D, the following quantities of foods would be needed:
- eggs - one and a half daily per rat, or
- mackerel - 8g, or
- salmon flesh - 3g, or
- beef liver - 50g

It's easy to see how a rat can easily become depleted if vitamin D is not supplemented!

PROS AND CONS OF METHODS OF SUPPLEMENTATION
FISH FLESH OIL - these oils tend to have variable amounts of vitamin D and A in them, depending on quality and source. Salmon flesh has the highest naturally occurring levels of vitamin D, however, if you use salmon oil produced for the pet market you may find the manufacturers do not list

vitamin content. I contacted both Salmopet and Fish4Dogs about their salmon oil and neither could tell me how much vitamin D or A was in their product. Since neither extracts the vitamins there will be some present, but the amount is uncertain and possibly variable. An alternative is sourcing fish oil aimed at the human market; a typical fish oil capsule containing 100 IU of vitamin D per gram is useful. Each gram of oil is approximately half a millilitre, so the daily dose is about 0.15ml. However, using fish oil as the *only* dietary source of vitamin D will provide a rat with more than twice as much vitamin A as is needed.

FISH LIVER OIL - the oil from fish liver is high in both vitamin D and A, and because of a rat's proportionately lower vitamin A requirements (in comparison to a human's) overuse of liver oils could potentially lead to vitamin A toxicity. Cod liver oils vary enormously in strength and vitamin content so you would need to check the labelling and work out a suitable dose. Some pet grade cod liver oils are not really suitable as you would need to give too much oil on a daily basis to get an adequate dose of vitamin D. For instance the Solvitax brand cod liver oil contains 200 IU per 5ml so the daily dose would be around 0.5ml (per rat), which is a lot of extra oil in the diet and would also give ten times the required amount of vitamin A.

VITAMIN A EXTRACTED COD LIVER OIL - some companies extract the vitamin A from their fish oils so that they can be used alongside multivitamin, and this provides a really useful alternative. One such product is Seven Seas high strength pure cod liver oil with vitamin D and E. If a product aimed at the human market is vitamin A extracted, there will be no vitamin A listed in the nutritional information; be sure to check the packaging. Because the Seven Seas product is high strength only a 10th of the capsule will provide the daily dose of vitamin D. The capsules contain 0.5ml oil, so a daily dose would be 0.05ml, which is a manageable amount that can be given on a little cube of wholegrain bread. One capsule can be shared between 10 rats if you are mixing it into fresh food.

LIQUID CALCIUM AND VITAMIN D SUPPLEMENTS - these are aimed at the pet market and are water soluble preparations, that provide a readily absorbed form of calcium along with vitamin D. They are efficient supplements and *shouldn't be given every day*, because regular provision of too much calcium can cause problems. These include a reduced ability to move calcium in and out of the bones, (which is how the body copes with normal periods of increased or decreased demand), kidney stones and anaemia. Using a product like Calcivet or Calciform two to three times a week is adequate, except to support lactation, when up to five times a week is more suitable. The dose of Calcivet per rat is between 0.5 and 1ml over 24 hours in water, or in food, with higher dose being used for lactation and rapid growth, or where no other dietary source of vitamin D is used. If you are using it in water, try adding 1ml to approximately 50ml water for two rats at the maintenance dose, or 2ml to roughly 50ml water for two rats to support reproduction and growth. Calciform is approximately only a third of the strength of Calcivet, so should be given at a higher rate. Since Calciform is designed for avian use, the doses on the packaging are not appropriate for rats and doses three times higher than those given for Calcivet will need to be used to achieve the same result - that is 3ml to 50ml water for 2 rats for a maintenance dose, or 6ml to 50ml water for two rats to support growth and reproduction. Calcivet has a strong taste and may be rejected in plain water, so most people add it along with Dr Squiggles Daily Essentials.

CALCIUM AND VITAMIN D TABLETS - chewable tablets are widely available and are palatable. Giving about a 10th of the daily human dose per rat, provides (in theory) the required vitamin D plus 88mg calcium and 6.66 micrograms of vitamin K. However, in this form the absorption of calcium from the gut is less efficient and as much as two thirds of the content may be lost.

MULTIVITAMIN AND MINERAL SUPPLEMENTS - example are Dr Squiggles Daily Essentials, Bio Plus and Tiny Animal Essentials, SF50 (used to be SA37), Senior Aid and Nutrical, all of which are useful in different circumstances. Daily Essentials does not contain any calcium so it is best used alongside Calcivet for greatest effect.

It should be noted that Vitamin D deficiency can lead to calcium deficiency

as it is required for absorption of this mineral, but the two deficiencies
don't always occur together. Shortfall is most likely during reproduction,
rapid growth and old age, when requirements are increased, but adults may
become deficient if their diet is low in Vitamin D over longer periods. Signs
of deficiency (regardless of calcium status) would include poor growth,
weakened bones that are more prone to injury and teeth problems.[8]

Vitamin D deficiency is thought to exacerbate a number of illnesses and
may also increase the likelihood of them happening in the first place. These
include cancers, autoimmune diseases, bone disease, infectious illness and
heart disease. There is a demonstrated link between chronic vitamin D
deficiency and shortened lifespan in male rats.[9] Interestingly, chronic
vitamin D shortage in early life is thought to be linked to an increased risk
of multiple sclerosis in humans. Hind leg degeneration is caused by a
similar process of de-myelination, and it is possible that lack of vitamin D
might have a causative effect.[10]

Personally, I feel that it is unwise to rely on one source of vitamin D since
most of the supplements have their own unique issues, or may not offer
sufficient vitamin D without over doing other nutrients. Therefore using a
variety of methods of adding it to the diet is more likely to keep a rat at
optimum levels, without any detrimental effects. My own regime is not
rigid, but for maintenance I give Dr Squiggles Daily Essentials and Calcivet
in their water every 3rd day or so, Tiny Animal Essentials once a week on
fresh food, a dose of Seven Seas High Strength cod liver oil once a week, a
small portion of mackerel once a week as part of their fresh meal and liver
biscuit treats (recipe: page 284) once a week. Sick and undernourished rats
also get Nutrical and they, along with the very old get egg based fresh food
and wet dog food, both of which contain vitamin D. Lactating does and
rapidly growing kittens also get these extras, plus Insectivorous Feast and
Lactol, which also have vitamin D added. Vitamin D is stored well in the
body and deficiencies only tend to occur after long periods of inadequate
diet.

CALCIUM

Rats require 5g calcium per kg of feed for growth and somewhat more for reproduction, which equates to at least 125mg of calcium a day for a rat consuming 25g food. Maintenance levels are lower, but older rats require good levels and 3g per kg of feed (75mg/day) is quoted as optimal for the elderly. A varied grain mix (grains only) gives about a tenth of the daily calcium requirement, so clearly rats need to receive the majority of their calcium from other sources.

When levels of calcium in the blood are low it is drawn out of the bones; a process called demineralisation. When supplies are in surplus it is pushed back into the bones, and this natural cycling is perfectly healthy so long as the overall balance isn't in constant deficit. If this occurs, bones can become weakened and fragile. Chronic calcium deficiency is a serious problem and signs may include anaemia (pale ears, feet and gums), lethargy, 'lightweight' feel (even when well nourished in terms of calories), poor bone development, accidental bone fractures, tooth problems, muscle twitching and spasm.

SOURCES OF CALCIUM

To provide the average rat with its daily requirement for calcium (75mg) the following quantities of foods would be needed:
* sesame seeds - 7.5g (about 2 teaspoons), or
* dried fish - 9g, or
* sardines - 19g, or
* flax seeds - 30g, or
* kale - 50g, or
* chicken bones - roughly a quarter of a gram.

From this information we can see that other than chicken bones there is no realistic dietary source that would meet all the needs of a rat, in a quantity of food that it could eat daily, even for maintenance, let alone reproduction and growth. However, because calcium is stored well, giving a varied diet with some calcium rich food sources and intermittent supplementation, should be sufficient to maintain bone health, with extra care being given during pregnancy, lactation and growth. Some of the foods that we often add to the diet to support reproduction are already enriched with calcium, such as Lactol, Complan and Burns fish and rice kibble. Intake can also be boosted if you add some powdered calcium (crushed chewable tablets) to any baking that you do for the rats, for instance the liver biscuits that are mentioned above. Most commercial mixes already have calcium added, so supplementation during maintenance is only necessary if you feed straight grains, or you use a commercial feed that is low in calcium (less than 3 to 5g/kg feed). Calcium digestibility is never close to 100%, so a diet should provide more than a rat actually requires.

Supplementation can be with either inorganic or organic calcium; tablets, capsules and milky suspensions, such as calcium carbonate are inorganic, and liquid supplements where the calcium is fully dissolved in fluid (like Calcivet) are organic. Organic calcium is much more readily available to the body during digestion, (only about a third of the calcium in a tablet would be absorbed). For this reason if you are going to supplement it may be preferable to use something like Calcivet or Senior Aid, depending on the other needs of the rat. These supplements are discussed in more detail on pages 139 and 182.

CALCIUM SUPPLEMENTATION AND ANTIBIOTIC THERAPY

Calcium (as well as other minerals) can bind to quinolone and tetracycline based antibiotics, (such as Baytril, ciprofloxacin and doxycycline) in the gut, making them less efficient at normal doses as less of the medication will be absorbed. It is important to remember this when supplementing calcium, and antibiotic doses should not be given within two hours either side of feeding the supplement. If you are using Calcivet (or the equivalent) in the water, simply remove the bottle a couple of hours before dosing and replace it with plain water. The bottle with the Calcivet in it can be kept and returned about 2 hours after the medication is given.

COPPER

Copper is one mineral that is often talked about in terms of deficiency in rats. Rats need around 8 mg/kg of feed for reproduction and 5mg/kg for growth, and since maintenance levels are not certain the 5mg/kg of feed is generally taken as a baseline. As a rough guide this equates to around 125 micrograms in 25g of daily food. Higher levels are often quoted for commercial feeds (usually around 15mg/kg), which is because of issues absorbing copper from un-purified dietary sources. Like other minerals, the absorption of copper is affected by antinutrients in whole grains, legumes and vegetables, high dietary fibre and it may also be decreased by high zinc levels in the diet.

Copper is required for a wide range of functions including, fixing calcium in bones, energy production, resistance to infection, thyroid function and all aspects of a healthy nervous system. Reproduction is highly dependent on adequate copper levels, and lack of copper in the diet during pregnancy can result in dead or deformed babies. Rats who are chronically copper deficient simply fail to reproduce, and it can probably be assumed that females who reproduce normally are unlikely to be copper deficient.[10]

One of the major effects of copper deficiency is iron deficiency anaemia, because one is needed for the absorption of the other. Anaemia shows in rats as pale ears, feet and gums. Paling of the fur is another common sign of copper deficiency, but not *loss* of fur from around the eyes as is often stated. Pale eye rings where the fur is present but paler in colour is one possible symptom, as is paling of the coat over the rump (rusting).

To provide an average rat with its daily copper requirement, the following quantities of foods would be needed (assuming that all the copper was absorbed):
* lamb's liver - 2g would provide 140 micrograms copper
* sesame seeds - 3g
* dry shrimps - 8g
* oyster - 8g (this is about half an oyster)
* soya - 11g
* chickpeas (soaked and roasted) - 15g
* millet - 17g
* crimini mushrooms (slightly matured button mushrooms as they grow

and the flesh darkens) - 25g
* kale - 41g

25g of mixed grains would provide a rat with the required 125 micrograms
of copper if all of the copper was absorbed. Due to antinutrients, fibre
content and the nature of digestion, this is extremely unlikely and some
copper rich foods should be provided as part of a mix. A daily little cube of
liver biscuit (page 284) would wipe out any guesswork, or try a freeze dried
liver treat (sold as dog treats) cut to size a couple of times a week. Copper is
stored well in the body, so daily supplementation is rarely necessary,
however, a good all round multivitamin and mineral mix used once or
twice a week provides an extra safety net. It is also excreted well in excess so
toxicity is unlikely to occur.

SELENIUM
Selenium is a mineral that is needed in tiny quantities for the functioning
of several metabolic processes. It is thought to promote antioxidant activity
in the body through a selenium dependant enzyme. This micro-mineral
occurs naturally in all plants and animals, but at extremely varied levels,
and it may be reduced or removed by processing. Brazil nuts are an
outstanding source of selenium, with only one fifth of a gram of nut
needed to supply a rat's daily requirement.

The amount of selenium in grains and seeds depends to a large degree on
the amount occurring naturally in the soil where they were grown, and the
level of selenium in UK soil is low. It is quite possible that a rat who
receives a grain and seed based diet plus UK grown vegetables could be
deficient in this mineral, however, giving adequate selenium is not difficult.
Sesame seeds, mussels, egg yolk and liver are all good sources (4 to 5g of
these foods would supply daily needs), and Kamut wheat, which is grown in
the selenium rich soil of the American Midwest, has certified useful
amounts. Some multivitamin and mineral supplements contain selenium,
including Dr Squiggles Essentials products.

It should be noted that the needs of a female rat to support reproduction

1.   *Burgess Supa Fruitti Rabbit Food* (see page 95)
2.   *Jollyes Fruitti Guinea Pig Food* (see page 98)
3.   *Shunamite style straight grain mix* (see page 121)

The Burgess feed is representative of the kind of feeds that are made up primarily of micronized flaked grains, legumes and extruded wheat biscuits. It is not highly coloured; the wheat biscuits are brown and the orange you can see is carrot. The Jollyes feed is similar, but has no extrusions - instead it has lots of micronized beans and more fruit. It is uncoloured. Both feeds contain alfalfa pellets which are often wasted. The straights mix is hugely varied, but primarily whole or micronized grains and legumes. It is free from colours and contains no unpalatable ingredients, so no waste.

1.   *Burgess Supa Rabbit Deluxe (see page 93)*
2.   *A selection of high fibre alfalfa, grass, wheatfeed and oatfeed pellets*
3.   *Chudley's Rabbit Royale (see page 96)*

The Burgess feed is typical of many rabbit foods that combine grass pellets and extruded biscuits to make up the bulk of the mix, though this feed also has quite a lots of whole grains. Not too highly coloured, though it does contain a few lurid greed biscuits. High fibre pellets represent waste and where mixes have a high proportion of these pellets, you effectively pay twice as much for the food your rats do eat. The Chudley's feed also has a high pellet content, but is otherwise interesting, though it is sprayed with glucose for palatability, which adds sugar. No colourants - it's the marigold's that make it look so pretty.

(Above) *Brandywine Brent,* beautifully demonstrating the art of pea fishing (see page 253). Photograph reproduced by kind permission: Annette Rand.
(Below left) *Hakuna Matata Some like it Hot (India),* offering a working solution to the challenge of getting the food out! Photograph reproduced by kind permission: lilladysez.
(Below right) A Brandywine baby and his own take on the problem of a vege-basket. Photograph reproduced by kind permission: Annette Rand.

From top left clockwise: rat biscuit (page 286), rat cake, rat scones (page 285), pizza swirls (page 287). Baked and beautifully presented by Neil Turner - photograph reproduced with his kind permission.

Close-up of pizza swirls. Photograph reproduced by kind permission: Neil Turner

Banana heart rat cakes (page 287). Photograph reproduced by kind permission: Trudy Hurdman

1.   *Boredom Breaker Naturals range - Wood Picnic (see page 260)*
2.   *Boredom Breakers Naturals range - Herb Plus (see page 259)*
3.   *Sunny Brunch Garden-Snack (see page 264)*

A selection of interesting treat products. Wood Picnic is full of goodies that would be found naturally, foraging in a wood. Provides enrichment and variation on the usual treat themes. Herbs Plus has a long ingredients list and is almost a mini-feed. It has some interesting ingredients and smells fabulous. It does contain a few highly coloured biscuits (deep red) but these are coloured with beetroot. The Garden-Snack is an ingenious edible bowl made from grains, vegetables and parsley, which comes full of carrots, but these can be replaced with other nibbles when these have been eaten. The bowl itself is quite substantial and offers great chewing potential!

A lovely round tail on a well nourished young rat. The appearance of the tail is a good indicator of overall nutrition and (in the short term), hydration.

A square tail on a severely undernourished rat. You can clearly see the 'edges' and ridges where the tail is no longer cylindrical.

Waste from a straight grain mix consists entirely of empty seed cases or 'chaff'. Buckwheat hulls retain their shape but they can be easily squashed to check that they are empty.

rocket to almost 3 times the maintenance level. Small pieces of Brazil nut could be a useful addition to the diet at this time.

BEYOND BASIC RATIONS
FEEDING FOR HEALTH

For maximum benefit a dry mix should always be accompanied by fresh vegetables. Plants in the form of vegetables, herbs, seed sprouts and legumes contain phytochemicals and are generally rich in vitamins and minerals. They can have a positive influence on well-being and immune system health, and can help to fight the ageing process.

PHYTOCHEMICALS EXPLAINED
Phytochemicals (sometimes called phytonutrients) are organic compounds that are found in plants and whilst they don't add to overall nutrition, they are thought to promote health, protect against cell damage and support repair within the body. These effects can slow down the aging process. The many phytochemicals include carotenoids, flavonoids (polyphenols), isoflavones (phytoestrogens), phytate, saponins and sulfides. They are found in varying amounts in vegetables, fruit, grains, seeds and herbs. Many studies have been carried out involving rats and it does appear that benefits extend to the species, though some phytochemicals - like the carotenoids, appear to be less well absorbed by rats.

CAROTENOIDS
Carotenoids provide the red, orange and yellow pigments in plants, and seem to protect against some cancers, heart disease and age related macular degeneration - a condition that causes loss of vision with age, that is known to affect rats. Good sources of carotenoids include carrots, green leafy vegetables, tomatoes, sweet potato and water melon.

POLYPHENOLS (flavonoids, lignans, tannins)
These compounds are found in a wide variety of plants and are natural antioxidants. They have been linked to providing protection from heart disease, some cancers, bone demineralisation and some neurodegenerative

diseases. Hind leg degeneration, often seen in elderly rats, falls into this category of diseases and it is possible that polyphenols could play a role in delaying this process. Sources include berries, fruits, soya and vegetables.[11]

PHYTATES

Phytic acid is an antioxidant, which is thought to protect against cancer in the intestines and aid bone health with aging. Sources include seeds, nuts, whole grains and legumes. The negative effects of phytates are discussed in chapters 2 and 13.

HOW DO PHYTOCHEMICALS PROMOTE HEALTH?

Phytochemicals are antioxidants that are thought to reduce oxidative stress. Oxidation is an essential chemical reaction that occurs within the body but can produce unwanted free radicals, which can then go on to damage body cells. Antioxidants within the body reduce this effect by helping to remove the free radicals. When the body is at rest this system is well balanced, but when certain stressors - for example, infection, ageing, inflammation, UV radiation, smoke inhalation and exercise - disturb the balance, the system's ability to mop up the free radicals (and so prevent damage), is unable to keep up. This insult to body cells is an important factor in many diseases, but also in the whole process of aging. Taking in antioxidants in the diet can help to restore the balance and prevent this damage, which may reduce the likelihood of disease developing and the rate of aging.

Free radicals depress immunity by damaging kappa B, a protein involved in gene expression (the process of extracting information from genes, in order to produce specific proteins in the body). This affects everything from the productions of cytokines - the chemical messengers that tell the immune system what to do - to the production of antimicrobial proteins, and the efficient functioning of the inflammatory response. In mopping up the free radicals, antioxidants can help to reverse this effect.

Apoptosis is the programme of cellular death within the body, which is necessary to get rid of damaged or infected cells. When maintained at the correct rate, apoptosis allows cells to die and be cleared from body tissue without any negative effect. When the rate is too slow, body cells are able to reproduce and grow without adequate controls, and the end result of this is cancer. Phytochemicals can help to normalise the rate of apoptosis, by chemically triggering the process of cellular death and arresting the cycle of cell growth in cancer cells.[12] They are also thought to detoxify some known carcinogens (substances that cause cancer).

DNA within cells contains the genetic instructions that are responsible for all of the development and function of living organisms. Exposure to toxins, such as chemicals and smoke, can lead to damaged DNA and antioxidants are thought to facilitate its repair. The mechanisms by which this repair takes place are not entirely understood, but one study showed that the antioxidants in kiwi fruit were able to increase the ability of lymphocytes to repair DNA base oxidation damage.[13]

Phytochemicals in the carotenoids group can boost vitamin A levels in the body - beta-carotene is metabolized into vitamin A, effectively increasing the levels provided by the diet.

High levels of oestrogen in the rat are known to be linked to an increased risk of mammary tumours and other hormone related illnesses. Balancing oestrogen levels in the body is a complex subject, but phytoestrogens and antioxidants can alter oestrogen metabolism and help to normalise high oestrogen levels, and thus reduce mammary tumour occurrence.

BOOSTING THE IMMUNE SYSTEM

Immune system health is an extremely complex issue and influenced by many factors including stress, sleep, activity and genetics. Diet plays an important part in maintaining a fully functional system of defence against infection and disease, but no one food acts alone to make *the* difference. The most effective approach is to include as much variety in the diet as possible, including some foods that are known to stimulate a particular aspect of immune system health.

As wide groups of foods these are:
- dark green leafy vegetables
- red/orange/yellow vegetables
- onions and garlic
- berries and some other fruits
- whole grains
- oily fish
- nuts and seeds

Adequate levels of all vitamins and minerals are important and some will help in greater abundance.
These are primarily:
- vitamin A
- vitamin C
- vitamin E
- zinc
- selenium.

SUPERFOODS FOR RATS

The term "superfoods" has rightly received a degree of negative publicity due to the unreasonable claims that some food manufacturers make on behalf of their products. However, there are indeed some fresh foods that are more suited to supplying a range of minerals, phytochemicals and vitamins, and I thought that it might be helpful to include my own top ten fresh foods for rats. These are not arranged in any order of preference.

- Kale - rich in vitamins, a good balance of calcium and phosphorus, other minerals (including copper) and phytonutrients.
- Dandelion - as for kale.
- Salmon flesh or oil - rich source of essential fatty acids and vitamin D.
- Chick peas - good source of copper, folate, iron, zinc and manganese. Soak, then cook or sprout.
- Fresh garlic - excellent antioxidant properties, may increase resistance to infection as well as reducing cancer growth.
- Carrot - range of vitamins and minerals including vitamin A and

calcium. Rich in carotenoids.

- Millet - possibly the king of grains for a rat having perfect levels of protein and fat, good quantities of B vitamins, copper, manganese, magnesium and zinc, and in addition, excellent antioxidant properties.
- Red pepper - range of vitamins including excellent amounts of the antioxidant vitamins (A, C, E), plus a small amount of most minerals and plenty of carotenoids.
- Flax seed or oil - rich source of the phytochemical lignan and omega-3 fatty acids. Flax is linked to reduced levels of some cancers, stabilisation of blood sugar levels and a reduction in the rate of decline in kidney disease.
- Egg - probably the best protein source for rats in terms of reducing the toxin load for the kidneys. Good source of carotenoids in an accessible form, vitamin D and B_{12}, essential fatty acids, sulphur, iodine, zinc and phosphorus.

This is not a definitive list, but foods that I prefer. Arguably berries could easily have been included, but I don't tend to feed them very often, and some of the foods listed have similar properties. Chicken or lamb's liver narrowly escaped inclusion, on the grounds that if you fed the rest of these foods - and a rich mixture of grains - you could probably do without it. But it is an easy means to an end if you need to boost nutritional status, perhaps after a significant blood loss, or at times of increased demand.

IMMUNE SYSTEM BOOSTER DIET

This mix is designed as a short term diet to help boost immune system health. It may be useful to feed to any rat who is having antibiotics, surgery or likely to be experiencing sustained stress, and is designed to be fed daily as a short term boost at times of illness, alongside (perhaps 50/50) a good quality grain mix. The completed mixture can be stored for up to 48 hours in a refrigerator, in an airtight container.

RECIPE

- 2 tbsp cooked brown rice [selenium, zinc and vitamin E]
- 2 tbsp millet, soaked if desired

- 1 tbsp oily fish: fresh tuna, mackerel, sardines, salmon, trout or tinned sardines or mackerel *or* 1 tbsp boiled or scrambled egg plus ½ tsp salmon flesh oil
- 1tbsp carrot, grated
- 1 tsp flaked almonds [vitamin E and zinc]
- 1 small floret broccoli, chopped [vitamin C, flavonoids and carotenoids]
- 1 clove garlic, raw, finely chopped, crushed or grated
- 2-6 berries depending on size, chopped [very high levels of antioxidants] *or* 1 tbsp red pepper finely chopped
- ½ tsp flax oil *or* 1 tsp of flax seeds

METHOD

Mix all the ingredients together and sprinkle on a multivitamin and a probiotic if desired. The volumes above will feed approximately 5 or 6 rats, as half their diet.

The ingredients of this mix are chosen for their high levels of the following nutrients: selenium, omega 3 fatty acids, vitamin E, vitamin C, flavonoids, zinc, carotenoids and other antioxidants. All of these nutrients and phytochemicals have been shown to support immune system health. The body can be viewed as having a microscopic army, which is both defensive and offensive - creating barriers to viruses, killing bacteria both chemically and by engulfing them, and maintaining normal flora (good bacteria) that are responsible for creating an environment that is hostile to any invasive bacteria. The immune system is complex and has many weapons of attack, as well as defensive tactics. Many micronutrients have been found to help support a strong immune system by increasing antibody production, aiding the manufacture of white cells, protecting the body against toxins and environmental pollutants, or supporting the production of other elements of the immune system such as cytokine, T-cells and B-cells. It should be noted that whilst rats can manufacture their own vitamin C, research seems to indicate that there are still benefits to be gained from high levels of dietary vitamin C, especially for elderly rats.[14]

CALORIES AND LIFESPAN
FEEDING FOR LONGEVITY

Discussions that centre on extending lifespan define the term in two ways. They either speak about average lifespan, which is the average age that rats in a particular line or strain will reach, or maximum lifespan, which is the oldest any rat in a particular line or strain will reach. Average lifespan can then be use to mean two different things. The mean (average) lifespan of a strain is worked out by adding all the ages at time of death together and dividing by the number of rats involved. This average is, however, skewed by individual rats who died very young, or lived unusually long lives. A more meaningful average is to work out the age by which 50% of the line has died, and 50% remain alive. As a general rule it is much easier to extend average lifespan than maximum lifespan within a line, because the number of factors that can extend lifespan towards the maximum are many and varied, while very few things are known to extend actual maximum lifespan.

Factors that affect longevity include a genetic predisposition for any life shortening illness, environmental hazards, medical and surgical resources and expertise, diet, exercise, breeding practices, general husbandry and stress factors.

Dietary factors have been shown to strongly influence lifespan in rats, and there are three main principles of rat nutrition that will serve to extend the duration of life in an individual. These are:

1. Good maternal nutrition (especially meeting protein needs) during pregnancy and also for the kittens during the rapid growth phase.
2. Slow growth through puberty and into maturity - this varies from line to line but is also affected by early nutrition.
3. Reduced volume of feed overall from the maturation phase (about 8-10 weeks onwards) to less than 80% of what would be taken if fed ad lib.

"In general, an early adult death age is associated with a high food intake prior to

adulthood particularly when coupled with a high efficiency of food utilization during the post-puberty period, a rapid growth rate and early attainment of mature weight. Deviations from this pattern serve to increase the duration of life of the individual.[15]

The trend within the fancy over recent years has probably been to over feed our rats. This trend has a number of possible causes which include:

- The increase in no-cull breeders who then had to learn to raise large litters successfully, in terms of adequate nutritional support.
- The desire to produce lovely big kittens, that go on to mature early into lovely big adults. These rats can be bred from at quite an early age, and often succeed from a young age when shown (if good examples of their variety).
- The tendency to feed kitten diet on into early adulthood.
- The tendency to feed the same diet throughout life without considering the changing needs of the individual, as growth slows down and stops.
- Following diet plans prescriptively, without tailoring them to the way individual rats grow and gain weight. This varies greatly from strain to strain and also depends on early feeding and environmental factors.
- Ad lib feeding and the human trend to overfeed and 'treat' our pets in terms of quantity, whatever diet is chosen.
- A preference amongst many owners for large squishy adult rats; bucks in particular.

Most of these tendencies are borne out of sound motivation, but all of these trends are likely to lead to overweight middle-aged rats who may have a shortened life expectancy. Radical calorie restrictions (up to 50% less than ad lib intake) from post-weaning age have been shown to increase both maximum and average lifespan in mice and rats.[16] However, they are rightly rejected by pet owners as they effectively chronically under nourish the rats, sometimes to the extent of causing lethargy, poor condition and stunted growth. However, some studies have looked at more moderate restrictions of around 70-80% of the volume of food taken if fed ad lib, and these restrictions also extend lifespan (just by a lesser degree). It seems that the tendency of a rat that is fed ad lib, is to overeat and put on weight and this can increase disease occurrence and reduce longevity. Hence, modest restrictions can have a positive effect.

It should be noted that commencing restrictions in middle age may still bring about a moderate extension in lifespan. Certainly obese rats who are then calorie restricted will often go on to live significantly longer lives than those who remain obese. Good feeding practices should ideally begin before birth and where this is not feasible, should start as soon as possible after weaning age.

When many breeders began to raise whole (often large) litters, there was a need to learn to feed them well in order to meet their nutritional needs. The pendulum swung too far the other way, with overfeeding becoming more of a problem than under-nutrition. Neither is desirable and restraint to promote slow and steady growth, with reduction in food intake as soon as the rapid growth phase begins to slow down is ideal, at least in terms of longevity.

Reducing intake in a pet colony can't be done 'scientifically', but it is still possible for our rats to have a lean, active period over the evening (without available food) by feeding late in the evening before we go to bed. This coupled with moderate amounts of food, which they are expected to finish before their lean hours, will effectively reduce overall calorie intake. When feeding fresh food, always reduce the quantity of dry food available to compensate.

The problem with suggesting a move towards less food is that there will always be people who take advice to the extreme, and some rats may become undernourished. Please be careful about any restriction on diet. Observing a rat's tail for signs of thinness/square edges (as well as their overall fitness and condition), can help to determine the nutritional status of an individual rat. It is, however, normal for a kitten or young adult who is not being fed to its maximum growth rate to have periods of slight squareness of the tail set (where it attaches to the body) during growth spurts. Photographs comparing square and round tails can be found on page 164. It is important to remember that where diet is restricted the quality of the feed has to be excellent, as it is only calories that you are aiming to restrict, not nutrients.

Scatter feeding can be used as an aid to restricting calories as the food must be found by digging and foraging and intake overall is generally reduced. It is particularly useful for mixed aged groups, or groups with some thin and some overweight rats. The rat who has greater calorie needs (or who is less food oriented), will have a better chance of getting their fair share of food when their more food-obsessed cage mates can't sit with their head in a food bowl. When feeding by this method it is important not to throw in an extra handful of food just in case they don't find everything. This will lead to overfeeding; a rat is a natural forager and will work hard to find food when necessary. A full discussion of scatter feeding can be found in Chapter 8.

OTHER DIETARY INFLUENCES ON LIFESPAN

Antioxidants in the diet (primarily from fresh vegetables, herbs, grains, fruit, seeds and nuts) have been shown to extend average lifespan, but not maximum lifespan. Blueberries alone, for example, have been linked to a reduction in brain aging in rats.

Low protein diets (around 9%) given to pregnant and lactating does, have been shown to cause a reduction in average lifespan of around 11% in the offspring.[17] Protein levels to maintain reproduction should be nearer 20 to 25%. Protein for maintenance (crude not pure) should ideally be between 10% and 14%, with the lower values being helpful in older rats. Rats have a natural susceptibility to kidney disease as they age, and high protein diets tend to hasten the progress of this degeneration once it has begun. This will shorten average lifespan. Egg protein is considered to be a good protein to support kidney health and soya seems to have a protective effect on the kidneys, which can enhance longevity (see page 143). Kidney issues and related diet are discussed more fully in Chapter 8.

Any illness can limit longevity and many illnesses do have a strong dietary influence beyond general immune system health and well-being. The most common of these are expanded in the next chapter.

FEEDING ELDERLY RATS

Elderly rats do not necessarily have the same dietary needs for maintenance as those who are younger and fitter. Rats age at different rates so it is hard to give an arbitrary value for 'elderly', but since one study puts the average lifespan of the UK pet rat at 21.6 months, I am going to define 'elderly' as over 18 months, though many rats will not begin to age until much later than this.[18]

These are some of the signs you may observe as a rat begins to age:
• Reduced muscle tone or 'firmness'.
• A 'drop' in the abdomen which leads to the rat looking lower to the ground and leaves the spine more prominent.
• Slightly slower, waddling gait, which can progress to weakness of the hind legs and reduced muscle bulk around the haunches.
• Letting the tail drag on the ground rather than holding it up off the ground when moving.
• A less sleek and shiny coat in both genders, less orange buck grease in males (at skin level), and a softening of any coarseness in the male coat.
• Coat may not be as thick.
• Changes in the teeth which can become slightly translucent, or lose some of their orange colouration.
• General decrease in activity.

It is not unreasonable to assume that all elderly rats have a degree of kidney damage (remember, they need to lose 75% of kidney function before they will show any signs). By reducing the protein and phosphate load of the diet at this time, it is likely that you will reduce the rate at which damage occurs once the process has begun.

When our rats reached this age I used to change their overall diet to follow the principles of a kidney friendly diet (Chapter 8), although I would not necessarily give all of the supplements (particularly the phosphate binders) if they were fit and well. I changed the grain mix, fed a small amount of Naturediet Lite - or an egg and rice mixture - with flax oil and vitamin B supplements. When the rats began to age visibly or lose condition for no apparent reason I would add the phosphate binders. This is one perfectly valid approach.

More recently I have changed my entire mix to be more 'kidney friendly' using mainly lower phosphate cereals, some soya protein and flax seed, and this is fed throughout their lives except for when supporting reproduction and rapid growth. This type of diet is explained in Chapter 5 along with a recipe of our current mix. As the rats age their mix can be modified to reduce phosphorus further and supplements can be added. The kidney diet is fully described in Chapter 8.

In contrast to the need for less protein and phosphorus in the diet of elderly rats, some nutrients are needed in increasing amounts, primarily because the body becomes less efficient at absorbing nutrients with age. These include most vitamins and minerals, but especially the antioxidant vitamins C and E and beta-carotene (precursor of vitamin A), vitamin D and calcium. Aged rats become less able to produce their own vitamin C and other natural antioxidant activity within the body is also reduced, so dietary antioxidants become increasingly important. Adequate calcium and vitamin D levels need to be maintained throughout life, or elderly rats will lose bone mass. However, over supplementation of calcium should be avoided, because very high calcium intake at the same time as a low phosphorus diet can lead to soft tissue calcification. Calcivet and Daily Essentials three times a week in water is sufficient in addition to a nutrient rich diet, which includes plenty of fresh vegetables.

SUPPLEMENTS THAT MAY HELP OLDER RATS

FLAX OIL - rich in omega-3, antioxidants and shown to slow down the progression of kidney degeneration. Flax can also be added to a dry mix in the form of seeds. If you are feeding the oil daily, I would suggest about

0.1ml for each rat. Flax is also called linseed.

FISH OIL - contains some vitamin D which when lacking may contribute to hind leg degeneration. These oils are also rich in omega-3. If you feed daily, I would suggest using a human grade fish oil, which lists the amount of vitamin A and D it contains, and will allow you to work out a suitable dose (see page 152). This will help to avoid any potential issues with over supplementing vitamin A.

FISH LIVER OIL - depending on the quality, this can have excellent levels of fat soluble vitamins including vitamin A and D, so it is good to use a little less frequently to boost vitamin D. If you select vitamin A extracted oil, such as Seven Seas high strength pure cod liver oil, you can avoid worries about vitamin A toxicity and give it daily. More information can be found earlier in this chapter.

VITAMIN B COMPLEX - vitamin B_{12} deficiency in particular, has been linked to demyelination of nerves in humans, similar to what is thought to be the main cause of hind leg degeneration in older rats. The body's ability to absorb B_{12} gets worse with age and even with the practice of coprophagy, it is possible that older rats are more likely to be deficient.

CHROMIUM PICOLINATE - has been shown to have a beneficial effect on glucose metabolism, cardiovascular health and one study showed that rats who were given this supplement significantly outlived those who did not receive it. Chromium picolinate has been used with good effect in type 2 diabetes in humans, to enhance the metabolism of glucose. It may also be useful in aiding weight control in obese rats (along with healthy diet and exercise it has been shown to enhance weight loss). The dose for rats should be approximately 200 micrograms per 500g of body weight (40mcg per 100g). Good food sources of chromium include meat, whole grains, sweet potato and lentils, but even where diet is adequate, supplementation may be beneficial to older rats.

CO-ENZYME 10 - produced by the body itself and needed for cell growth and maintenance. It is also a powerful antioxidant. As the body ages, its ability to manufacture co-enzyme 10 is reduced. Supplementation can provide many health benefits, and research involving aged rats showed anti aging effects when co-enzyme 10 and was given.

SENIOR AID - a liquid formula manufactured specifically to support aging pets. It contains a selection of amino acids, glucosamine (an amino-sugar that may help to maintain healthy joints) and a wide range of vitamins and minerals. Recommended dosage is 0.5ml per kg of body weight, so a 500g rat would have 0.25ml. Ingredients: taurine, l-carnitine, methionine, arginine, glucosamine HCL, ascorbic acid, thiamine HCL, riboflavine, niacin, vitamins A, B12, B6, D3 and E, biotin, folic acid, zinc oxide, iron, d-calcium pantothenate, iodine, potassium, copper (gluconate), manganese sulphate, selenium, choline and palmitate, in a caramel flavour suspension.

NUTRICAL - a high calorie, low volume nutritional supplement for ailing, convalescing or ageing rats. It looks a bit like gel toothpaste, only brown. Most rats seem to love its taste (a bit like malt extract), and only a large pea sized blob is needed daily, so even a rat with a very poor appetite can often be tempted to take it. It contains a wide selection of vitamins and minerals, plus essential fatty acids. Other similar pastes are available but most contain less nutrients, and some like Beaphar malt paste are quite limited and not a comparable product.

CALCIVET AND DAILY ESSENTIALS - general supplements suitable for all rats, but especially important for those feeding a straights based diet. Used together in the water every 2nd or 3rd day they will help to ensure that micronutrients are present in adequate amounts. This is less important if your rats are fed a commercial rat food as this will already be supplemented.

IMMUNE BOOSTER RECIPE (see page 173).

IPAKITINE - a phosphate binder with chitosan that also helps to reduce urea levels in rats with deteriorating kidney function. Presented as a powder, the dose is 1g (the size of the little spoon provided) per 5kg body weight, so most rats will need about a tenth of a spoonful but it's not critical to be entirely accurate. Available online from vet suppliers.

RUBENAL - medicinal rhubarb extract which has been found to help protect healthy renal tissue in rats with induced nephropathy. Presentation 75mg tablets, and suggested dose is about 55mg a day, this is about two thirds of a tablet crushed, but it is not critical to be entirely accurate. Available online from vet suppliers.

BUYING SUPPLEMENTS ONLINE
http://www.ratwarehouse.com - A good variety of rattie supplements, plus help and advice about which products would be most helpful in your circumstances
http://www.vetuk.co.uk - Vet supplies, good for sourcing non-prescription medications, such as Ipakitine.
http://www.birdcareco.com - Dr Squiggles full range and larger sizes.

Review - The Rat Warehouse online shop
"The Rat Warehouse is a small, home based online retailer, with whom I have often done business in the past. I have always found them to be efficient and helpful, and if you have a sick rat they will endeavour to get supplies out to you as quickly as possible. The shop sells a wide range of rat related products, including food, treats, supplements, toys and a variety of homemade, well constructed hammocks and sleep sacks. The owner has kept rats herself for many years and has a good deal of expertise and understanding of her products, which is extremely helpful if you need advice on which supplements to buy in a particular situation." (AC)

FEEDING A SOFT DIET

Elderly rats – amongst others – will sometimes benefit from a diet based entirely on soft foods over extended periods of time. Such a diet would also be useful for certain tooth problems, pituitary tumours and advanced hind leg degeneration, amongst other conditions. Meeting nutritional needs over long periods of time using only fresh foods, requires a little thought and a lot of variety.

MAKING GRAINS, LEGUMES AND SEEDS EASIER TO EAT

Most grain mixes can be soaked in boiling water to soften them and make them easier to eat, but small grains often remain quite hard. Generic mixes and nuggets can also be treated in this way, but always make sure the grain mixture has cooled adequately before feeding. Cold water can also be used, although soaking times will be longer. Feeding soaked grain mix is a good interim step between a dry mix and wet food and is useful during periods of decline or recovery.

If you are selecting individual grains to make a soaking mix you will have the greatest success if you avoid grains that are still in their husk (hull). The following grains all soak very well: millet (human grade), quinoa, flaked barley, rolled oats, bulgur wheat, couscous, flaked rice, egg food (EMP or CeDe) and human breakfast cereals. Split or flakes peas, soya flakes, lentils, flaked corn, rice, dog kibble and dried vegetables all soak well if boiling water is used, but will generally maintain their shape (with the exception of kibble).

SPROUTING WHOLE GRAINS, SEEDS AND LEGUMES

Another method of making these whole plant seeds easier to eat is to soak and sprout them. Almost all whole seeds (includes grains and legumes in this context) can be sprouted, though some species are easier than others to achieve good, consistent results.

Sprouts are super little packages of nutrition. They contain all of the seeds goodness, but less antinutrients, which enables the nutrients to be more readily absorbed. They are also actively growing, rather than their dormant state, which means that stored proteins, fats and carbohydrates are broken down into amino acids, fatty acids and sugars, making them easier to digest. They are also packed full of plant enzymes that are activated during the sprouting process, which can also aid digestion. Conversely the enzyme inhibitors (antinutrients) present in dormant seeds are inactivated. These nutritional benefits make sprouted seeds an excellent choice for rats at any stage of their lives, and invaluable during times when a dry mix is refused. Because they are soaked they are softer and easier to eat, though can be liquidised just prior to feeding if necessary.

GENERAL PRINCIPLES OF SPROUTING

Before you start you need to decide on which seeds to sprout and the container you will use to sprout them. It is easier to sprout seeds of one variety only, as you won't have to consider varying sprouting times, and I would recommend starting off with chick peas, as they are easy to sprout and extremely nutritious. As you sprout different seeds, keep a note of how long they take and you will soon work out what kinds of seeds can be easily sprouted together. Differences of 2 or 3 days are not really relevant, but long differences will mean some seeds are still 'closed' when others are ready.

The container you use can be a sieve over a bowl, or a large plastic bottle like an over-sized juice bottle. If the neck is narrow you will make things easier on yourself by cutting it off to make a wider opening. I usually use a colander as this requires a really simple technique and still achieves good results.

Seeds only need air and water to sprout, but too much pooled water and they will die and rot. If you want to green up your sprouts before feeding they will also need exposure to sunlight towards the end of sprouting.

HOW TO SPROUT

Rinse the seeds thoroughly in a sieve, using cold running water and at the same time remove any obvious debris, stones and the like. Then soak the seeds for 8 to 12 hours before sprouting, in 2-3 times more cold water than you have volume of seeds. Dry seeds won't sprout because they are dormant and soaking them wakes them up. Lukewarm (never hot) water can be used to speed things up, or to get obstinate seeds to take up water. If the water is too hot (above about 45°C) the enzymes that enable the seed to sprout will be denatured and it won't be able to grow. If you are sprouting legumes then change the soaking water two or three times during the soaking period.

Agitate the seeds within the soaking water from time to time, to ensure that the whole surface of each seed remains wet. This is especially important with small seeds.

Drain and rinse your seeds in fast running water (the higher pressure the better) in a colander or sieve, depending on the size of the seeds. Shake the colander vigorously while rinsing to ensure the whole of the surface of each seed is exposed to the fresh water. Never skimp on the rinsing stage.

SIEVE (COLANDER) METHOD

After a thorough rinsing, agitate the sieve to drain the seeds well and once you have shaken the bulk of the water off, leave it sitting over a small bowl on a bench or table where air can circulate around it. The bowl needs to be small enough to leave most of the holes of the sieve sitting above it - so that air can easily reach the seeds through them - and make sure the seeds at the bottom of the sieve are not sitting in pooled water. Cover the top of the sieve with a small, preferably plastic plate, but don't try to make it a snug fit.

Twice a day, throughout the sprouting period, repeat this vigorous rinsing and draining procedure. Use cold running water at a good pressure and lots of it! Rinsing not only hydrates the seeds but helps to supply them with oxygen, so keep the seeds moving by flipping them in the sieve as you rinse. Seeds and sprouts are robust and aren't easily damaged.

After each rinsing session, drain the seeds well and return them to rest on the bowl. Cover as before. Continue to repeat the rinse and drain cycle until the sprouts are ready to eat.

THE BOTTLE METHOD

If you are using a bottle you will need to transfer the seeds to this after they have been soaked, rinsed and well drained. I then store the bottle on its side so that the seeds are more spread out (better aeration), on a bench or window sill. If you have cut the bottle down to widen the neck and are in danger of losing the seeds cut a section from a pair of tights and fix this as a lid over the neck of the bottle with an elastic band.

You will need to rinse the seeds thoroughly twice a day until they are ready to eat using one of two methods. Either decant the seeds into a sieve and rinse as above before returning to the bottle, or rinse them in the bottle through a mesh nylon 'lid' as described. To do this simply run the water in through the mesh until the bottle is about two thirds full, then shake the whole bottle vigorously to rinse and aerate. Tip it upside down and drain the water out through the mesh. Providing your 'lid' is well secured with the elastic band, you can squeeze and release the bottle to help expel the water. Repeat at least three times.

After the final rinse take extra pains to remove as much water as possible from the bottle by shaking, squeezing and releasing. When the seeds are well drained tip the bottle onto its side and return to its resting place.

WHEN ARE THEY READY?
Deciding when to harvest the sprouts is not a precise science; it depends how long you want the sprouts to be. I normally leave them until the sprouts are about a cm long, less for tiny seeds. Sprouts can be eaten when they have just begun to grow, or left until they grow a full shoot with leaves (or anywhere in between). If you are trying to green up your new shoots they will need sunlight as well as air and water.
Sprouted seeds can be stored for 1-2 weeks in the fridge so long as they are dry before storage.

GRAINS - Sprout quickly (2 to 4 days), taste slightly sweet and are highly nutritious. Look for naked grains or groats.

SEEDS - sometimes quite slow to sprout, some take up to 2 weeks. Pre soaking in lukewarm water can hasten the process. Variable taste, some are quite spicy.

LEGUMES - relatively fast to sprout, generally taking between 2 and 5 days. Only the following legume sprouts should be fed raw (larger beans can be sprouted and then cooked once sprouted); adzuki beans, mung beans, chick peas, green peas, yellow peas, marrowfat peas, whole lentils. If a bean needs to be boiled rapidly, followed by an extended cooking time to render it safe to eat, this would still apply after sprouting. Split peas and lentil will not sprout successfully.

For more information about successful sprouting take a look at the Sprout People website.[19]

SUGGESTIONS FOR SOFT FOOD DIETS

There are many possibilities for providing good nutrition over time using soft foods, but whatever combination you choose the diet as a whole should be planned to avoid deficiencies. The base food should make up the main bulk of the diet and should be varied to include maximum nutrients. The base food replaces the cereal, seeds and legume element of a dry diet.

POSSIBLE BASE FOODS

* Cereal mix - combine 1 cup oats, 2 broken Weetabix biscuits, 1 cup puffed rice, I cup puffed millet, 1 cup cornflakes. Store in an airtight container. Serve by soaking in goat, cow, soya or rice milk. Use more milk if a really sloppy food is required.
* Grain mix - in a small pan of boiling water cook 1 tbsp barley and 1 tbsp brown rice, after 20 minutes add 1 tbsp buck wheat, 1 tbsp bulgur wheat and 1 tbsp quinoa. Boil for a further 15 to 20 minutes. Drain and mix in half a small can chickpeas which can be mashed a little first. Cool quickly and store in the fridge for up to 48 hours. Can be frozen. To increase palatability mash a little and mix through a beaten egg then microwave until set or add some grated fresh garlic and a little flax (linseed) or salmon oil.
* Sprout mix - a selection of soaked and sprouted grains, seeds and legumes.
* Good quality soft dog food - choose the ones made for elderly or over weight dogs if you want lower protein and fat values. Burns Penlan Farm range or Naturediet are particularly suitable.
* Vitalin Original - soaked in hot water and, once soaked, mixed with any

one or more of cooked rice, soaked couscous, soaked bulgur wheat, cooked buckwheat, cooked quinoa, cooked mashed sweet potato, cooked millet. This will help to enrich the food and reduce the overall protein content.

- Soaked rat nuggets - can be used if desired but be wary of those that contain low quality ingredients.
- Savoury 2nd or 3rd stage human baby food - add in extras to what is a quick and easy base food. Try mixing into soaked couscous and add one or more of mashed avocado, oily fish or scrambled egg.

POSSIBLE PROTEIN SOURCES

Foods such as Vitalin, NatureDiet and nuggets already contain adequate protein, but a grain based mixture will benefit from some extra protein, especially when rats are young or sick, as healing, inflammatory and immune responses all rely heavily on adequate protein. Suggestions for the addition of protein include:

- Egg - scrambled, boiled/poached and mashed.
- Chicken - great to add to broth or puree up with vegetables.
- Liver - gives a vitamin and iron boost maybe once a week. Liquidises easily, or chop finely and mix into other food. One option is to bake liver biscuit (see page 284), which can then be frozen in portion sizes until required; soften in milk before feeding.
- Oily fish - fresh or tinned
- Shellfish, especially shrimps, prawns or mussels.
- Sprouted or cooked (tinned) legumes.
- Good quality dog kibble (like Burns) soaked.
- Insectivorous feast or EMP soaked and mixed into other food.

It is best to aim at as much variety as possible and two or three of the staple foods can be used in rotation, with various protein additions.

MICRONUTRIENTS AND PHYTOCHEMICALS

These can be provided in a soft diet with a little planning.

- A daily serving of vegetables - these may need to be cooked, mashed or finely diced/chopped, to be easily accepted into a soft diet. Mix in with other foods. Vegetable puree can be made from cooking some curly kale, broccoli and carrots and then liquidising with a little water if required. If you want to give the puree more substance add mashed sweet potato which is starchy, low fat and contains an excellent range of vitamins and minerals, including A, B group, C, E, K, calcium, iron, magnesium, copper and manganese. The puree can then be frozen or stored in the fridge for a few days.

- Mashed berries - excellent for vitamin C and antioxidants.
- Flax (linseed) oil.
- Salmon oil.
- Weekly fish liver oil if not using liver.
- Grated garlic.
- Nutrical as required.
- A good all round multivitamin and mineral supplement such as Dr Squiggles Daily Essentials may be useful when feeding this kind of diet, but do not use every day if you are also feeding daily Nutrical.

PUREED DIET

If necessary the carbohydrate, vegetable and protein foods can be pureed together with any supplements in a batch, and portions can be frozen for future use. Make sure that any pureed food is of a fairly sloppy consistency to avoid gagging. Soups and broth are excellent in this regard - just add some barley, lentils, mixed vegetables, tomatoes and a chicken thigh to water and simmer until the barley is soft. At the end of cooking remove the chicken thigh and chop finely before returning it to the broth, or blend with a hand blender if desired.

EXAMPLE OF A WEEKLY DIET PLAN

Monday - mixed breakfast cereals as listed, scrambled egg and vegetable puree. Drop or two of salmon oil and flax oil. A few mashed berries.

Tuesday - portion of Naturediet Lite. Cooked mashed sweet potato, carrot and fresh grated garlic. Drop or two of salmon oil and flax oil.

Wednesday - mixed cooked (tinned) pulses mashed and mixed with oily fish and vegetable puree. Drop or two of flax oil. Mashed banana.

Thursday - cooked mixed grain, egg and vegetables. Drop or two of salmon oil and flax oil. A few mashed berries.

Friday- Insectivorous Feast, cooked millet, grated fresh garlic and vegetable puree. Drop or two of salmon oil and flax oil.

Saturday- portion of Burns Penlan Farm Range egg based dog food. Soaked sprouted mixed seeds. Cod liver oil. Mashed avocado.

Sunday- chicken, lentil and barley broth made with mixed vegetables. Drop or two of salmon oil and flax oil. Mashed banana.

Where extra calories are required, use Lactol (puppy milk) or coconut milk wherever possible in the mixing of foods. Lactol is best made up to the strength listed on the tin for feline kittens when feeding to rats. Mashed avocado, mashed banana and Nutrical are also useful in this regard. If you need to top up quantity, give some additional porridge or 'souped-up' baby food. Where the soft diet is for a rat with other underlying health issues you should try to maintain the best diet for that illness as well as soft food. Details of specialised diets are in Chapter 8.

REFERENCES

[1]The Journal of Nutrition Jan 1947
Growth and longevity of rats fed omnivorous and vegetarian diets
Anton J. Carlson, Frederick Hoelzel
[2]The American Journal of Clinical Nutrition 2004;80:550 -9.
Saturated fats: what dietary intake?
J Bruce German and Cora J Dillard
[3]International Journal of Food Sciences and Nutrition 1996, Vol. 47, No. 5, Pages 417-425
Influence of Dietary Fats Upon Systolic Blood Pressure in the Rat
Simon C. Langley-Evans1, Alan G. Clamp, Robert F. Grimble and Alan A. Jackson
[4]Handbook of laboratory animal science: Animal models, Volume 2
By G. L. Van Hoosier, Per Svendsen
[5]Cancer Research. 1975; 35(11 Pt. 2):3384-6 (ISSN: 0008-5472)
Dietary fat and growth promotion of rat mammary tumours.
Chan PC; Cohen LA
[6]British Journal of Nutrition (1964), 18, 595
Coprophagy and vitamin B_{12} in the rat

T. B. Morgan
[7]The American journal of Clinical Nutrition - Vol. 83, No. 2, 191-201, February 2006
The acute and chronic toxic effects of vitamin A
K.L. Penniston and S.A. Tanumihardjo
[8]Proceedings of the National Academy of Sciences of the United States of America
Vitamin D deficiency in rats with normal serum calcium concentrations
G E Lester, C J VanderWiel, T K Gray, R V Talmage
[9]Mechanisms of Ageing and Development 1984 Apr-May;25(1-2):161-75.
Effects of long-term vitamin D deficiency and response to vitamin D repletion in the mature and aging male and female rat.
Thomas ML, Armbrecht HJ, Forte LR.
[10]The Lancet Neurology, Volume 3, Issue 12, December 2004, Pages 709-718
Environmental risk factors in multiple sclerosis aetiology
Dr Ruth Ann Marrie
[11]British Journal of Nutrition (1973), 29, 95
Lesions produced by copper deficiency in neonate and older rats
G. A. Hall, J. Mcc. Howell
[12]American Journal Clinical Nutrition 2005 Jan;81(1 Suppl):215S-217S.
Polyphenols: antioxidants and beyond.
Scalbert A, Johnson IT, Saltmarsh M.
[13]Cancer Cell International 2004
Potential mechanism of phytochemical-induced apoptosis in human prostate adenocarcinoma cells: Therapeutic synergy in genistein and β-lapachone combination treatment
James Kumi-Diaka, Simone Saddler-Shawnette, Alex Aller and Jayann Brown
[13]International Society for Horticultural Science: VI International Symposium on Kiwifruit
Antioxidant and other effects of phytochemicals on DNA integrity
A.R. Collins and M. Aisch
[14]Biochemical and Biophysical Research Communications Vol 303, Issue 2, 4 April 2003, Pages 483-487
Decreased plasma and tissue levels of vitamin C in a rat model of aging: implications for antioxidative defence.
B. van der Looa, M. Bachschmidc, et al
[15]American Journal of Clinical Nutrition, Vol 41, 1332-1344
Dietary habits and the prediction of life span of rats: a prospective test
MH Ross, ED Lustbader, G Bras
[16]Toxicologic Pathology. 1995 Sep-Oct;23(5):570-82

Longevity, body weight, and neoplasia in ad libitum-fed and diet-restricted C57BL6 mice fed NIH-31 open formula diet.
Blackwell BN, Bucci TJ, Hart RW, Turturro A.
[17]Gerontology Vol. 47, No. 1, 2001
Prenatal Exposure to a Maternal Low Protein Diet Shortens Life Span in Rats
A. A. Sayera, R. Dunnc, S. Langley-Evansd, C. Coopera
[18] Life expectancy survey - Angela Clarke. Results can be found on the Fancy Rats website: http://www.fancy-rats.co.uk
[19]http://www.sproutpeople.com/index.html

"Old rats shouldn't eat health foods. They need all the preservatives they can get."

Based on a quotation from Robert Orben

Chapter eight - overview

Feeding for health
Calorie restriction
    How to achieve calorie restriction
In sickness and in health
    Kidney disease - prevention
    Kidney disease - treatment
    Mammary and pituitary tumours - prevention
    Mammary and pituitary tumours - treatment
    Skin problems - prevention and treatment
    Spinal nerve (hind leg) degeneration - prevention and treatment
    Diabetes mellitus - prevention
    Diabetes mellitus - treatment
    Gluten free diet
Feeding sick rats
    Useful foods for younger sick rats
    Useful foods where kidney disease is a consideration
Rehydration
Syringe feeding
Giving medication
The affects of antibiotic therapy.

Chapter eight
Feeding for health:
prevention and treatment

FEEDING FOR HEALTH

Diet can play an important role in maintaining the health of a rat, in terms of both the prevention and management of illness. Without doubt, the most effective way that you can help your rat in terms of long-term health is to keep their food rationed and prevent them from becoming overweight. Lifelong weight is affected by early overfeeding, as this permanently changes aspects of fat metabolism, making it easier for the rat to put on weight.[1] For this reason, breeders have a role in long term weight control, as slimmer babies who have not been fed to their maximum capacity for growth will have a greater chance of remaining slim into adulthood. It is also recognised that there are genes that influence appetite, activity levels and the propensity to put on weight, and some rats will be naturally more prone to obesity than others.[2]

CALORIE RESTRICTIONS

As outlined in chapter seven, calorie restricted diets have been shown to extend lifespan in rats. The reason for this is thought (at least in part) to be due to these diets having a positive effect on kidney health. They delay the onset of deterioration in kidney function, and slow the pace of decline once it begins. Protein restricted diets have the same effect, but to a much lesser degree.[3]

Other reasons for increased longevity when calories are restricted are thought to include a greater resistance to stress and an increased ability to prevent the cell damage that leads to aging. This may be due, at least to some degree, to reduced metabolic rate and the resulting reduction in the free radicals that damage body cells, but the theories as to why restricting calories is so effective remain subject to further research and debate.

Some of the diets tested on rats and mice have been so restricted that the animals became unhealthy and lethargic. Clearly this is unacceptable and lifespan should always be a secondary issue to the *quality* of that life. However, it seems that moderate restrictions (of about 70 to 80%) have measurable benefits while still allowing the rat to function normally. It is important to realise that a calorie restricted diet should be just that; restricted in calories (energy) but not in nutrients. When feeding a reduced quantity it is obviously more important to make sure that the food given is rich in nutrients and will meet the rat's requirements. If there is any doubt about this, it is advisable to give a good general vitamin and mineral supplement (like Dr Squiggles Daily Essentials) regularly.

HOW TO ACHIEVE CALORIE RESTRICTION

There are a number of ways to achieve calorie restriction that are within the reach of the average pet owner. The most obvious is to simply feed fewer calories by feeding less food. Since a low fat, moderate protein diet is recommended for rats, most of their calories are coming from carbohydrate rich foods like grain and legumes. So in order to reduce calorie intake, less grain mix needs to be offered than would be eaten if the rat had free access to the mix at all times. One way of achieving this is to work out roughly how much a group eats when fed ad lib (freely), by varying the amount in the food dish until you find the point where the amount of food offered is generally cleared in 24 hours, (just a very small amount of undesirable food left in the dish at feeding time). You will of course need to be sure that the rats are not stashing quantities of food around the cage for later! Once you work out this volume you have the 'ad lib' volume for that group. Then you would feed about one fifth less than that every 24 hours.

Another method is to have an evening 'active fast' period. This involves making sure that your rats have no access to food from waking after their daytime sleep period, to when you feed them (late evening). You can achieve this by removing the food bowl, giving them time out, or only feeding enough food to last them until they go to sleep after their morning period of activity. There is no point in making their fast period a time when they are naturally sleepy. They have to be awake and active - and fasting.

Alternatively you can feed the same volume of food, but less grain mix and replace this with low calorie vegetables. There is a list of suggested foods for this method on page 231, in the section on weight reduction. If you choose this method, do watch your rats for loose faeces while they get used to the change. You will also need to remember that they will probably drink less, as there is more fluid in their diet.

Some people prefer to think less about volumes of feed on a daily basis and use the regular fast method. Rats are not grazers, but opportunistic foragers who are well adapted to have longer periods without food. One method of (incomplete) fasting is to not feed at all the night before you clean out the cage. This works particularly well if you scatter feed. The rats will then clear up any morsels of food left around the cage and - if you can resist the temptation to overfeed for the rest of the week - will have a naturally lean, but not entirely food-free extended period. Another method is to clean out in the morning, then not put any food in the cage until late the same evening. None of these systems will work if you over feed in between; daily volume should always be at least on the lean side of ad lib volume.

I tend to use a combination of these methods and try to keep the regular volume of dry mix a little under ad lib amounts, while having regular lean days (usually every third day) when I feed about half of the volume I do on other days. Also, on clean out days, I leave no food in the cage from late afternoon through to late evening when I feed as normal. Finally I scatter feed.

OUR FEEDING 'REGIME':
Monday - dry mix to about 85% ad lib amount
Tuesday - dry mix to about 85% ad lib amount
Wednesday - half rations of dry mix
Thursday - dry mix to about 85% ad lib amount
Friday - dry mix to about 85% ad lib amount
Saturday - half rations of dry mix
Sunday - fresh meal (including Dr Squiggles Tiny Animal Essentials, salmon oil and seaweed powder) - no dry mix.

I also feed fresh vegetables most days, Dr Squiggles Daily Essentials and Calcivet 2 times a week in their water and liver cake once a week.

While not in itself able to reduce the amount of food given (that's up to us), I find that scatter feeding is probably the single most effective measure in helping me not to over feed my rats. Having no food bowl means that there is no focus for me as a human to feel I ought to be replenishing it when empty, or keeping it topped up. Scatter feeding replicates (as closely as possible in a caged environment) the natural foraging behaviour of the rat, and it requires determination, time and energy to find food, especially once the initial flurry of activity at feeding time is over. For every calorie consumed, energy is also expended, making calorie restrictions easier to maintain. You do have to be able to trust your rats to do what millions of years of evolution have equipped them to do admirably - find food. Adding an extra scoop to make it easy for them will just set you back to square one. The 'how to' of scatter feeding is expanded in Chapter 9.

IN SICKNESS AND IN HEALTH

With all rat illnesses that are related in some way to diet, there are two elements to providing dietary solutions; prevention and treatment. Health relies on us taking preventative measures before illness occurs, but even so, all rats eventually succumb to something and a well planned diet can often help in supporting rats in ill-health, and minimising the effects of illness.

KIDNEY DISEASE - PREVENTION

It cannot be overstated how common kidney disease is in older rats, as almost all rats will be affected to some degree. The only questions are "how early?" and "how badly?" With this in mind many people will wish to feed a preventative diet to their rats, in terms of minimising kidney damage over the majority of their lives. Factors that have been shown to delay or slow the rate of degeneration are:

- Calorie restriction.
- Protein restriction.
- Soya or egg protein sources (rather than other vegetable sources, milk or flesh).
- Low phosphorus diet.
- Inclusion of flax/linseed oil.

It can be deduced that there are certain methods of feeding that are likely to delay the effects of kidney problems, and therefore extend well-being and lifespan. Feeding a diet for maintenance that is lower in protein, where the main protein source is soya or egg, and feeding reduced volumes overall will help to postpone the onset of kidney disease. Then, later in life adding in flax seed or oil and selecting lower phosphorus grains and fresh foods will slow down the progression of the disease process once it has begun. Other supplements like vitamin B complex help to reduce anaemia (an effect of kidney failure and of B_{12}/folate deficiency), and may help slow hind leg degeneration.

KIDNEY DISEASE – TREATMENT
Kidney failure accounts for many of the deaths where rats just gradually decline and die for no apparent reason, but for many other rats it will weaken them sufficiently for another illness or infection to end their life. Treatment in humans is dialysis and transplantation, which are obviously unavailable to our small pets, but diet also plays a large role in maintaining balanced blood chemistry and slowing the rate of decline. Since rats can lose 75% of their kidney function before actively displaying signs of illness, the following treatments should be considered palliative for all older rats that are already showing symptoms, and preventative for those who aren't. They should improve quality of life and slow down the progression of the disease process, but there is no cure.

Much of the malaise that accompanies kidney failure is due to high levels of toxins circulating in the blood. This is called uraemia. Protein is broken down in the liver and this process produces waste products (particularly urea) which are then excreted by the kidneys. When the kidneys are failing, the urea level builds up in the blood as a result.

Symptoms of uraemia are:
• Tiredness
• Itching
• Loss of appetite
• Nausea

- Breathlessness
- Fluid retention
- Weakness
- Encephalopathy (toxicity of the brain causing confusion/clumsiness and eventually coma, leading to death).

It has been found that controlling protein intake does not always slow down the progression of the disease, but will significantly improve comfort and well-being by reducing uraemia. It is not simply a matter of feeding a low protein diet, but it is important to consider the quality of the protein and how easily it is broken down, as some protein sources yield larger amounts of toxins. With this in mind, the best sources of protein are egg, soya, then fish, chicken and finally the red meats. Of the vegetable protein sources, soya is the most useful and least taxing on the kidneys. Indeed research has shown that soya actively helps to maintain kidney health in comparison to milk protein.

It has traditionally been the case that when a rat is elderly and 'failing', we increase the protein load they have to deal with by feeding foods such as EMP, porridge and scrambled egg, and I would suggest that it might be more helpful to consider an alternative approach. Even in the absence of obvious symptoms, it is wise to assume that all elderly rats in decline have a degree of kidney damage. For many, this will be serious enough to be the cause of their decline. For the rest, feeding a 'kidney-friendly' diet will serve to protect their kidneys from further damage.

As well as considering the amount and quality of the protein given, the other main factor affecting the progression of the disease is phosphorus intake. When the kidneys begin to fail, phosphorus (which is a component of all foods) isn't excreted as efficiently and blood levels begin to rise. Calcium and phosphorus are closely linked, and as the phosphorus level rises calcium is pulled out of the bones. This not only weakens the bones, but increases the levels circulating in the blood. These minerals can then be deposited in soft tissue around the body where they cause inflammation and discomfort. When they are deposited in the soft tissue of the kidneys they will serve to increase the rate at which they fail.

Reducing dietary intake of phosphorus is critical to slowing the progression of the disease process. This can be done in two ways: avoiding foods that are high in phosphorus and giving phosphate binders along with food. The 'old fashioned' medications that we take as antacids, (those made of calcium carbonate), work well as phosphate binders and are safe, however, I would only recommend giving phosphate binders to rats who are showing signs of general decline or once kidney disease becomes apparent. Ipakitine is a more effective alternative to antacids, being both a phosphate binder and also binding with some uraemic toxins, thereby increasing feelings of well-being. Some people have also reported improved hind leg function where degeneration is associated with kidney disease. Ipakitine should be available from your vet or via some vet suppliers and the dose is 1g per 5kg of body weight – so 0.1g for a 500g rat. It is a palatable powder that can easily be added to soft food.

Calcium balance is also affected by a drop in available vitamin D, which occurs because the kidneys are responsible for producing the active (usable) form of this vitamin within the body. As the kidneys become less efficient, the available vitamin D decreases and this leads to a reduction of the absorption of calcium from food, since vitamin D is required for this process. It is therefore essential to ensure that levels of active (usable) vitamin D are high in the diet, in the form of D3 (calciferol). This will help to increase the absorption of calcium from food and reduce the risk of serious bone disease.

The following diet is one that I have devised to support kidney function and am now feeding to all my elderly rats, unless they live in groups with those who are still growing. Whole grains (especially wheat, oats and rye) are high in phosphorus and a base food should be selected with this in mind. Once grains are processed, phosphorus is reduced and 'white' versions of grains have very little phosphorus at all, but are also stripped of much of their nutrition except for energy.

SUITABLE COMMERCIAL BASE FOODS FOR USE IN KIDNEY FAILURE:

Rat Rations - Geriatric and kidney support mix. Sold as a complete food and could reasonably be used as such with necessary supplements, but most people will wish to add further variety, micronutrients and interest. At approximately £1.50 per kg it is an inexpensive and highly suitable base, even with postage included.

Harrison's Banana Rabbit Bunch - one of the more suitable commercial feeds as it is does not contain wheat or oats as primary ingredients. Unless the rat already has polyuria (passes large volumes of urine), you should pick out most of the banana chips and feed them as treats to younger rats. Where urine volumes are increased, potassium levels in the body can become depleted, as potassium is lost along with the large volumes of fluid. The banana can help to boost potassium levels in these circumstances.

Hills Prescription Diet k/d Canine. Whilst not suitable to be used alone as base food this dog kibble, which is designed to support chronic renal failure, is suitable to be added to a kidney support base. It is low in phosphorus, has restricted protein (primarily egg based) and is a useful source of copper in this diet too (14 mg/kg). It has a high fat content, but I feel the other benefits outweigh this at this time in a rat's life and much of the rest of the dry mix is very low fat. A 2 kg bag costs about £12 from a vet but will last you a good while.

PROPORTIONS IF USING RAT RATIONS MIX AS A BASE FOOD:

'Scoop' simply represents one measure, and can be replaced by cup, jug or similar, depending on how much feed is required.

6 scoops Rat Rations mix
2 scoops Hills k/d Prescription Diet (can be omitted if preferred).
½ scoop corn flakes/corn cakes
½ scoop puffed rice/rice cakes/white rice
½scoop puffed wheat/Shredded wheat
½ scoop of flax/hemp/pumpkin seeds

¼ scoop corn or rice pasta/egg noodles (optional)
¼ scoop carrots
Garlic and seaweed if desired (can be omitted if preferred).

PROPORTIONS IF USING HARRISON'S AS A BASE FOOD:
3 scoops base food
2 scoops Hills k/d Prescription Diet
1 scoop corn flakes/corn cakes
½ scoop corn kernels (e.g. popping corn)
1 scoop puffed rice/rice cakes or ½ scoop white rice
½ scoop puffed wheat/Shredded Wheat Bitesize (broken)
½ scoop of pearl barley
1 scoop flaked barley
½ scoop of flax/hemp/pumpkin seeds
¼ scoop corn or rice pasta/egg noodles (optional)
Garlic and seaweed if desired

A 'kidney friendly' mix (like the one detailed on page 121) can be used throughout adult life as a protective measure, and increasingly modified into old age to further reduce phosphorus levels. This can be achieved by removing the wheat, oats, Ryvita and river shrimps and adding a little extra soya.

USING STRAIGHT GRAINS FOR SUPPORTING RATS WITH KIDNEY DISEASE:
Some people who are already feeding their other rats on straight grains may prefer to make up their kidney friendly diet from scratch, from the ingredients they already have available. Here is an example of a suitable recipe:

2 scoops barley flakes
1 scoop pearl barley
1 scoop paddy rice
½ scoop white rice
1 scoop broken rice cakes

1 scoop flaked maize
1 scoop flaked peas
1 scoop soya flakes
½ a scoop of dried split peas
1 scoop mixed millet
1 scoop buck wheat [this isn't wheat]
1 scoop puffed wheat
1 scoop broken corn cakes or low sugar corn flakes
½ scoop seeds; hemp, linseed (flax), pumpkin etc.
half a scoop of broken noodles
Some dried vegetables, especially carrot
Garlic and seaweed if desired
This mix can be used with - or without - the addition of up to 3 scoops of Hills k/d Prescription Diet.

WET FOOD AND SUPPLEMENTS

As well as the dried mix I would recommend one of the following 'wet' foods, shared between about 10 rats:

- Half a pack of Burns Penlan Farm Range - egg, brown rice and vegetables.
- Half a pack of Naturediet lite.
- A little of the eggy rice mixture detailed below .

This 'wet' food is simply a vehicle for delivering some or all of the following supplements (doses for 10 rats):

- ½ teaspoon of flax oil (shown to slow progression of kidney disease).
- 1 capsule of Seven Seas High Strength Cod liver oil (vitamin A extracted; boosts omega 3 and Vitamin D).
- 2 crushed antacid tablets, for example Rennie (binds phosphate in the diet) or 1.0g Ipakitine.
- 1 crushed high dose vitamin B complex tablet (improves associated anaemia and may help slow spinal nerve degeneration).
- 1 teaspoon Senior Aid (supplement for elderly animals).
- 550mg Rubenal (see page 183).

I tend not to give these rats too many other 'treats', though they do get a small amount of fresh vegetables, however most mineral rich vegetables (such as kale, broccoli, pak choi) also contain fair amounts of phosphorus. As with everything you need to weigh the balance of the benefit over the cost. I feel the benefits of a small amount in the diet probably outweigh the extra phosphorus. If fed at the same time as the wet food above, some of the phosphorus would be 'removed' by the phosphate binders. Of the green leafy vegetables, kale performs best for highest copper (advantageous) and lowest phosphorus. Carrot is a vegetable with lower levels of phosphorus and good levels of other micronutrients. Apples, berries, grapes, plums, pineapple, peaches are all fine to feed in moderation in this situation.

Foods that are particularly high in phosphorus and should be avoided when treating kidney problems are unprocessed whole-wheat, bran, oats, rye, spelt, dairy (soya products are better), some fruit, such as avocado and nuts. Banana is high in potassium but contains relatively little phosphorus.

If you are feeding this diet as a *preventative* measure, you may choose not to be so strict about the higher phosphorus grains, or not to use the wet food daily, as this is really a medium for adding the supplements to the diet. Flax oil, fish oil and vitamin B complex remain useful supplements for any rats, and you might still want to give these. In a mixed aged colony where younger rats (1 year to approx 20 months) are being fed this diet, it is probably wise to reduce the amount of Prescription Diet to 10% (1 scoop for every 9 scoops of other ingredients) of the overall mix, or use soya alone. This will reduce the overall fat level of the mix. If feeding a group with a wide age spread (rats who are still growing alongside those who have active kidney problems), then feed the kidney friendly dry mix with reduced or no prescription diet. Then separately supplement the older rats with something like Burns Penlan Farm Range egg, brown rice and vegetables dog food and the youngsters with mixed fresh foods. See Chapter 12 for more ideas.

EGGY RICE RECIPE
I often use this as an alternative to Naturediet or Burns Penlan Farm and as

a means for giving supplements.

Half fill a pudding bowl with cooked white rice, beat through one egg, add a little fresh garlic or seaweed if desired. Microwave for 30 seconds then remove and stir. Add the supplements and stir well. Return the mixture to the microwave for 20-30 seconds until set. Break up to serve.

Essential fatty acids like those in flax and fish oil are sensitive to heat and need to be treated gently in that regard. Mixing into egg and rice buffers them a little and this degree of heating should not cause chemical changes. If you are in doubt you can add them to the mixture at the end of cooking and cooling, and then stir thoroughly.

FLUID AND OTHER LOSSES
Once in kidney failure, most rats produce large amounts of dilute urine and drink furiously as a result. Adequate quantities of fresh water should be available at all times. Where urinary output is high, you need to realise that minerals, protein and water soluble vitamins are also flushed out of the body in greater quantities. A good multivitamin and mineral mixture is a good idea at this point, regardless of your diet.

MAMMARY AND PITUITARY TUMOURS - PREVENTION
Beyond genetic predisposition, increased occurrence of mammary and pituitary tumours has been directly linked to ad lib feeding, rapid maturing into adulthood, fatness and high fat diets. They tend to be reduced by not feeding to maximum capacity for growth, calorie restricted diets, low protein,[4] low fat diets and possibly feeding a diet high in antioxidants and some fermented soya (like miso paste, which can be softened in a little warm water and then mixed into any soft food). There is more information on soya in Chapter 6.

MAMMARY AND PITUITARY TUMOURS - TREATMENT
The principal treatment for mammary tumours is removal, with or without an accompanying spay. Very occasionally a rat is too sick for surgery, or a mammary lump is inoperable. All pituitary tumours are inoperable. In

these cases, and as a preventative measure for rats who have already had a mammary tumour removed, some of the following supplements can be tried:

- CLA (Conjugated Linoleic Acid) - 1000mg capsules - antioxidant that hinders the growth of mammary tumours.[5] Daily dose would be approximately one third of one capsule.
- Shark cartilage - 650mg capsules - some indication that this slows angiogenesis (the growth of new blood vessels), and as mammary tumours are extremely vascular this may help to reduce the rate of growth.[6] Daily dose approximately one third of one capsule. Many people have ethical objections to using shark cartilage and the active ingredient of turmeric (curcumin) may make a viable alternative.
- Curcumin - 500mg capsules - antioxidant with anti-inflammatory properties, that reduces tumour growth.[7] Might be helpful in slowing the growth of any tumour. Daily dose approximately one quarter of a capsule. Bioavailability (absorption from the gut) is not good, but may be improved by feeding mixed into flax oil.
- Co-enzyme Q10 - 10mg - antioxidant which potentially has many beneficial properties, including reducing oxidation and DNA damage.[8] Daily dose one 10th of a capsule.
- Echinacea/goldenseal liquid herbal extract - herbal preparation considered to have some immune system benefits.[9] Daily dose 1 drop. There is some evidence to suggest that the benefits are short term and immunity may become depressed with long-term use, but views are mixed and more research is needed. Short pulses of treatment may be better than long term daily use.
- Sublingual B vitamin complex liquid - required for metabolism and the healthy functioning of the immune system. Daily dose 0.1ml.
- Super antioxidant formula (has an number of vitamins and minerals including vitamin C, E, beta-carotene and selenium - do not give this if you are using Dr Squiggles Daily Essentials, Essentials Plus, Senior Aid, Nutrical, or similar multivitamin preparations - promotes immune system health, including mopping up free radicals and promoting apoptosis (see page 170). Daily dose one 10th human dose.

- Flaxseed/linseed oil - omega 3 fatty acids and may help to reduce tumour growth.[10] Daily dose one 10th human dose.

These supplements can be mixed together and fed in a little Nutrical or yoghurt. If you mix a few doses up at the same time, they will keep for up to a week in the fridge. *Please be cautious about giving some of these supplements around the time of tumour surgery, because of their effects on the growth of new blood vessels. If in doubt ask your vet.*

Some lump mixes include Pau d'arco which does have the widely accepted property of destroying cancer cells (active ingredient lapachol, present at levels of less than 4%). Lapachol is well researched and a single dose of 365mg produced clastogenic effects in rats (disruption of chromosomes).[11] Repeated doses can have cumulative effects, that is, lower doses can cause the same effect if given regularly. However, at the highest recommended dose of Pau d'arco that I have seen for rats (around 400mg/kg/day) the amount of lapachol will be less than 16mg/kg/day, well below the level needed to produce a clastogenic effect, but above the level seen to cause gastro-intestinal side effects in humans, such as nausea and diarrhoea. The problem with Pau d'arco is that the doses needed to be effective against cancer cells are toxic, often causing severe anaemia amongst other issues. For this reason while it is recognised as a useful antioxidant (at lower doses) for human use, it is not considered to have a viable role in treating cancer.

Medical treatments are available for pituitary tumours, which may also be helpful in the treatment of some specific types of mammary tumour. *I do not recommend the use of supplements for these conditions without first discussing appropriate treatment with your vet.*

SKIN PROBLEMS - PREVENTION AND TREATMENT
Some skin lesions, excessive scratching and loss of hair can be related to dietary issues. Diets that are deficient in essential fatty acids, essential amino acids or micronutrients, can lead to skin lesions and poor coat quality. The most striking cases I have seen have been when the rat has been on a very restricted diet (e.g. all sweetcorn), or on a diet that contains

a large amount of one problematic ingredient (e.g. peanuts or sunflower seeds). Deficiency related issues are unusual in a rat who receives a varied diet, but they should be considered in all cases after parasites and infection have been excluded. Potential problems include a lack of omega 3 fatty acids, essential amino acids, zinc and vitamins A, B_2, B_6, C and E. Treatment is supplementation in the short term and the re-introduction of a widely varied diet where this is not already being fed.

It has often been quoted historically that high protein diets cause scabs, but this seems to be well accepted now as a myth. Likely, there are some high protein foods that may cause allergic skin reactions (e.g. sunflower seeds), but protein levels alone do not seem to produce this effect. Rats may succumb to various food allergies that can have wide-ranging effects. At their most serious, allergies can be lethal because the tongue and airways swell and block off air flow, but occasionally an allergy will show as a dermatitis type reaction. The prevention of allergies relies of avoiding large quantities of allergenic-type foods, such as sunflower seeds, peanuts, dairy products or food dye, but even so, allergies may still sometimes occur. Where this is the case, you will need work out what the allergen is (using an exclusion diet if necessary), and then exclude any traces of the problematic food or additive from the diet.

A full exclusion diet should begin by being pared back to just cooked rice and millet, with a good vitamin and mineral supplement. Flax seed oil can also be added as allergies to this are rare. If the cause is a food allergy, the rat's skin should improve over a period of days, and once this is happening you can begin re-introducing food items, always one at a time and always leaving a gap of a few days in between. Chicken (another low risk food) should be added as soon as possible to provide an adequate protein source, and help support repair and healing of the skin.

SPINAL NERVE (HIND LEG) DEGENERATION PREVENTION AND TREATMENT

Hind leg degeneration (HLD) is a recognised feature of aging in rats, and is commonly due to a gradual process of demyelination of the spinal nerves, though there are thought to be other disease processes that produce similar signs. The demyelination means that the nerves can no longer function properly to supply the feet, legs and tail with sensation and movement. As the disease progresses, the severity of the signs increase, until eventually all of the nerve tissue is replaced with connective tissue and paralysis of the hind quarters is complete. Affected rats often lose weight rapidly because of muscle wasting of their rump and hind legs and the resulting difficulty in balancing to eat. Both genders are affected, though bucks more often than does. This may be due to the fact that there seems to be some correlation with kidney disease in rats, and this is more common in bucks.

Age at onset and rate of progression seem to be influenced primarily by genetic factors and to a lesser degree by activity levels; rats with high activity levels tend to remain mobile for longer, once HLD has become established. Apart from retrospective breeding away from badly affected rats, or those who get the disease at an earlier age, little can be done to reduce occurrence, however, it is thought that encouraging activity, alongside high dose B group vitamins, may slow the progression. Supplementation of the B group vitamins, including B_{12} may help, as vitamin B_{12} deficiency in particular has been linked to demyelination of nerves in humans. The body's ability to absorb B_{12} decreases with age and even with the practice of coprophagy, it is possible that older rats are more likely to be deficient.

Another factor which could potentially have an effect is a chronic shortage of vitamin D, as this again has been linked to the occurrence of a similar demyelination disease in humans. Various methods of supplementing vitamin D are discussed at length on pages 153 to 155, but it is important to realise that this is not a short term measure, to be used as the rat ages, but something that may have an effect throughout life. This means that a lack of vitamin D in the first six months of life could potentially affect demyelination in old age.

Chondroitin may also help at about a tenth of the adult human dose; it has been shown to delay the onset of demyelination in a similar, but induced disease in mice.[12]

One way of combining these supplements is to use Senior Aid daily, though it should be noted that the amount of some of these supplements in Senior Aid does not offer a therapeutic dose, and separate administration of Vitamin B_{12} and chondroitin should probably still be considered. Feed all of these supplements alongside a varied, low phosphorus diet that includes flax seed.

Many people refer to a link between HLD and kidney disease, but there is little research into this association. Both conditions occur in elderly rats and both conditions are common, therefore both will often occur in the same rat. However, it is difficult to know if this is cause and effect, or two unrelated issues, but there is anecdotal evidence, such as improvement in HLD in some cases with the use of Ipakitine, which is a phosphate and urea binder, but more research is needed. Since poor kidney function can lead to low levels of blood proteins (because they are lost in the urine), increased oedema can result (as fluid moves into the tissues of the body by osmosis) and the increased pressure caused by this on the spinal nerves could serve to exacerbate any hind leg weakness. Thus, feeding a kidney supportive diet and associated supplements, could feasibly help to relieve some HLD symptoms in rats who have both conditions.

DIABETES MELLITUS - PREVENTION
The main thing that can be done to prevent diabetes in rats is to breed away from large, obesity prone animals and encourage slow growth into adulthood. Calorie restriction will help achieve this and it is also wise to avoid anything more than treat levels of processed foods and sugar.

DIABETES MELLITUS - TREATMENT
Rats can develop both type 1 and type 2 diabetes, just as humans can and while type 1 will often require insulin injections, type 2 can often be treated with diet alone. In order to stabilise the blood glucose as much as possible

the diet should be high in unrefined carbohydrates and fibre. All refined carbohydrates and sugary treats should be avoided, and fruit given sparingly.

POSSIBLE MIX FOR A DIABETIC RAT

'Scoop' simply represents one measure, and can be replaced by cup, jug etc depending on how much feed is required.

9 scoops of mixed whole grains/straight cereals/legumes, for example, flaked whole grain barley, whole oats, wheat groats, oat groats, millet, milo, whole corn, pea flakes, soya flakes, paddy rice, buckwheat.
1 scoop Burns high oats kibble (recommended for diabetic dogs because it has low levels of rapid glucose-releasing carbohydrates).
1½ scoops high fibre human cereals, for example, Shredded Wheat, spelt flakes, quinoa, pearl barley.
½ scoop of mixed seeds - flax, hemp, pumpkin.
1 scoop dried mixed vegetables and rabbit herbs.
1 scoop soaked and roasted chick peas.

This mix is entirely suitable for any other adult rats who share the cage with the diabetic rat, unless they are very old, have kidney disease or have other specific dietary needs.

If you wish to replace the straight grains with a commercial feed try to combine two or three that have a relatively high fibre content and no sugar (fruit, glucose syrup, molasses) added. Mr Johnson's Supreme Rabbit, Supa Natural and Xtra Vital rat food are all suitable in this regard. Combining a few feeds helps to overcome their individual shortfalls.

Diabetic rats can be given nutritious low carbohydrate treats, or treats with low levels of rapid glucose-releasing carbohydrates, such as kale, spring greens, broccoli, carrot, pulses, nuts, whole grain pasta/bread/rice. Small amounts of protein foods (oily fish, chicken, egg) are fine, in line with a healthy diet for any adult rat.

USEFUL SUPPLEMENTS

There are definitely a few supplements that are worth trying with diabetic rats, as there is some evidence that they might be useful in helping to maintain healthy glucose metabolism.

ALPHA-LIPOIC ACID (ALA) - this is a compound that is similar to a vitamin. It is an antioxidant; a substance that prevents cell damage and there have been studies in animals and people that have suggested beneficial effects, such as increased glucose uptake in muscle, sensitivity of the body to insulin and reduced diabetic neuropathy. Dose approximately 80mg daily.

BIOTIN (VITAMIN B7) - increases the activity of the enzyme glucokinase. This enzyme is responsible for the first step of glucose use within the body. Supplements of biotin may cause a fall in blood glucose levels in diabetics. Dose approximately 1.6mg daily

CHROMIUM - may improve glucose tolerance, achieve lower fasting glucose levels and decrease insulin levels. Brewer's yeast contains high levels of chromium or you can buy chromium as a supplement. Dose is between 5 and 20 micrograms daily.

COENZYME Q10 - a compound that occurs naturally in the body, and may be able to help with carbohydrate metabolism. It is has been proven that animals suffering from diabetes are often coenzyme Q10 deficient. Research to date shows that coenzyme Q10 supplementation may lower blood sugar levels. Dose approximately 6 to 15mg daily.

FENUGREEK - in animal and several small, human trials, fenugreek has been found to lower fasting serum glucose levels, both acutely and long term. It is easy to give in powdered form or you can feed the whole seed. Holland and Barret sell a powder in capsule form, but the capsules can be opened to release the powder. Dose ⅓ to ⅔ of one 610mg capsule daily. Fenugreek seeds are widely available and could usefully be added to the diet but it may be harder to achieve a therapeutic dose in this way.

MAGNESIUM AND MANGANESE - diabetics are commonly deficient in these minerals, both of which directly influence glucose metabolism. Human diabetics supplemented with magnesium have even sometimes been able to reduce their dose of insulin. The dose is approximately 0.2 to 0.5mg manganese, and 30 to 40mg of magnesium daily. Both minerals are included in wide-ranging multivitamin and mineral supplements, such as Dr Squiggles Essentials range.

ZINC - thought to be crucial to insulin metabolism and can be lost with increased urination so supplementation is recommended. Also in Dr Squiggles Essentials range.

All doses quoted here are based on a tenth of the human dose. Although the daily amounts are quoted, because of the nature of metabolism, it may be wise to split the daily dose into at least two smaller doses spread across the day.

GLUTEN FREE DIET

I include this diet in case it turns out to be useful to anyone, as I worked it out recently for a rat-owning human who was very allergic to gluten, and was concerned about the effects of handling cereals containing it, and breathing in the dust.

It is possible to create a gluten free mix by making up your own food based on rice and corn, plus some of the less obvious grains like millet, quinoa, buckwheat (which is gluten free) and dari (milo).

Barley is a great staple grain for rats, but barley contains gluten, however, I understand that many people who are allergic to wheat are not necessarily allergic to barley - so it really depends on the individual. If you can't use barley, then view rice and corn as your base grains.

Suitable human grade cereals include pot or pearl barley (if possible), brown or wild rice, wholegrain rice cakes, whole grain puffed rice, pasta (corn/rice based), low sugar cornflakes (usually organic or supermarket budget range have least sugar), corn cakes, gluten free muesli or similar cereals.

Animal protein can be a rice based dog kibble (wheat and oat free) such as Burns, or freeze dried shrimps, insects or fish. Legumes are also encouraged and are gluten free. Herbs and vegetables, dried fruit, berries, seeds and nuts can all be added as to any mix.

QUANTITIES
So long as you have plenty of variety don't worry too much about exact amounts, but major on grains and vegetables/greens with smaller amounts of seeds, animal protein and only a very small amount of fruit and nuts.

For example:
2 cups paddy rice
½ a cup of whole grain rice
3 broken rice cakes
2 cups buckwheat
1 cup flaked corn
1 cup whole corn
1 cup corn flakes
2 cups mixed millets
1 cup white milo
1 cup quinoa
1 cup pea flakes
1 cup mixed vegetables
¼ cup hemp seeds
third cup pumpkin seeds
3 cups barley flakes (if using)
1 cup burns dog kibble or shrimps
½ cup dried banana
½ packet of dandelion mix*
½ packet of wood picnic mix.*
*These are just specific herbal blends from Burns and the Naturals range, but they can be substituted with any similar product.

Another time you might drop the whole corn and add in broken corn cakes or corn based pasta, so you can just mix and change as you please, but the main base should be the unrefined grains like paddy rice, buckwheat (the unprocessed grains, not the human grade equivalent), flaked/whole corn, millets/dari/quinoa and flaked barley (if allowed).

FEEDING SICK RATS

Sick rats often don't eat well, and lose weight rapidly. Their requirements for energy can in fact be raised as a result of raised body temperature, an increased heart rate, respiratory effort or supporting a large tumour. It is therefore important for sick rats to receive a diet that is rich in calories, but low in volume. If the sick rat is also elderly or has kidney problems, the principles of a kidney friendly diet should be applied.

This is the time to reduce the usual cereal based dry rat mix, in favour of moist highly nutritious foods that are easy to eat. Leave a small bowl of dry mix in the cage so that the rat can nibble on this if they wish, but also provide frequent small meals of fresh food. It is easy to increase the food value and energy content of 'wet food', by adding extras like Nutrical, Lactol, human infant soya milk or tinned coconut milk.

USEFUL FOOD FOR YOUNGER SICK RATS

- EMP made with Lactol or human infant soya milk.
- Porridge made as above (can add Nutrical and egg to this).
- High quality wet dog/cat food (Naturediet, Burns, Applaws).
- Wholemeal bread soaked in Lactol or human infant soya milk.
- Scrambled egg (made with Lactol or human infant soya milk and a little olive oil).
- Live (bio) yoghurt.
- Human baby foods (these can be 'souped-up' by adding Nutrical, coconut milk, mashed avocado or tinned fish).
- Mashed or sliced avocado.
- A little fresh or lightly cooked broccoli, kale and carrot. Cooking will make digestion a little easier.

- Human complete nutrition drinks for example Complan or Build Up.
- Coconut milk (tinned) can be mixed into other foods.
- Oily fish (fresh or tinned cooked trout, salmon, mackerel).

USEFUL FOODS FOR SICK RATS WHERE KIDNEY DISEASE IS A CONSIDERATION

- 'Porridge' made with standard soya milk and couscous (you can add Nutrical and egg to this).
- Naturediet Lite or Burns Penlan Farm range dog food.
- Puffed rice or puffed millet in soya milk (don't substitute other cereals).
- Live (bio) yoghurt, preferably soya.
- Human baby foods (these can be 'souped-up' by adding Nutrical, coconut milk or mashed banana).
- Mashed or sliced banana.
- A little fresh or lightly cooked broccoli, kale and carrot. Cooking will make digestion a little easier.
- Human complete nutrition drinks, for example. Complan or Build Up.
- Coconut milk (tinned) can be mixed into other foods.
- Processed grain products (cooked) like noodles, white rice and couscous (choose these in preference to pasta), mixed with egg.

HELPING SICK RATS TO EAT

"If you're struggling to get sick rats to eat at all, then Nutrical can be mixed with some water, sucked up into a syringe and syringe-fed, as that way you get some nutrition and fluids down them. Nutrical is fab generally for poorly/underweight rats. Also, when we had SDAV and they were all miserable and not really wanting to eat, Ready Brek with some honey and Lactol mixed in went down a treat. Obviously it's not something we'd give regularly, but when it was a choice of that or nothing, then there wasn't much of a choice in it at all." (Kate Rattray)

"I must have fussy rats as mine never liked Nutrical, but I did try Nurishum on the off chance and the rats love it! I can't squeeze it out quick enough for them." (Rhi01)

Rehydration

Many sick rats become dehydrated and need encouragement to drink. There are various ways of encouraging a rat to take extra fluids and if one doesn't work, simply try another. Regardless of the underlying cause, simply rehydrating the rat will make him feel better, after which, other problems can be addressed. If a rat persistently refuses oral fluids he may need subcutaneous or intra-peritoneal fluids, administered by a vet.

Tactics to try
- Lace the water with apple, cranberry or grape juice. This can be added to a gravity fed bottle, but be aware that mould spores will quickly build up unless the bottle is cleaned out thoroughly (hot soapy water and a bottle brush), every 24 hours.
- Sweeten the water with glucose powder, or a little honey.
- Add Dr Squiggles Daily Essentials powder to water. This multivitamin and mineral powder seems to be very pleasant to a rat's taste.
- Warm the fluid to around body temperature.
- Offer the fluid from a small syringe (1 ml is most successful as you can give it really slowly and there is no chance of you pushing the fluid faster than the rat can lick and swallow).
- Try really high fluid foods... sloppy baby food, melon, jelly made up to a fairly sloppy consistency (rats seem to love jelly!)
- Offer Lactol, human infant soya milk or soya milk in a gravity bottle.

NB If you are putting anything other than plain water into the water bottle, be sure to add a second water bottle to the cage, so that plain water is always available.

Syringe feeding

Very sick rats may be too weak, or sick, to want to eat or drink. Syringe feeding can help to support them at this time, but it is just that: supportive, and you are not force-feeding. If you approach syringe feeding with this attitude then you will not run the risk of causing your rat further problems through over vigorous feeding (such as choking or aspiration pneumonia).

You will find it easiest to use a small syringe; 1 ml is the easiest to control, and can be obtained online, or from your vet. The amount taken will vary from rat to rat, but will probably be between one and five millilitres. Hold the rat in a comfortable position on your knee, and offer the loaded syringe. Squeezing a droplet of the contents out onto the syringe tip may help the rat to get the idea, and begin licking the syringe. As the rat licks, slowly push the contents out of the syringe, stopping as often as necessary for the rat to keep up with you. If the rat is reluctant, then you can try tucking the syringe tip into one side of his mouth and pushing a couple of drops of the fluid in; hopefully he will get the idea. One final tactic is to hold the syringe tip against your own finger or palm and drip the fluid out slowly, while the rat licks it from your skin.

How often you have to repeat the procedure will depend on how much the rat is able to take in one sitting. As a general rule - the less taken, the more often you need to offer the syringe. But a rat taking 5 ml of fluid/food in one sitting should be offered more approximately every 3-4 hours or so.

Warmed fluid is often more acceptable than cold fluid, and if the rat refuses something from a syringe, don't give up - simply try something else. All of the 'hydration' fluids mentioned above can be given from a syringe, as can complete food drinks (e.g. Complan, Build Up), soft baby food, yoghurt, human infant soya milk and watered down Nutrical. If you are trying to hydrate the rat use the clear fluids, and if you are 'feeding' the rat, choose a higher calorie, liquid food. Nutrical can be added to any of these suggested feeds to increase the calorific and nutritional value.

GIVING MEDICATION

As a general rule it is usually less stressful for a rat to take medicine hidden in food, rather than squirted straight into the mouth. Each rat will have individual tastes and there are no universal foods for disguising medicines, but there are a number of foods that are widely tried and tested, and seem to be palatable for many rats.

My personal favourite for powders and Baytril is Nutrical, and it has the advantage of giving the rat a multivitamin and mineral boost too. The minerals present in Nutrical are at relatively low levels and unlikely to greatly impact on the absorption of the antibiotics. Certainly, (albeit anecdotally), I know of many people who use this method and still get the expected response to the antibiotic. Powders will mix in easily, whereas Baytril takes a little extra encouragement to mix in fully - but I just work it, and stir vigorously on a dessertspoon with a knife, until they are completely combined (it ends up as a thick liquid).

Another almost universally effective method is to use Heinz Oats and Apple baby breakfast. I begin by making up a small bowl of the cereal, by adding a small amount of boiling water - just enough to thicken the cereal to a paste. Then I gradually add milk and stir thoroughly to a thick, sloppy consistency. If you make it too thick the rat won't eat it, and if it is too thin it won't hide the flavour of the medicine well. This is the reason I use mainly milk to make the cereal - it gives a more substantial flavour to mask the drug. Measure the dose of medication onto a dessertspoon and if giving Baytril, sprinkle a little sugar over it so that the sugar soaks up the fluid. Baytril is incredibly bitter and rats hate bitterness, so a little extra sweetness can make all the difference to success with a reluctant rat. Even so - you should be able to drop it from the concoction after a few doses. Next, spoon on a small teaspoonful of the made up cereal and mix really well. The rest of the cereal can be stored for a few days in the fridge. It may thicken further on storage, so just soften it with a little extra milk as needed. The cereal can also be flavoured with a sprinkle of drinking choco-late   powder or a dollop of Nutrical stirred in when warm, if necessary, but I find most rats are happy to take it plain.

OTHER RECOMMENDATIONS
Seafood sauce (wizzyjo)
Peanut butter (Lilly)
Banana milk soaked bread (Lilly)

Half a Malteser
Melted vanilla ice cream
Chocolate soya milk
Melted chocolate, mix the medicine in while still warm and then put into
the fridge to set.
Mashed up warm baked beans. (Alison T)
Live yoghurt and honey. (Alison T)
Liquid from tinned fish in oil or tomato sauce. (Alison T)
Marmite on a piece of toast. (Alison T)
Neat or barely diluted Ribena for direct syringing. (Alison T)

THE EFFECTS OF ANTIBIOTIC THERAPY

Using antibiotics destroys the normal gut bacteria and can also cause the
lining of the bowel to become more 'leaky', (as can anti-inflammatories and
steroids). Both of these factors can influence the absorption of vitamins and
minerals (as well as other nutrients) and it is advisable to give probiotics to
counteract this effect, at the end of a course of antibiotics. Live yoghurts
generally do not contain enough live bacteria to be effective in this sort of
situation, and it is preferable to use a specially prepared probiotic powder,
sprinkled over food. It may also be helpful to supplement vitamins and
minerals when using these medications, but the absorption of some
antibiotics (particularly tetracycline and its derivatives, which include
doxycycline, and the fluoroquinolones, including Baytril and ciprofloxacin),
is affected by the presence of large quantities of some minerals in the gut.
Therefore, it is recommended that they are best given about 2 hours before
feeding time, and any water bottles with minerals added should be removed
2 hours before giving the medication, and returned at feeding time. Plain
water should be available at all times.

REFERENCES

[1]Paediatric Research November 2000 - Volume 48 - Issue 5
Perinatal Feedings Adversely Affect Lipogenic Activities but Not Glucose Handling
in Adult Rats

Balonan, Lino C.; Sheng, Hwai-ping
[2]http://www.timesonline.co.uk/tol/news/uk/health/article1647517.ece
[3]Toxicology and Applied Pharmacology,Volume 6, Issue 3, May 1964, Pages 247 to 262
Kidney disease and nutrition in the rat
Gerrit Bras, Morris H. Ross
[4]The Journal of Nutrition (Feb 1965)
Tumor Incidence Patterns and Nutrition in the Rat
Morris H. Ross and Gerrit Bras
[5]Alternative Medicine Review. 2001 Aug;6(4):367-82.
Conjugated Linoleic Acid: A Review
Gregory S. Kelly, ND
[6]Clinical and Experimaental Metastasis 2002;19(2):145-153.
Antiangiogenic and antimetastatic properties of Neovastat (AE-941), an orally active extract derived from cartilage tissue.
Dupont E, Falardeau P, Mousa SA, et al.
[7]Molecular Pharmacology November 2006 vol. 70 no. 5 1664-1671
Curcumin Inhibits Hypoxia-Inducible Factor-1 by Degrading Aryl Hydrocarbon Receptor Nuclear Translocator: A Mechanism of Tumor Growth Inhibition
Hyunsung Choi, Yang-Sook Chun, Seung-Won Kim, Myung-Suk Kim and Jong-Wan Park
[8]Experimental Gerontology, Volume 39, Issue 2, February 2004, Pages 189-194
Coenzyme Q supplementation protects from age-related DNA double-strand breaks and increases lifespan in rats fed on a PUFA-rich diet
José L. Quiles, Julio J. Ochoa, Jesús R. Huertas and José Mataix
[9]Clinical Infectious Diseases Mar 2005 (6): 807–10.
Treatment of the common cold with echinacea: a structured review.
Caruso TJ, Gwaltney JM
[10]Clinical Cancer Research May 2005 11; 3828
Dietary Flaxseed Alters Tumor Biological Markers in Postmenopausal Breast Cancer
Lilian U. Thompson1, Jian Min Chen1 et al
[11]Planta Medica. 2010 Jan 28
Lapachol Induces Clastogenic Effects in Rats.
Maistro EL, Fernandes DM, Pereira FM, Andrade SF.
[12]The Journal of Immunology, 2005, 175: 7202-7208.
Glucosamine Abrogates the Acute Phase of Experimental Autoimmune Encephalomyelitis by Induction of Th2 Response
Guang-Xian Zhang

Chapter nine - overview

Weight management
    Preventing weight gain
    Diet and prevention
    Activity and prevention
    Environmental considerations
Weight reduction diet
    Choosing a grain mix for weight loss
    Low calorie filler foods
Scatter feeding
    Possible objections to scatter feeding
    Practicalities of scatter feeding
Diet to promote weight gain

Chapter nine
Weight management

WEIGHT MANAGEMENT

Rats as a species seem to be extremely susceptible to the effects of rapid growth rate, early maturation and excessive weight gain, therefore weight management is an important issue. A rat's propensity towards weight gain is also affected by maternal diet and early dietary influences. This is because early overfeeding permanently alters aspects of fat metabolism (making it more efficient), which often results in fatter adult rats.[1] Some rats may also have specific genes that predispose them to obesity, usually by affecting appetite control, but these are less common.

Regardless of your rats' early kittenhood, you will also have a major effect in determining adult weight, according to how much you feed as they grow. Rats fed to their maximum growth potential, tend to grow quickly and reach maturity early, both of which are linked to reduced lifespan.[2]

Fat deposition seems to follow the same pattern in rats as it does in humans. Some seem to primarily lay down their fat underneath their skin. These rats tend to feel soft and squishy and when they become overweight you can clearly see and feel this. Other rats may actually have very little subcutaneous fat (beneath their skin) and tend to deposit fat within their abdominal cavity, around the organs. These rats are normally big rats who still feel firm to the touch. This kind of fat deposition is actually more detrimental to health, so don't rely on squishiness alone to decide whether your rats are overweight.

PREVENTING WEIGHT GAIN
It is much easier to prevent rats from getting overweight in the first place, than it is to get them to lose weight once obese. Prevention involves a combination of dietary consideration and activity.

DIET AND PREVENTION
The key to preventing obesity in rats is to encourage a slower path to maturity, by not over feeding the juvenile rat. This can be achieved by giving a diet full of necessary nutrients, but fewer calories. When feeding

kittens at the end of their rapid growth phase (around 8 to 10 weeks) you may find that this is best achieved by limiting their dry mix - as for adult rats - though they will need roughly the same volume of food as an adult rat, to account for growth. You can then supplement the dry mix with fresh vegetables, a little extra protein, and a good vitamin and mineral mix.

Once the rapid growth phase is over (10 weeks plus), an adult diet with some calorie restriction (say from a daily evening fast period, or feeding half rations every third day) is sufficient, so long as you remember not to offer too much volume overall. The diet by this stage can be primarily grain mix, with some fresh vegetables. If you want to continue feeding more fresh food the easiest way to do this without overfeeding, is to make a meal (perhaps once a week) based on a whole grain carbohydrate food, with some added protein and vegetables, and feed this *instead* of their dry food. Remember when feeding fresh foods the volume should be increased, as fresh food is largely made up of water.

Scatter feeding is also extremely effective as a means of weight management. Within groups where the rats differ greatly in size and weight, it can help underweight rats to thrive, whilst at the same time 'dieting' those who are overweight. When using a bowl, those rats who are more driven to eat have easy access to the food and often stash, dominate the food bowl and overeat. With scatter feeding, all of the rats have an equal chance of finding food, and lean rats are often fitter and more willing to actively work to this end. Hence the weights at both extremes begin to normalise. This method of food delivery will be discussed fully later in this chapter.

One group of rats who merit special attention in terms of preventing weight gain are those who are post neuter, be that a castration or spay. These rats are generally prone to putting on weight after the operation, and will benefit from reduced rations or extended lean periods, once they have recovered from the surgery. The propensity to gain weight post-neuter is thought to be due to a reduction in metabolic rate, secondary to alterations in hormone levels.[3] This means that most rats will gain weight following a neuter if they eat the *same amount* of food as they did before the surgery.

ACTIVITY AND PREVENTION

Physical activity is fundamental to fitness and long term health. Many caged animals are under exercised, partly due to poor cage design, with the routine use of shelving with ramps. In-cage exercise can be encouraged from infancy with varied climbing opportunities and cage set-ups that do not allow easy access from one level to another. If your cage came with ramps or ladders between levels, you could consider removing these to encourage the rats to climb up the cage bars, as this is probably the most vigorous form of in cage activity available to them, other than wheel running. Obviously some adaptations will be needed in the case of disability and old age.

Many rats will wheel run if given access to a wheel from infancy. I find that if a wheel is provided from about 3 weeks of age, it doesn't really matter whether the mother uses it or not, the babies will still do so. How long they continue to do this into adult life varies, with some rats stopping as they mature into adulthood and others continuing on into old age. This activity is to be encouraged as studies show voluntary wheel running alone can raise average life span by almost 10%. Interestingly, this level of exercise had a detrimental effect on average lifespan when rats were also subjected to more stringent calorie restrictions (around 70% of ad lib volumes),[4] so as always, balance is the key to positive results.

Out of cage activity is best designed to tie in with a rat's normal diurnal wakeful periods, (early morning or evening), as far as is possible. Not only will the rats be more active and alert, but their rest periods won't be artificially disrupted. Try to give plenty of free range time, and if your lazy bucks explore for 10 minutes and then find a corner to sleep, try giving them a number of short (10 minute) sessions outside of the cage, rather than one long one. Playing on the stairs is great exercise if you can engage your rats in such activity. Try giving them a hard boiled egg (in its shell) to play with on the stairs.

ENVIRONMENTAL CONSIDERATIONS

As well as the opportunity for activity, the environment that a rat lives in may also have an effect on weight management. Brown rats (*Rattus norvegicus*) are, as a species, hardy creatures who are naturally adapted to living outside, and well able to cope with colder temperatures. This was one of the advantages they had over the Black rat (*Rattus rattus*), who colonised the UK first, but have now been effectively eradicated from this island. While humans played a part in this, the Brown rat was certainly better adapted for over-wintering here, and our inclement weather.

Our rats thrive in cooler conditions and tolerate a cold environment much better than a hot one. Environmental temperature has a big influence on weight gain, and managing weight is easier when the rats are kept in cool surroundings. Because of their rapid metabolism, rats produce a lot of internal heat and in a cool environment this is easily lost. This results in the rat feeling comfortable, energetic and able to engage fully in activity without overheating. Even when the environmental temperature drops to the point where the rat feels cold, it can easily produce the energy needed to keep it's temperature at a comfortable level. All of this conspires to keep the rat fit and lean.

In a warm environment the rat's internal heat cannot easily be lost. The rat feels less comfortable, conserves energy so as not to generate more heat and as a result becomes less active. Less calories are burnt overall, both as a result of reduced activity and not needing to create energy to keep warm.

The amount of food offered needs to be adjusted to account for changes in environmental temperature, meaning we should feed less in the summer than in the winter, unless our rats are kept in a warm, heated room, in which case it may be necessary to feed less all year round to maintain normal weight.

WEIGHT REDUCTION DIET

Despite our best efforts, some rats seem predisposed to becoming obese, and these rats have a shortened life expectancy and a less active and rich life, because their size often makes them lazy and slow. Overweight rats are more prone to many illnesses such as diabetes, bumblefoot, mammary lumps, strokes, pituitary tumours and respiratory problems. It is also more likely that their kidneys will lose function earlier and more rapidly than their slim friends and relations. Obesity cannot really be ignored as it is likely to lead to future health problems and an early death.

If despite your best efforts you realise that a number of rats in a colony are becoming overweight it is very likely that you are simply feeding too much. Cut the diet right back to the quantity of dry mix that they will eat in about 20 hours, and less than this if they are still gaining weight on that amount. Use a dish to begin with to settle on the right quantity; they should clear all the edible food in the dish and if there is edible food left after the 20 hours simply reduce the amount given. Once you have determined how much is needed in terms of volume, stick to that amount and try scatter feeding, as weight control is much easier using this method. Make sure that they are only fed once a day (late in the evening), and that they have a lean period in the afternoon when there are only scraps in the cage. Don't give any treats or fresh food except for a small amount of low calorie vegetables, but not peas and sweetcorn, because of their higher energy content.

If you already feed a restricted amount and are still seeing weight gain, cut amounts further and replace some dry mix with low calorie vegetables, and employ scatter feeding as your most effective weapon in the battle to keep your rats lean.

You can extend this regime further by introducing lean days (when you feed half rations), or not feeding the night before a cage clean out, so that any missed food within the bedding is eaten. On these days you can feed extra vegetables. I tend not to recommend complete fasts, as these can tip the rat into 'starvation' mode, so that their metabolism slows and they become even more efficient at using calories and holding onto fat.

If only one rat in a colony is getting obese, the easiest thing to do it to remove that rat from the cage at feeding time. Encourage him to exercise and give him some vegetable treats. Only put him back with the others when they have had the opportunity to consume a proportion of the food.

Use this method alongside increased activity and scatter feeding. It may take weeks, or even months to make a real impact, but perseverance should eventually result in overall weight loss and will bring health benefits to your rat.

CHOOSING A GRAIN MIX FOR WEIGHT LOSS

Weight reduction is best achieved on a diet that is high in unrefined carbohydrates, but whatever mix you choose success relies heavily on restricting quantities. Rats are extremely efficient at processing and digesting food and can gain weight on most diets, if over fed. A mix based on straight grains and minimally processed human cereals, (such as those used in Alison Blyth's mix on page 114), a low fat protein source and vegetables is ideal. You will find it easier to succeed in helping your rats to lose weight if you also choose a low fat mix and stay away from starchy, fatty or sugary fresh foods, including quantities of fruit. Scatter feeding is the one single most effective tool that I have found in the management of weight, and it is helpful regardless of which grain mix you use.

LOW CALORIE 'FILLER' FOODS

Some rats, especially those with genetic factors that influence appetite, may be driven to eat almost continually. For these rats, the usual diet should still be restricted to normal levels as far as is possible without the other rats starting to lose weight. Scatter feeding will help this, however, these obesity prone rats will benefit from being offered an extra supply of low calorie foods to satisfy their constant appetite.

Possible low calorie fillers include:

Cucumber	Water melon	Celery
Rice cakes	Plain (fat free) popped corn	Broccoli
Kale	Red pepper	Pak choi
Dandelion leaves	Tomatoes	Frozen prawns

Also try ice cubes made from plain water or Daily Essentials, with pieces of fruit or vegetable in them.

SCATTER FEEDING

Foraging is the act of searching for food and for the non-domesticated rat, successful foraging is a key element of survival. For this reason a wild rat employs the vast majority of its time in this pursuit. By necessity, foraging involves many natural behaviours including, rummaging, digging, whisking (the act of scanning the environment using whisker sweeps), hunting and climbing. As well as the whiskers, a rat's sense of smell is the primary sense engaged in finding food, and in choosing what to eat and what to leave.

Domesticated rats have been traditionally fed from bowls or hoppers, which provide a ready supply of food, in a given location, at all times. For many years I fed like this and never considered an alternative, until that is, I started to read about and research scatter feeding. Some rat owners have been feeding like this for many years, and as attitudes have evolved on the subject of environmental enrichment, and efforts have been made to provide opportunities for the expression of natural behaviours, it was only a matter of time before scatter feeding made it onto the rattie agenda.

Initially I heard reports from a number of people who always scatter fed and whose rats seemed happy and healthy, so I began to look for research into the area of enriched feeding opportunities for caged rats. Everything I read was positive, including evidence that scatter feeding can help a rat to maintain a normal weight, and that it increases the amount of time spent in food seeking (natural) behaviours. I then found myself in an interesting position; intellectually I was convinced that this was a positive change in husbandry, which was of benefit to the rat and seemed to have no real 'down-side', yet I still felt reluctant to give it a try.

I had a number of reservations, which might be common to anyone who is considering scatter feeding for the first time. It took me months to decide to give it a go - and now I wouldn't choose to feed any other way, although I do feel it is probably best used in conjunction with "hide and seek" type techniques (for example, piñatas, toilet roll 'crackers' and treat balls) for extra challenges.

Scatter feeding tends to be used to refer to feeding the dry elements of a rat's diet, but it can be extended to some fresh foods too.

POSSIBLE OBJECTIONS TO SCATTER FEEDING

How will I know they are getting enough?

Before beginning to scatter feed it is worth getting a good feel for how much a particular group of rats should eat in a 24 hour period. Rats tend to be healthiest when not fed ad lib, that is when fed less than the amount they would eat if they have free access to food at all times, and also when a comprehensive, varied diet is consumed. For most rats, their day should generally include a lean period, when the rat is awake and active but does not have food available. However, the primary way of getting the volume of food just right for a particular group of rats is to look at the rats over a period of time. They should be active and in good condition and neither under, nor over weight. Once the required volume is discovered, you can simply dispense with the food bowl and scatter feed the same amount of food. You don't need to add extra to compensate (so tempting to do), and you can check under the cage litter from time to time, where you should find nothing edible - just chaff and food dust - if you are getting it right. Nutritional needs do vary with stage of life and environmental temperature (amongst other things) so monitoring your rats' nutritional status is an ongoing affair.

What if the rats don't find everything and eat an imbalanced diet?

This is where you need to believe in your rats. They are designed for the job, and will spend earnest hours in search of food if they are hungry. I feel we have all been successful if I clean out the cage and don't find any wasted food; I have got the volume right, and the rats have done what they have evolved to do best. Bear in mind that if you clean out only part way through your 24 hour feeding period there may well be a little food left from the previous night's feed - but only a very little. If you find lots of edible stuff under the bedding you are feeding too much, your rats will feed selectively, and may become fat and malnourished on an imbalanced diet.

How will the skinny/elderly/sick rats fare in competition with their stronger, or more healthy cage mates?
Skinny rats seem to fare really well, even in colonies of mixed size, probably because they have as much chance of finding food (and the higher calorie more desirable components of a mix), as their fatter cage mates who can no longer hog the food dish, but have to work hard to eat. If you are at all worried you can feed on multiple levels and you will find the leaner (generally fitter and more agile rats) can source food in the higher levels more easily. I have to say that variations in the weight of cagemates in my groups have decreased since I began scatter feeding. The rats more likely to get fat, stay leaner, and the leaner rats maintain a good weight. Sick and elderly rats generally need some extra nutritional support, and often more soft food. In this scenario I continue to scatter feed dry food and bowl feed just the fresh food for the elderly and moderately disabled or sick. If a rat is struggling to maintain weight I put all their food into dishes, but you have to work with what is best for the colony, and sometimes feeding a needy rat separately works well and prevents obesity in younger friends.

Won't the food get soiled amongst the litter?
With the use of litter trays, a thick layer of bedding shouldn't get too soiled in a week or so. It might help to bear in mind that rats often mark their food with urine, to signal it as safe to eat, and are also designed to practice coprophagia - that is, eating their own faeces and gaining extra nutrition from it. The issue of food mixing with the odd poo in the cage litter is really only a problem to us, as humans.

PRACTICALITIES OF SCATTER FEEDING
Do:
- Use as deep a layer of substrate as possible.
- Scatter as widely as possible. If your scatter area is too small, the main principle of scatter feeding (the need to work to find food), is lost.
- Vary your technique. Newness is extremely stimulating to a rat and having to solve new problems relieves boredom and sharpens a variety of skills.
- Try hanging a plastic 'planter' from the cage roof and filling it with cross cut shredded paper, into which some food is mixed, alongside scattering

on the cage floor.
- Scatter feed on different levels.
- Experiment with a variety of substrates. Even if you always use (say) chipped card, you can add an extra layer of shredded paper, or good quality soft hay.
- Scatter feed alongside hidden food games such as placing some of the mix inside a toilet roll cracker, or small cardboard box (like a toothpaste box).
- Check you're not over-feeding by looking at what is left under the substrate before you feed, and especially when you clean the cage out. There is a photograph on page 167, of the kind of waste I would expect from my mix after scatter feeding.

Don't:
- Feed extra "just in case" - the rats will find it. If there is more than the odd morsel of edible food left over under the bedding when you clean out, you are feeding too much overall.
- Worry if you can't see any food in the cage within a few minutes of feeding.
- Scatter only in a very limited area, for example, a small tray.
- Feed in the same place, in the same way every day.

Diet to promote weight gain

Sometimes a rat becomes undernourished, perhaps before it comes into rescue, or during a period of ill health. Many rats also lose weight as they age. When trying to increase the weight of a group of rats who can eat normally, it is best to rely to a large extent on a good quality, varied grain based mix, fed ad libitum. A daily portion of fresh, higher calorie, nutrient rich foods can be given, such as banana, avocado or nuts, as well as the usual vegetables. Where there is not a pressing reason to normalise weight, this approach is preferable to overfeeding lots of high fat, high calorie foods; weight gain will be slower, but the negative impact on long term health will be much less.

Interestingly, I have found that in a group of rats of mixed weights scatter feeding helps the underweight gain weight, just as surely as the overweight lose weight. This seems to be because the food is not readily available in a dish for the over-eater to 'hoover up' and the leaner rats have an equal chance of finding the food they need, before it is eaten by someone else!

In the case of sick or elderly rats a move towards a higher calorie softer diet will often help. This kind of diet is expanded at the end of Chapter 7. It may also be helpful to supplement the diet with a high calorie nutrient paste, such as Nutrical, which not only boosts calorie intake but helps to stimulate appetite.

REFERENCES

[1]Paediatric Research November 2000 - Volume 48 - Issue 5
Perinatal Feedings Adversely Affect Lipogenic Activities but Not Glucose Handling in Adult Rats
Balonan, Lino C.; Sheng, Hwai-ping
[2]American Journal of Clinical Nutrition, Vol 41, 1332-1344
Dietary habits and the prediction of life span of rats: a prospective test
MH Ross, ED Lustbader, G Bras
[3]Physiology & Behaviour, Volume 22, Issue 3, March 1979, Pages 583-593
Gonadal effects on food intake and adiposity: A metabolic hypothesis
George N. Wadea and Janet M. Gray
[4]Journal of Nutrition Vol. 122 No. 3_Suppl March 1992, pp. 774-777
Exercise and Food Restriction in Rats.
John O. Holloszy.

"Only Irish coffee provides
in a single glass all four
essential food groups:
alcohol, caffeine,
sugar and fat."

Alex Levin

CHAPTER TEN - OVERVIEW

Feeding for condition
  Condition and vitality
  The biology of skin and hair
  Useful supplements for coat condition

Chapter ten
Feeding for vitality and condition

Feeding for condition

Condition and vitality

The skin, coat and body condition of a rat can tell you a great deal about its overall health, well-being and nutritional status. Condition (in the rat) may be defined as:

- Having good muscle tone and moderate weight for build; neither skinny nor overweight.
- Being bright and alert, with abundant energy and vitality.
- Having a short, smooth and glossy coat (except for rex, hairless etc).
- Showing clear skin, free from dryness, flakiness or sores. Some orange buck grease at skin level is normal for males.
- Having bright, shiny eyes.

The skin is the largest organ in the body and its demands on metabolism are huge. It is thought that about a quarter of all protein intake is used to regenerate hair and skin, and to produce secretions from the skin's many glands. Fats, vitamins and minerals are also required for this, therefore, the skin and hair are good indicators of the quality of nutrition.[1] A variety of skin conditions (for instance, dandruff, irritation, lesions and poor healing) and many problems with the coat (including thinning, patchiness, dryness, very long hair, a greasy feel, faded and patchy colouring or dullness) can all be the result of inadequate diet and lack - or excess - of nutrients. These signs can occur in isolation, or a number of issues might arise at the same time.

The biology of the skin and hair

Hair (fur) is an anatomical feature that is unique to mammals and has a variety of functions, such as insulation, waterproofing, improving the sense of touch, display (e.g. increasing physical 'size') and colour patterning (e.g. camouflage).

Hair grows out of follicles in the lower layer of the skin (dermis) and each follicle normally grows one hair. The part of the hair below the surface is called the root, while the part that is seen above the skin is the shaft. The activity of the hair follicle is cyclical and each period of activity and growth is followed by a resting period. After the resting period, a new cycle begins and a new hair is formed, which pushes the old hair out from below and the hair is shed (moulting).[2]

The length of a hair is determined by both the length of the resting phase and how long the active growing period lasts. These vary from species to species and, within an individual, may vary between different types of hair and this explains why humans can have notably longer hair on their heads than on their arms. Despite the differences in hair length not being as striking in rats, there is some regional variation, with shorter hairs on the head and belly in comparison to the rump. The hairs covering the chest and abdomen of the rat have a resting period of about two weeks and a growing period that lasts roughly as long, whereas in the centre of the back the resting period is about four weeks and the growing period lasts for three. This accounts for the spine and rump always being the last area to moult out, and also for the fact that hair in this region shows lack of condition more dramatically than other areas; put simply, the hair there is older.[3]

In most animals the cycles are synchronised to some degree so that the hairs are all due to be shed at around the same time (a moult). If the cycles are not synchronised then hair is lost continually, but never in large amounts; this is the pattern that is seen in humans.

In the rat, the active growing period for each hair is approximately two to three weeks and the resting period, two to four weeks and cycles do occur at roughly the same time, but in a pattern of progression across the body. This means that rats moult out fully approximately every six to seven weeks, and the moult always begins at the belly, progresses up the sides of the body to the spine and moves from the back of the neck towards the tail. This can lead to some very bizarre coat 'patterns' as the new hairs replace the old. Interestingly, in female rats the growth cycle is slower than in males, and the length of the hair in all regions is shorter.

There are a number of factors that are thought to affect the rate at which moults occur and the speed at which cycles of growth repeat. These include hormones, nutritional status, stress, disease and environmental factors such as heat (a warmer environment may shorten the cycle). These effects can be seen most notably in kittens who are stuck in moult; those who do not moult out into adult coats for unusually long periods of time. These kittens are generally ill, undernourished or experiencing stress. However, delayed moulting can occur throughout a rat's life, which can lead to a coat that looks long and out of condition.

Poor coat quality and condition may indicate underlying illness, or even a hormone deficiency (such as hypothyroidism). It may also result from stress, for example, when a rat loses a cage mate or there are changes within group structure. The most likely cause, however, is also the easiest to rectify; inadequate nutrition.

Hair, though dead throughout the majority of its length, is composed mainly of protein. The active growth cycle involves rapid cell division, which depends on many micronutrients and hormones. The benefits of an excellent diet cannot be overstated, but at times when coat quality and condition are lost, extra supplements may also be of benefit (see below). One should remember that during the moult all coats will tend to look a little patchy and below peak condition. Excellent nutrition and lack of stress will help the rat to pass through this phase as quickly as possible, and this can be helpful for those who wish to exhibit their pets.

For a rat's coat to look its best and gleam with health and condition, its overall diet needs to be adequate in protein (requirements vary with age) and essential fatty acids (EFA). EFA are needed in cell division by all animal cells, but the hairs are also 'oiled' by sebaceous glands, which secrete an oily substance (sebum). Too much oil in the diet isn't helpful for many reasons, including the coat becoming greasy, but where dietary fat is low, a drop or two of fish oil, flaxseed oil or olive oil (or some seeds or oily fish) a few times a week will help to boost condition. Vitamins, particularly A, B_2, B_6, C and E, and minerals, such as zinc are essential for healthy skin, and healthy skin is essential for good hair growth. Thyroxin is a hormone which is required anywhere where rapid cell division occurs, as in the skin, and iodine is needed for the production of thyroxin.

Clearly the relationship between good nutrition and condition is crucial and cannot be ignored. The more varied and appropriate your diet is, the better condition your rats will be in. Good condition is fuelled by adequate protein, essential fatty acids, vitamins and minerals, so if your rats don't seem to be gleaming, look at your diet for any possible gaps. If the quality seems good overall then try adding in some hemp and flax seeds and supplementing with a little extra fish oil, some seaweed and a multivitamin and mineral powder for a week or two. It might just be that the rats are experiencing an underlying stress (such as building noise, extreme weather, disruptions in cage hierarchy, your own stress or ill health) and just need some extra nutrients to boost them at a difficult time.

Part of healthy hair growth is pigmentation, and minerals such as iodine and copper will also improve colour. Hair colour has been shown to be changed by free radicals (highly reactive molecules that can cause damage within the body), exposure to sunlight and certain chemicals. Free radicals can be neutralised to some extent by giving antioxidants, (such as vitamin C and E), which occur naturally in many fruits and vegetables. As rats are most comfortable at low light levels, avoiding direct sunlight will generally be an integral part of their care.

In elderly rats the coat tends to thin and lose condition, which may in part be due to underlying disease processes, less efficient uptake of nutrients, increased cellular damage, and changes in the growth cycles of the hair. Many elderly males get softer, shorter coats particularly over their back as they age, probably due to hormonal changes. The prominence of guard hairs diminishes, which can lead to an apparent lightening of colour in ticked rats, and the shorter base fur can look wavy but these changes are unlikely to be a cause for dietary concern.

USEFUL SUPPLEMENTS FOR COAT CONDITION

Seaweed powder or unsalted seaweed - contains iodine and many other trace minerals.

Omega-3 fatty acids - fish oil or linseed (flax) oil. Hemp seed seems to be particularly helpful in improving coat condition.

Dr Squiggles Tiny Animal Essentials (multivitamin and mineral powder) or Daily Essentials (multivitamin and mineral for use in the water).

REFERENCES

[1]Optimizing skin and coat condition in the dog
D. H. Lloyd PhD, B VetMed, FRCVS, DipECVD Royal Veterinary College, UK
K. A. Marsh BSc, PhD WALTHAM Centre for Pet Nutrition, UK
[2]British Medical Journal, 1965, 1, 609-614
Endocrine Influences on Hair Growth
Arthur Rook M.D., F.R.C.P.
[3]Journal of Endocrinology (1958) 16, 337-NP
Quantitative studies of hair growth in the albino rat
Elizabeth Johnson

"Cooking is like love.
It should be entered
into with abandon
or not at all."

Harriet Van Horne

Chapter eleven - overview

Feeding for pleasure and enrichment
    Foraging behaviours
    Food related foraging activities
    Digging behaviour
    Food related digging activities
    Carrying and manipulating objects
    Food related manipulation activities
    Chewing behaviours
    Food related chewing activities
Games that involve food
Treats
    Making healthy choices
    Fruit
    Vegetables
    Legumes
    Dog biscuits
    Nuts
    Seeds
    Coconut
    Bones
Shop bought treats and reviews

Chapter eleven
Feeding for pleasure,
interest and enrichment

FEEDING FOR PLEASURE AND ENRICHMENT

With a little imagination it is possible to use food to give our caged rats an opportunity for carrying out natural behaviours, while at the same time enriching their environment and increasing pleasure. I have no doubt that rats derive enjoyment from food and are therefore, frequently motivated by it. This, along with their natural curiosity, will most likely assure your success with food based activities however wild your imagination!

FORAGING BEHAVIOURS

A great deal of a wild rat's day is consumed by looking for food, and foraging has been correlated (in laboratory rats) to other positive outcomes such at the consumption of less food, and better weight control. This is obvious really, as a foraging rat will spend more time active and looking for food.

FOOD RELATED FORAGING ACTIVITIES
SCATTER FEEDING

I have had great success using a scatter feeding method in deep litter. I use a chopped card substrate and I cover the cage base with a thick layer of this, so that the rats can dig. Each evening the ration for 24 hours is scattered at random over the cage floor and this quickly mixes into the substrate with the movement and activities of the rats. They then spend a great deal of time digging about in the litter looking for tasty morsels. This is much closer to a natural style of feeding than simply taking as much as they want from a filled dish.

Review: *"I swear by scatter feeding. Since I was introduced to the idea my rats, who were over-weight, now maintain a good healthy weight. I will never feed using bowls again. They love searching for the food and I can see trails in the litter where they have foraged every morning I look."* (Laura E)

HIDING FOOD

Food can be hidden around the cage and hiding places should vary. Consider placing food under mounds of shredded paper or soft hay, inside planters and hanging baskets, or scrunched inside paper, placed inside cheap plastic baskets.

BIRD FEEDERS AND VEGETABLE BASKETS
Many designs of these are available and they can be filled with vegetables and hung in the cage – or filled with paper strands and some interspersed treats.

BOXES
Larger cardboard boxes such as shoe boxes can be filled with shredded paper and food. You can even replace the lid and just cut a suitable opening. Cheap boxes of tissues (supermarket budget range) are another fun activity, which girls especially, really enjoy. Sprinkle a few treats amongst the layers and you'll soon find the tissues becomes bedding and the box a new den!

PAPER BAGS
These can be bought cheaply in bulk on the internet and are great for putting treats or dry mix into. You can create a few layers with little ones, or if you get really big ones – they can be opened up with shredded paper and you can then just throw some dry mix in there.

KABOBS
Commercially available hanging kebab type sticks, which can be used to hold pasta shapes, monkey nuts in their shells and a variety of fresh foods.

DIGGING BEHAVIOURS
Rats dig instinctively (given the opportunity), and in the wild they often live underground in self-made burrows. Rats tend to dig under something, and if you intend to create a digging box it is helpful to remember that this is the case, and provide a slate or ceramic tile on top of the dirt at one end.

FOOD RELATED DIGGING ACTIVITIES
SCATTER FEEDING
Scatter feeding in deep litter (for example, a deep layer of cardboard chips) encourages true digging behaviour. If your rat is displaying this behaviour

you will see both front leg and hind leg action; the front paws scrape and dig into the substrate whilst the hind legs flick the piles of dirt/card that are created out behind them, and away from the 'burrow' entrance. Lose the food bowl and scatter their ration of dry mix over the cage floor and mix into the bedding, though if you use a loose substrate like card chips they will quickly do this for themselves as they feed. With experienced scatter feeders try scattering and then covering with a layer of shredded paper or hay.

DIGGING BOXES
Digging boxes are often most successful as an in-cage activity. They can easily be made from a plastic storage tub, filled to two thirds with sterile potting compost and with a piece of slate or a ceramic tile placed at one end. Scattering a few seeds, bean sprouts or some dry mix into the soil can encourage digging. If you wish to contain the mess, use a lidded tub and cut away a large entry/exit hole in one corner.

LARGE PLASTIC COLANDERS
These can be found very cheaply in most supermarkets; a large plastic bowl would do just as well. I cable tie two clips to one side of these and attach to the cage bars at ground level. Because the clips are along the same segment of the circle, the attached colander easily tips forward. Then I fill it with a mound of cross cut shredded paper and mix in the rats' dry food. This offers an alternative to simple scatter feeding and it could equally be used for treats.

POTTED HERBS
These can be purchased for under a pound in most supermarkets and when attached inside the rats' cage, will provide a little digging, as well as a healthy treat. Basil, lemon thyme, lemon balm and mint are favourites here. Expect it to be trashed!

SPROUTED GRASS/SEEDS
Scatter a handful of barley grass or bird seed onto a tray of compost and water until the seeds sprout and begin to grow. Once the shoots have become established, place the tray into the cage, but beware - it is likely to

be completely destroyed!

CARRYING AND MANIPULATING OBJECTS
Another behaviour that can easily be overlooked within the cage is the need to carry and manipulate objects, which is closely linked to nest building (male rats nest, as well as females). Searching for suitable materials is part of the fun, as is working out how to get them from where they are found, to where they are needed. Rats in the wild have been seen to co-operate to manipulate difficult objects up and over walls and similar obstacles. Such activities allow them to problem solve as well as physically undertake the task.

FOOD RELATED MANIPULATION ACTIVITIES
HARDBOILED EGGS
These can be fed in their shells and give the rats the added problem of getting to the goodness. If they get too frustrated and lose interest then you can crack the shell to get them going again. Some rats have been found to roll eggs down ramps to try to break open the shell.

TREAT DISPENSERS
There are some excellent parrot toys and rat treat balls that require some manipulation in order to free the treats, though some rats will simply chew through the plastic!

CRACKERS
Treats can be hidden inside toilet roll inners, then wrapped around with a sheet of A4 paper and the ends twisted to make a cracker. These can be filled with the day's ration of dry mix, or perhaps a hazelnut in its shell for each rat. Or try filling with sprouted legumes and feeding immediately.

Review: *"Of all the things I buy my rats as presents (hammocks, toys, igloos) these go down the best. My girls love to open their own presents and there's nothing like a lovely treat of food at the end."* (Laura E)

HAZELNUT TREAT BALLS
A single hazel nut can be hidden inside a little treat ball, made by cutting a

toilet roll inner into rings, about 2cm wide. Then thread three rings over each other (in different orientations), around the nut to form a little ball.

RATTIE 'PASS THE PARCEL'
These can be made up from sheets of newspaper or tissue paper, with treats hidden within the layers.

EGG BOXES AND LITTLE BOXES
Dry or wet foods can be hidden in the compartments of an egg box, or inside a small box, like those used for toothpaste, stock cubes and the like. Close the box and seal if necessary.

CHEWING BEHAVIOURS
Often chewing has purpose for a rat, for example to get into something (or out of a cage), but it also appears that rats chew for pleasure (or without purpose). Contrary to what is often written, a rat does not need to chew in order to keep his teeth short, but chewing is still a natural behaviour that is very easy to provide for. Providing legitimate chewing opportunities can help to reduce unwanted chewing behaviour.

FOOD RELATED CHEWING ACTIVITIES
NUT KNOT NIBBLERS
A commercially available mesh of thick and thin wooden sticks that enclose a walnut. The wooden structure has to be dismantled by chewing and manipulation in order to get at the nut!

NUTS IN THEIR SHELLS
All nuts can be offered in their shells, but some are very hard to open up and all but the most determined rats will give up. Hazelnuts are my own favourite as they take a persistent rat about 10 minutes to chew into, and they are quite small, so they make an ideal treat. Once rats are more practised (or if you have accomplished chewers), pecan, almonds, walnuts, Brazil and macadamia nuts can be offered. The last three have very hard shells and some rats will give up before breaking them open.

DOG CHEWS

Some of these are suitable for rats such as the Nylabone edible range and the crocodile or hedgehog chews available from The Rat Warehouse. http://www.ratwarehouse.com

BONES

Because rats grind bones to a fine powder before swallowing, all kinds of cooked (and raw) animal bones are suitable for them. The favourites here include chicken bones, pork ribs and lamb bones.

GAMES THAT INVOLVE FOOD

The fact that rats are so food orientated can be used to provide them with stimulating entertainment.

When using fresh treats in these games, be sure to remove any leftovers from the cage after 12 to 24 hours (depending on the environmental temperature), before it has a chance to spoil.

PEA DIPPING

Take a large shallow tray such as a roasting tin or large dish. An unused paint roller tray is ideal for this, as you can have a shallow end and a deep end. Fill the tray with water and place in an open space on a large towel. Drop in a handful of frozen peas and maybe a few other items such as small stones. Allow the rats to investigate, paddle, fish and enjoy. This is an excellent activity for cooling rats on a hot day.

Variations: use frozen mixed vegetables or sweetcorn. You can also use the same food item but vary the environment, for example, deeper water, pebbles, a large stone 'fishing island' and even 'jug fishing' which I have only seen on video, but involves putting pebbles (to weight the jug) and peas into a glass or pot jug and filling about ¾ full with water.

"A game my girls enjoy: Ice cubes with food frozen inside - great for hot days. You need to run them under a cold tap to avoid fingers and tongues sticking to them. If the activity is carried out within the cage remember to check hammocks and bedding

afterwards to make sure they aren't too wet." (Phil G)

GLOVE PIÑATA (HELZIE)

Source some cheap fleece gloves (some supermarkets sell them for a pound a pair), and stuff the fingers with nuts or other dry treats, as well as paper. Tie up the open wrist end and hang from the cage roof or bars. Ideally the rats have to nibble through each of the fingers separately. The rats will love playing with this and will no doubt chew it down to get the treats out but it keeps them occupied for a little while. Many rats will also enjoy adding the glove material to their bedding.

Variations: use any small box and vary the treats given.

HANGING TREATS

Many treats lend themselves to being hung around the rats' cage - this adds interest to their environment, and helps them to work for their food. Here are some suggestions:

- Thread a length of garden wire with air popped popcorn, then loop and twist the ends together leaving enough free wire to attach to the cage roof/bars. Hang. Make sure that the loop is quite large so that there is no possibility of a rat becoming trapped in it.
- Wrap cotton string a number of times around the middle of a Nylabone (the edible range). Knot to secure and hang from the roof or bars.
- Plait three strips of material together to form a soft rope. Hang this from the cage bars and insert dog biscuits, pasta or other longish treats between the twists of the rope. A thicker, climbable rope can be made using denim strips and then plaiting three plaits together, to make the final rope. Fleece lends itself to making soft ropes suitable for hanging treats in and because of its elasticity it tends to cling onto the treat when the rat tries to pull it out, which extends the fun!

BREAD HOUSE

Take a whole (uncut) wholemeal, granary or seeded bread loaf, and tear away a small area in the middle of one side. Leave in the cage. The rats will eat and tunnel their way into the loaf, and maybe even take up residence there! Remember to remove the loaf before it gets too soiled or starts to mould.

BIG BOXES OF FUN

Beg or borrow (will they really want it back?) a large, heavy-duty cardboard box. Find a selection of smaller boxes, cardboard tubes, paper bags and similar. Using a few small paper bags make up 3 or 4 'treat bags' by filling the bags with some rattie treats and then loosely sealing the end. Randomly fill the large box with the smaller items and also piles of shredded paper. Somewhere in the process add the treat bags. Then let your rats in there to explore.

RAT RUGBY

"You will need a group of at least four rats, a large cage or free-range space and a walnut in its shell. To start the game, give the rats the walnut. Every rat for itself. Points scored by

- *length of time with walnut*
- *height of jump holding walnut*
- *any progress getting into the walnut!"* (Ros Jenkins)

TREATS

It is human nature to give our companion animals treats as a way of showing our love, but because rats are so affected by diet it is preferable to select treats that are a healthy, integral part of the diet. This is not difficult as rats are generally very food oriented and will appreciate a nut, or slice of melon, just as readily as a piece of chocolate.

MAKING HEALTHY CHOICES

I would define a treat as something that is given in small quantity to give pleasure to our rattie friends, but does not constitute part of their staple diet. However, the line between rat treats and rat diet is fuzzy and elusive, primarily because rats like food! Most fresh food is received gladly and as such, treats can simply be a part of the whole.

It is perfectly possible to feed rats treats that are in keeping with a healthy low fat, low sugar diet. Rats don't differentiate between treats that are healthy and those that aren't - so it's up to us to choose the best for them. Again it's the general principles that will help us. Try to choose treats that are low in fat, salt and sugar. However, a treat is a treat, and doesn't form a substantial part of the diet, and almost any food can be offered in very small quantities.

FRUIT

Many fruits are well received by rats, but due to their high sugar content should probably be seen as treats rather than staples. When choosing fruits it makes sense to go for those which can provide maximum benefit by adding vitamins and minerals to an already balanced diet. Most fruits contain vitamins A, C, E and some of the B group, alongside potassium, calcium, phosphorus, magnesium, iron, selenium and other trace elements. Their specific variances may make individual fruits particularly beneficial at different times of a rat's life. Young, growing rats will benefit from fruits that contain some protein, like avocado and banana, and those with higher levels of calcium, such as blackberries and kiwi. Adult rats are best given the lower calorie vitamin and mineral rich fruits such as water melon, kiwi, tomato, strawberry, peach, mango, blackberry, apple (not an exhaustive list). For elderly rats you may wish to avoid fruit that is particularly high in phosphorus such as avocado, but all fruits have phosphorus levels that are much lower than grains (weight for weight). Apples, bananas, berries, grapes, plums, pineapple and peaches are all fine to feed in moderation in this regard.

Dried fruit can also be given as a treat and a wide variety of fruits are suitable, but watch out for those with added sugar and those preserved in sulphur dioxide. This preservative can cause allergic-type reactions in humans, especially those with respiratory illness, but certainly in laboratory conditions (which usually involve pathogen free animals) regular intake of small amounts of sulphur dioxide didn't appear to cause any problems. However, if you want a preservative free, no added sugar product, check labelling carefully or go for organic suppliers. Further information about perceived issues related to fruit stones and pips is included in chapter 13.

VEGETABLES

Vegetables vary hugely in their value as foods. Most are received well by rats, though sometimes they can be rejected when fed whole. If your rats refuse to eat vegetables, you may find you can encourage them to do so by grating the vegetable (or chopping finely) and mixing it into cooked rice, drizzled with a little fish, olive or linseed (flax) oil.

Some vegetables (such as lettuce, cucumber and courgette) have very little nutritional value and are not terribly useful as a supplementary treat for this reason. However, rats seem to particularly enjoy cucumber, making it a great source of moisture, when travelling or showing. Vegetables that are mainly water are also useful as very low calorie treats for overweight rats.

LEGUMES

Rats seem very partial to peas and beans of many varieties and a cooked broad bean or chick pea, or a few garden peas makes a healthy treat. Peas can be offered raw and still in the pod, which not only provides enrichment getting the peas out, but some rats enjoy eating the pod too. Even where legumes are added to the dry mix, rats will often appreciate fresh or sprouted legumes as a treat.

DOG BISCUITS

Many of the mini sized biscuits produced as treats for dogs are suitable for rats too. Most are wheat based, with a protein level of about 10%, and many are available that are not highly coloured. If you want a quality dog biscuit try Kelties made by Burns or the Tiddlers range from Fish4dogs. If you want something organic, the Minis range by The Organic Pet are cute little bite-sized bones in a variety of interesting flavours.

NUTS

Because of their high fat and protein content, nuts are best only fed as treats. Ideally, feed them in their shells, as this not only provides the rat with a treat, but with the interest of excavating the nut. Nuts are a good source of copper, as well as essential fatty acids and other nutrients.

Review - nuts in shells: *"Although these aren't readily available in the stores except around the festive season the rats love them and it's an easy boredom breaker as it challenges them into thinking of ways to get to the nut inside."* (Rhi01)

SEEDS

Seeds are a great addition in small amounts to a dry mix, but many are also perfect as treats because they are treat-sized! Don't forget that seeds are often more than 50% fat, and for this reason alone intake should be restricted. Sesame, pumpkin and sunflower seeds are all fairly high in phosphorus, so should also be limited in relation to older rats.

COCONUT

Worthy of a special mention, coconut can be a useful treat to feed regularly to older and ailing rats. The raw flesh is approximately 30% fat, while dried or creamed coconut are nearer 65% fat. However, the fats in coconut, despite being saturated, are generally beneficial to health and are thought to have anti-viral and anti-fungal properties, stimulate thyroid function and lower cholesterol. A small cube of raw coconut on occasion makes a healthy treat for rats of all ages. If you are buying coconut in its husk, the rats will enjoy this too and you can hang part of the shell up in the cage with a little of the flesh still attached, or just give them the empty shell to play with.

BONES

Chewing bones seems to bring great pleasure to rats, and it is good that they are also a nutritious treat, especially for young, growing rats. The nutritional benefits of the bone itself are largely the inorganic mineral element (70%) of the bone, which is rich in calcium and phosphorus. For this reason bones are not really a suitable food to give to rats in old age, particularly when kidney disease is suspected. Rats grind their food to a powder before swallowing so there is no chance of them choking on bones. The best bones are cooked chicken bones (with a little meat attached), as they are lean, small and easily manipulated by a rat, but chop bones or ribs can also be given, though you might wish to remove any surplus fat first.

SHOP BOUGHT TREATS

BOREDOM BREAKER NATURALS RANGE
(representative examples of a large range)

Naturals rodent marbles
Ingredients: grains, carrots, alfalfa, beetroot, cheese
Analysis: protein 13.5%, oils 3%, fibre 9.5%, ash 5%

Naturals vegetable edges
Ingredients: grains, beetroot, alfalfa, vegetable protein, malt, minerals
Analysis: protein 14.5%, oils 5%, fibre 2%, ash 3.5%

Naturals sticks - strawberry, dandelion, rose petal, carrot and fennel.
Ingredients (carrot and fennel): cereals, seeds, fennel, nuts, eggs and egg products, carrots.
Analysis: protein 14.5%, oils 12.6%, fibre 8%, ash 4.4%

Naturals carrot pellets
Ingredients: carrots
Analysis: protein 7.3%, oils 1.5%, fibre 28.3%, ash 5.6%

Naturals mixed dairy drops
Ingredients: sugar, milk and dairy products, oils and fats, vegetable derivatives, fruits, dandelion, honey powder, woodberry powder
Analysis: protein 6.6%, oils 24.4%, fibre 3%, ash 4.5%, vitamin A, D_3, E and lecithin

Naturals Herb Plus
Ingredients: oat flakes, wheat flakes, pea flakes, carrot, beetroot, parsley, popped wheat, popped corn, alfalfa, grain extrusions, peppermint, dandelion, locust bean fruit, flaked corn, balm, marigold, red clover.
Analysis: protein 13.5%, oils 2.8%, fibre 13.6%, ash 5.5%

Review: *"I add a hand full to my dry mix and the boys love it! It smells lovely and herby too.*" (Louisap)

Naturals Wood Picnic
Ingredients: acorns, edible boletus, mushrooms, beechnuts, edible roots
Analysis: protein 7.7%, oils 2.3%, fibre 20.1%, ash 2.7%

Naturals Herbal Garden
Ingredients: green oat, green wheat, parsley, balm, peppermint, nettle, dandelion, camomile
Analysis: protein 16.4%, oils 2.4%, fibre 22%, ash 10.6%

Review: *"A lovely mix of garden herbs that can be added to a dry mix or mixed into shredded paper for edible bedding. Smells gorgeous."* (Alison C)

BURGESS EXCEL TREATS

Excel wild apple and carrot chunks
Ingredients: dried wild apple, dried carrots
Analysis: protein 4%, oil 0.02%, fibre 7%, ash 3%

Excel apple snacks
Ingredients: dried apple 98%, dried parsley and thyme 2%
Analysis: protein 4%, oil 0.02%, fibre 8%, ash 2.7%

Excel berry bites
Ingredients: rose hips, carrots, milk thistle, rose petals
Analysis: protein 4%, oil 0.01%, fibre 55%, ash 9%

Excel Mountain meadow Herbs
Ingredients: dandelion, milk thistle, coltsfoot leaf, chamomile, parsley, sage, hibiscus, fennel seeds, rose petals, sunflower petals.
Analysis: protein 13%, oil 1.4%, fibre 21%, ash 5%

Excel Country Garden Herbs
Ingredients: dandelion, plantain, chicory, mint, milk thistle, marigold, cornflower, Jerusalem artichoke.

Analysis: protein 10%, oil 1.5%, fibre 19%, ash 5%

NUTRI-CARE TREATS

Nutri-Care Treat-ums - rabbit (odour control)
Ingredients: wheat flour, sunflower oil, sugar, rice flour, wheat bran, dried skimmed milk, dried milk, water, flaxseed oil, brewers dried yeast, salt, artificial apple and other flavouring.
Analysis: protein 8%, fat 18%

Review: *"These treats are popular with my rats. Although they aren't very natural, I reckon they are okay as an occasional treat. They are a crunchy apple flavoured biscuit with a creamy savoury papaya filling. The odour control part is yucca, a plant extract. But I don't give them to mine for that aspect, just as a change from the handmade treats."* (Sab, The Rat Warehouse)

Nutri-Care Treat-ums - cat (cranberry)
Ingredients: sunflower oil, wheat flour, sugar, rice flour, wheat bran, dried skimmed milk, dried milk, water, natural flavouring, salt, maltose syrup, dried cranberry, taurine, vitamin A, D_3 and E, flaxseed oil, BHA, Red 40 (E129), biotin.
Analysis: protein 7.5%, fat 20%, fibre 2%, moisture 10%, ash 5%

Nutri-Care Treat-ums - ferret care
Ingredients: sunflower oil, wheat flour, sugar, rice flour, wheat bran, dry skimmed milk, dry milk, flaxseed oil, salt, water, artificial flavourings, BHA, vitamin A, D3 and E

VITAKRAFT TREATS
(representative examples of a large range)

Vitakraft nature cookies - carrot, beetroot
Ingredients (carrot variety): cereals, vegetables (10.5% carrot), oils and fats, seeds.

Vitakraft raviolis
Ingredients unavailable.

Review: *"My rats enjoy these (good for their teeth/jaw as they take a fair bit of chewing) – I only give them occasionally as one rat will try to eat the whole thing and they are quite big and hard to divide into smaller pieces."* (Laura E)

Vitakraft drops - strawberry, wildberry, carrot, milk and honey
Ingredients (milk and honey variety): sugar, vegetable oil, whey powder, dried skimmed milk, corn starch, honey, yogurt powder, riboflavin, lecithin, vanilla.
Analysis: protein 6%, fat 22%, fibre 1.7%, moisture 2.5%

Vitacraft Rat Corn and Fruit Sticks
Ingredients: cereals, fruits (3%), seeds, nuts, vegetables, honey.
Analysis: protein 8.8%, oil 4.9%, fibre 5.5%

Review: *"I've tried the rats on the range of these sticks all of which seem to have interesting and tasty ingredients which the rats seem to enjoy."* (Rhi01)

MISCELLANEOUS TREATS

Good Boy chocolate drops (dog)
Ingredients: oils and fats, milk and milk derivatives, cereals, various sugars, derivatives of vegetable origin.
Analysis: protein 6%, oil 25%, fibre 0.5%, ash 8%, vitamin A, D_3 and E

Review (dog sized chocolate drops in general): *"Although there are small animal sized drops available, I always found that these were eaten quite quickly with the rats coming back for more before I had time to shut the cage door. So I feed mine the dog sized ones instead, as the size means I can give one to all of them and shut the door before the first manages to eat it. Also some stores have a help yourself bit with dog biscuits, and a whole bag which lasts months would cost a fraction of what the smaller bags did, which lasted a lot less."* (Rhi01)

Pedigree Milky Biscuits (dog)
Ingredients: cereals, minerals, various sugars, oils and fats, milk and milk derivatives.
Analysis: protein 9%, oil 4%, ash 14%, calcium, omega 3, vitamin A and E, iron.

Review: *"Nice as an occasional low fat treat as they are perfect for threading through twisted ropes. Well received by most rats."* (Alison Campbell)

Rice Bites Natural Dog Treats
Ingredients (Adult variety): rice flour, dried brewer's yeast, alfalfa powder, wheatgrass powder, vitamin E, rosemary extract, selenium yeast.
Ingredients (Puppy variety): rice flour, calcium carbonate, vitamin E, rosemary extract.
Ingredients (Senior variety): ice flour, wheat bran, dried brewer's yeast, vitamin E, rosemary extract, selenium yeast.

Organic Pet Minis Mint Herb (dog)
Ingredients: organic wholemeal flour, organic margarine, organic egg, organic milk powder, organic parsley (2%), organic mint (2%), charcoal
Analysis: protein 10%, oil 12.2%, ash 2.2%, fibre 2.6%

Crocodile and Hedgehog chews (dog)
Ingredients: wheat starch, glycerine, vegetable fibres, lecithin, natural colourings and flavourings.
Analysis: protein 1.5%, fat/oil 3.2%, fibre 8.3%, ash 0.6%, moisture 7%.
Contains no animal products.

Reviews: *"These are one of my rats' favourite treats and are quickly gnawed and eaten."* (Rhi01)
"Crocodile chews (meant for dogs I believe) are thoroughly enjoyed by the boys. As far as I remember they're made from 100% cereal so don't have any strange or unhealthy additives either." (wizzyjo)
"I wrap these in paper so my girls have to open them first. They don't last long as they adore them. The hedgehog ones are thicker and larger so take longer to

chew." (Laura E)
"I cable tie them onto the cage - the crocodile ones are easiest to do this with. The rats have to then climb up and hang off the bars to chew it." (Alison T)

Johnsons Fruity Stick
Ingredients: seeds, nuts, cereals, honey, apple, apricot, banana, raisins, currants.

Review: *"This treat was ignored by my rats. Although it looked okay when I opened the packet it didn't seem to have many interesting ingredients to hold the rats' attention."* (Rhi01)

Shaws Egg Biscuits, original and wild berry flavour
Ingredients: whole eggs, wheat flour, sugar, natural flavours. Colours and preservatives.
Analysis: protein 11%, fat 4%, fibre 0.3%, moisture 13%, ash 0.95%.
All reviews were positive especially for the wild berry variety.

Review: *"They go wild over these treats, and get them fairly often. Because they're so big, I cut them into quarters before giving them any. These make good birthday cakes for ratties with natural yoghurt as icing, and yoggie drops for decorations!"* (Maria)

Strawberry Shortcake Egg Biscuit Treat
Ingredients: egg biscuit (whole egg, wheat flour, sugar), freeze dried strawberries, dehydrated cranberries, honey, de-hulled soybean meal, white millet.
Analysis: protein 12%, fat 3.5%, fibre 0.2%, ash 2.7%, moisture 10%

Review: *"I use this once a week as a quick way to sort dinner out for the rats. It can be sprinkled on food or made into a paste by adding warm water or soy milk. The rats love this and all dive for the dish when I put it in leaving nothing by the morning."* (Rhi01)

Sunny Brunch Garden-Snack (carrot)
Ingredients: grains, vegetables, vegetable derivatives,

Review: *"Entirely edible bowl of grains and parsley, filled with dried carrots. Good healthy chewable fun, and if they don't immediately demolish the bowl you can refill with tasty nibbles. The bowl is quite substantial, and at almost 8cm across and 5cm deep (with thick walls), this is probably a treat best given to larger groups of rats."* (AC)

The Rat Warehouse - selection of home made treats
Mediterranean Rat Loaf, Pizza Rat Loaf and Honey-Oats Crunchies, hand made using wholesome ingredients such as olives, garlic, thyme, tomatoes, herbs, cheese, oats, peanut butter and honey.

Bunny Bazaar herby wholemeal toast
Home baked herby wholemeal bread cut into bunny shapes – a lovely treat if you can't be bothered to make your own!

"Never eat more than you can lift."

(Miss Piggy)

CHAPTER TWELVE - OVERVIEW

Main meal dry mix substitutes
Egg based recipes
Celebrating couscous and bulgur wheat
'Souping up' baby food
Other savoury meals and mixes
Fruit based dishes
Cakes and biscuits
Milky puddings
Miscellaneous

Chapter twelve
Recipes

Main meal dry mix substitutes

You might like to replace the dry element of the diet with a fresh meal once a week, or so. This can be very easy to do and provides enrichment and often superior nutrients if the ingredients are carefully chosen. If you do this you shouldn't feed any dry food, but remember - however many rats you own they will need a greater quantity of fresh food than they would dry. This is because of the high water content of all fresh food.

Mix together:
At least one (preferably more) carbohydrate based food:
- Cooked brown rice
- Cooked quinoa
- Cooked millet
- Soaked whole grain or barley couscous
- Cooked, diced sweet potato
- Sweetcorn
- Cooked whole wheat pasta
- Soaked bulgur wheat

At least one legume:
- Soaked and cooked beans/chickpeas (any variety)
- Tinned beans/chickpeas (any variety)
- Garden peas
- Soaked and sprouted legumes

A protein food:
- Diced chicken
- Tinned fish
- Egg
- Mussels
- Prawns
- Insectivorous Feast
- Ready prepared dog food like Naturediet
- Diced cooked chicken liver

For vegetarian rats, use a double portion of legumes instead of animal protein.

Lots of mixed vegetables and herbs
A few seeds and/or chopped nuts

Supplements such as:
- Fish oil
- Linseed (flax) oil
- Olive oil
- Fresh garlic
- Seaweed powder or flakes
- Dr Squiggles Tiny Animals Essentials.

EXAMPLE MEALS
(serve approximately 15 rats):
1 mug dry bulgur wheat - soaked
1 mug sweetcorn - frozen or tinned
1 mug chickpeas - tinned
½ mug prawns - frozen or fresh, chopped
6 sprouts - chopped
1 red pepper - chopped
2 tbsp sesame seeds
2 tsp salmon oil
1 tbsp seaweed powder
1 level tsp Dr Squiggles Tiny Animal Essentials.

1 mug dry quinoa - cooked
1 mug naked barley - sprouted
1 mug peas - frozen
1 pack Naturediet - chopped
1 cup broccoli - chopped
1 apple chopped
2tbsp sesame seeds
2 tsp flax oil

2 cloves garlic finely chopped, and microwaved for a minute.
1 level tsp Dr Squiggles Tiny Animals Essentials.

RATTY STIR FRY
Ingredients:
Bean sprouts
Peas
Sweetcorn
Broccoli florets
Chickpeas
Chopped peppers
Small amount chopped onion
Kale or shredded spring greens
Fresh noodles
A few prawns

METHOD:
1. Use a good non-stick pan so you use no oil, but if you must use a tiny splash of good quality olive oil.
2. Heat the pan, throw in the ingredients adjusting quantities according to how many rats you have.
2. Cook and serve.

My girls love this and rattle the cage doors when they can see me bringing it to them. (Miss Muffet)

FISHY RICE
Ingredients:
Cooked brown rice
Tinned sardines in olive oil
Peas
Sweetcorn
Carrots
Green beans
Broad beans
Kale

Dandelion
Spearmint
Millet spray
Salmon oil

METHOD:
1. Chop the kale, dandelion and mint.
2. Mix all ingredients together and drizzle with oil.
3. Mix well and serve. (Mistress Sadako)

EGG BASED RECIPES

EGGY COUSCOUS
Ingredients:
Couscous (amount depends on how much other food you are giving your rats!)
Boiling water (enough to cover the couscous)
Egg, beaten with small amount of soya milk
Small handful of hempseeds
Sprinkle of linseeds
Splash of omega 3 rich oil (linseed or hempseed - cod liver oil would also be fine but smellier!)
Shredded greens (or spinach, peas or whatever else you have in the fridge or freezer)
Optional garlic

METHOD:
1. Pour the boiling water over the couscous, either in a pan over heat or in a microwavable bowl. Beat in the egg, add the garlic - if you have no guests visiting your house that day, and don't mind leaving the rat-room windows open!
2. Leave over a moderate heat until couscous has absorbed as much liquid as it is going to. If you are cooking in a microwave, this is best done by microwaving for 20 seconds, mixing and microwaving again.
3. Add greens and cook for a few seconds more.

4. Remove from heat and add some cold water to help it cool and to make sure the mixture doesn't dry up when cooling. This will prevent sticky eggy couscous from being picked up and mashed all over the cage!

5. Add the seeds and a small splash of omega oil if you have it - some of the benefits of omega oils are lost in heating, hence doing this at the end.

6. Mix. Hey presto.

To refresh eggy couscous for dinnertime, pour a small amount of boiling water over and mix until soft. You can also add Lactol instead of soya milk if you need to increase the calories. Sometimes we add cooked chick-peas or lentils if we have some leftover from something else. (Ros Jenkins)

BANANA, KALE AND GARLIC OMELETTE
Ingredients:
Banana (sliced)
Kale (shredded)
Egg (beaten)
Clove garlic (crushed)
Seaweed powder

METHOD:
1. Fry sliced banana in a very small amount of olive oil for a few minutes.
2. Next add torn up curly kale.
3. Then add a beaten egg(s) with added fresh crushed garlic and seaweed powder and cook through.

It smells awful due to the seaweed powder and it will fall apart when you try and slice it up, but the rats love it. (Gemma Driscoll)

EGGY BREAD
Ingredients:
Wholemeal or granary sliced bread
Beaten egg
Oil (tsp)

METHOD:

1. Cut each slice of bread into half or quarters.
2. Dip the bread into the beaten egg (both sides).
3. Using a heavy based frying pan, fry the pieces of bread in a teaspoon of olive oil (you can use a pastry brush to coat the whole pan base).
4. Once browned on both sides remove from pan and chop into small squares.

Some pans may allow you to dry fry these. (Alison Campbell)

EGGY POTATO

Ingredients:
Beaten egg
Cooked mashed potato or sweet potato
Oil

METHOD:

1. Stir the beaten egg into the mashed potato to give a soft consistency.
2. Heat a teaspoon of olive oil (use a pastry brush to coat the whole pan base) in a heavy bottomed frying pan and drop tablespoons of the mixture into the pan.
3. Once browned and cooked on one side, turn and brown on the other side.
4. Remove from pan and chop into small pieces.

You can add a variety of things to the potato mixture before cooking, for example, garlic, seaweed powder, tuna, peas, sweetcorn.

Some pans may allow you to dry fry these patties. (Alison Campbell)

HIGH CALORIE EGGY POTATO

Ingredients:
¼ cup coconut milk
1 egg
Portion of cooked, mashed potato or sweet potato
Oil

METHOD:

1. Beat coconut milk and egg into mashed potato until you have a soft consistency.
2. Heat a teaspoon of oil (use a pastry brush to coat the whole pan base) in a heavy bottomed frying pan and drop tablespoons of the mixture into the pan.
3. Once browned and cooked on one side, turn and brown on the other side.
4. Remove from pan and chop into small pieces.

You can add any supplements of your choosing to the mixture before cooking. (Alison Campbell)

SCRAMBLED EGG SPECIAL

Ingredients:
2 eggs
Coconut milk
½ cup of finely chopped kale
Oil

METHOD:

Beat 2 eggs with a little coconut milk.
Add finely chopped kale.
Cook in a little oil stirring constantly to 'scramble'.
Cool and add a sprinkling of shelled pumpkin seeds before serving. (AC)

SCRUMMY OMELETTE

Ingredients:
2 medium free range eggs
½ cup of soya milk
A handful of fresh curly kale
½ red pepper cut into small pieces
Half a small packet of smoked salmon, though any fish/meat that your ratties love can replace this.

METHOD:
1. Beat the eggs and soya milk together and pour into a hot pan.
2. Add the curly kale, red pepper pieces and salmon (or alternative).
3. Stir the mixture over a gentle heat until it is all mixed together and scrambled.
4. Once cooked leave a few minutes to cool down and then serve to your ratties.

I find this will serve a large group of rats - this quantity feeds my 20 ratties. The recipe can also be made without the fish/meat, but with additional vegetables, as well as cooked pasta. Scrummy omelette is a massive hit with my ratty clan and they will all go in mad rush to be the first to get to a bit of egg with curly kale attached - the bowl is usually   completely clean within 15 minutes and leaves some very content ratties. (Katie Findlay)

CELEBRATING COUSCOUS AND BULGUR WHEAT

Most couscous, (like white rice and pasta) has been stripped of many of its nutrients by processing. It is derived from wheat, and while whole-wheat products are rich in B vitamins, plus a number of essential minerals including iron, zinc and copper, but processing reduces nutritional value. Nevertheless, the product becomes highly digestible, and remains an excellent source of starchy carbohydrate. If you look around, you can buy whole grain couscous, and I have also found barley couscous. It is an excellent addition to a rat's diet in a number of situations; particularly useful for feeding babies, elderly and sick rats. It is easy to prepare - just cover with boiling water and leave to soak for a few minutes - and can be added to many other ingredients. The couscous itself shouldn't be wet and sloppy, but rather dry and 'fluffy'. Drain in a sieve if you have added too much water.

Bulgur wheat is a whole grain that is parboiled and then dried. It contains more nutrients than standard couscous which is a 'white' grain product. It is prepared in the same way, so is quick and easy to use, though it has a longer soaking time than couscous.

COUSCOUS AND BULGUR WHEAT MIXES

To your prepared grain add:

1. Tinned sardines, mackerel or tuna I use the tomato sauce varieties as they tend to have less oil added. Avoid fish in brine wherever possible. Adult rats should really only be having a taste of fish; I use one small tin of sardines amongst 25 rats. If feeding youngsters use more fish per rat.

2. Chopped butter beans, chick peas or other tinned beans. Again, look for brands that do not have salt added wherever possible. Rinse the beans prior to use in a sieve or colander.

3. Any chopped fruit or vegetables suitable for rats.

4. Chopped hardboiled egg.

5. About the same volume of Insectivorous Feast or EMP

6. A beaten egg and then microwave for a minute until set.

'SOUPING UP' BABY FOOD

The better quality jars that are prepared for human infants (2nd or 3rd stage) can be an excellent resource for elderly rats and those needing a soft diet. Alone they lack calories, but as a base food they have perfect consistency and can be easily improved.

Select a jar of savoury baby food and one that has some texture (for example, little pieces of cooked pasta). Tip this into a medium sized bowl and add a combination of the following:

• A large blob of Nutrical let back with a little water for easy mixing.
• A tbsp of soaked Insectivorous Feast or EMP.
• 2 tbsp mashed chickpeas (skins removed if possible).
• Soft scrambled egg.
• Mashed avocado or banana.
• Soaked wholegrain couscous.
• Cooked millet or quinoa.
• A little mashed, tinned fish.
• Geek yoghurt or soya yoghurt.
• Coconut milk.

- Salmon or linseed (flax) oil.
- Grated garlic, microwaved for a few seconds.
- A teaspoonful of puppy milk powder.
- A teaspoonful of Complan.

Pureed fruit puddings are also useful and you can add some Greek yoghurt, avocado or coconut milk for a high calorie palatable meal.

OTHER SAVOURY MEALS AND MIXES

PUREED ROASTED BUTTERNUT SQUASH
Ingredients:
One butternut squash
A little coconut milk or Lactol

METHOD:
1. Cut butternut squash (without peeling) in half lengthwise and scoop out seeds.
2. Place squash face down on baking sheet.
3. Bake at 230°C for about 50 minutes or until the skin puckers and halves feel soft.
4. Scoop the baked squash out of the skins.
5. Place the squash flesh in blender or food processor and puree.
6. Add coconut milk or Lactol if necessary to make a smooth consistency (roguez).

ROAST VEGETABLE SOUP
(feeds about 20 rats)
Ingredients:
2 medium potatoes
1 parsnip
1 carrot
1 butternut squash
A handful of small mushrooms
Dry or fresh herbs (I used mixed dry and some mint or parsley).

METHOD:
1. Chop the root vegetables and potatoes up into roughly same sized chunks and spread over a baking tray (or use an oven proof pan).
2. Spray with Frylight (1cal vegetable oil spray) and then add the chopped herbs.
3. Toss to coat in the herbs.
4. Cook at 200°C until soft, which can take anything from 40-60mins.
5. Blend with a little liquid - either water, milk/Lactol or coconut milk.

The Frylight will prevent the vegetables from sticking to the bottom of the pan or tray (roguez).

PASTA SALAD
Ingredients:
Enough cooked whole wheat pasta to feed your rats
Cucumber - cut into small squares
Seedless red grapes - halved
Cherry tomatoes - quartered
Small tin low salt sweet corn - drained
Cooked chicken - finely diced
Red pepper - cut into small squares
Any fresh herbs - chopped
Salmon or linseed (flax) oil

METHOD
1. Put drained cooled pasta into a large bowl.
2. Drizzle with the salmon oil or linseed (flax) oil.
3. Add all other ingredients and mix well. (Alison Campbell)

CRAMMED COURGETTE
Ingredients:
Courgette
Potato
Butternut squash
Carrot or parsnip

METHOD:
1. Split a courgette in half lengthways and scoop out soft middle leaving a 'boat'.
2. Put scooped flesh into a bowl with the chopped vegetables (small cubes).
3. Add a tablespoon of cooked rice and a small handful of shredded kale.
4. Mix together and stuff the courgette with this mixture.
5. Add a fine drizzle of olive oil, wrap in foil and bake at 190°C until tender.
6. Allow to cool to a sensible temperature and serve.

If you find that the 'boat' rocks use a potato peeler to cut a strip off the bottom to stabilise. (Miss Muffet)

SAVOURY RICE PUDDING
Ingredients:
1½ cups pudding rice
1 tin tuna
1 tsp seaweed powder
2 grated cloves fresh garlic
3 eggs
1 pint of soya or puppy milk.

METHOD:
1. Mix the tuna, garlic and uncooked rice in a large oven-proof dish.
2. Sprinkle over the seaweed powder.
3. Beat the eggs into the milk and pour over the rice and tuna.
4. Stir.
5. Bake at Gas Mark 4, 180°C, 350°F for 1 hour or until set.
6. Cool and serve.

VEGGIE BURGERS
My rats are quite fussy when it comes to their vegetables, they will only eat peas, sweetcorn, broad beans and cucumber. I've managed to find a way round this by making them veggie burgers!

Ingredients:
Selection of vegetables finely chopped or grated
Fresh wholemeal breadcrumbs
2 cloves garlic
1 beaten egg
(optional) A little grated cheese

METHOD:
1. Mix all ingredients together.
2. Brush a teaspoonful of oil over the base of a heavy frying pan.
3. Cook small spoonfuls on one side until browned.
4. Flip and flatten and cook the other side. (Fiona)

FRUIT BASED DISHES

SPECIAL FRUIT SALAD
Ingredients:
Apple (pips removed)
Banana
Pear
Blueberries
Strawberries (if there is any spare, which doesn't happen often)
Grapes
Natural yoghurt

METHOD:
1. Chop the fruit
2. Mix in the natural yoghurt – enough to coat thinly.
3. Serve

Divides easily between multiple cages. It's probably advisable to only use yoghurt just before clean out, as it does get everywhere as the fruit is hoarded so that they can go back for more.

VARIATION: Another option is to use vegetables such as carrots, broccoli, corn cob slices, etc and instead of using yoghurt, make up (or use up) your own home made gravy. I started making my own gravy for my baby's meals so knew exactly what was going in it. If you don't want to serve in a dish, it is all easily mounted on a kabob stick or string "necklace". (jolandra)

PUREED PEACHES
Ingredients:
A peach
Apple juice

METHOD:
1. Peel the peach and take out the stone. Chop.
2. Steam for about 4 minutes.
3. Put peach flesh into blender with some apple juice and blend till smooth (roguez).

CRANBERRY PUREE (GOOD FOR CYSTITIS)
Ingredients:
Fresh cranberries
¼ cup of water per 100g fruit

METHOD:
1. Add the water to a pan and bring to the boil.
2. Add cranberries and simmer over medium-low heat until the berries burst.
3. Puree in blender or food processor until desired texture is reached.

You can strain through a sieve or strainer if you wish before pureeing (roguez).

FRUITY YOGURT
Ingredients:
Plain yoghurt
Fruit of choice

METHOD:
1. Put the fresh plain yogurt into a blender.
2. Add mixed fruit of choice.
3. Blend till smooth for sick rats, or just mix mashed fruit in for healthy rats (roguez).

FRUIT SPLAT
Ingredients:
Apple
Peach or apricot
Blackberries
Cranberries (cook better if you split the skin)
Mango (females only)
Plums
Strawberries
Raspberries
Choose all, or at least 3 fruits from the list above.

METHOD:
1. Chop into equal sized pieces and throw into a saucepan.
2. Simmer until fruit is soft and squishy, then remove from the heat and mash a little, but leave a few lumps.
3. To serve, splat a blob onto a rice cake – edible plates!

This fruit sauce will freeze for up to 3 months or keep in the fridge for 2 days. You can add banana, but my girls aren't keen. (Miss Muffet)

BAKED BANANA
Ingredients:
1 banana per 4 to 6 rats

METHOD:
1. Take the banana(s) and bake in a fairly hot oven (Gas Mark 5, 190°C, 375°F) in the skin for approximately 20 minutes, or until black.
2. Leave to cool.
3. Split open and serve to ratties. You can serve it in its skin and the rats

will leave this. (Jen)

STUFFED APPLE
Ingredients:
1 apple per cage of rats
Seedless red grapes - quartered
Chopped banana
A little human cereal such as Weetabix or rolled oats
Ingredients can be varied depending on your rats' tastes.

METHOD:
1. Take the apple(s) and cut the top(s) off.
2. Scoop out the inside (like you do with a pumpkin), discarding the core.
3. You can use a corer to remove the core if it's easier before scooping out the flesh. Leave a thick shell.
4. Cut up the apple flesh and mix with the grapes, banana and cereals.
5. Add a little water to mix if necessary.
6. Stuff the filling into the apple and feed to ratties.

My rats love it. They pick out their favourite bits and then if they are still hungry they eat the apple bowl! (Sara)

KIDNEY FRIENDLY STUFFED APPLE
Ingredients:
1 apple per cage of rats
Seedless red grapes - quartered
Grated carrot
A few cornflakes and puffed rice

METHOD:
1. Take the apple(s) and cut the top(s) off
2. Scoop out the inside (like you do with a pumpkin), discarding the core.
3. You can use a corer to remove the core if it's easier before scooping out the flesh. Leave a thick shell.
4. Cut up the apple flesh and mix with the grapes, avocado and cereals.

5. Add a little water to mix if necessary.
6. Stuff the filling into the apple and feed to ratties. (AC)

CAKES AND BISCUITS

LIVER BISCUITS
Ingredients:
8oz chicken liver
2 eggs
4 good sized cloves garlic
1 large apple grated
1 tbsp peanut butter
Enough wholemeal flour to create a soft, biscuit dough

METHOD:
1. Preheat the oven to 180°C.
2. Lightly grease a flat baking tray
3. Place the chicken liver (including juices) into a liquidiser or food processor. Add the eggs, garlic, apple and peanut butter, and process until liquefied.
4. Pour the liver mixture into a large bowl and stir in the flour until you have a soft dough.
5. Roll/pat the dough into a flat rectangle that will fit onto the baking sheet.
6. Bake for 30 minutes.
7. Remove from the oven and allow to cool a little, then cut into small treat sized squares.

Freeze in usable quantities depending on the number of rats you are feeding. You can add crushed calcium and vitamin D tablets to the biscuits if you want to increase the amount in the diet. (AC)

LIVER CAKE
Ingredients:
1 or 2 livers (pork/lamb)

2-3 eggs
2 cloves garlic
Wholemeal flour

METHOD
1. Puree the liver in a food blender.
2. Beat in the eggs.
3. Mix in the garlic.
4. Mix all together with wholemeal flour to thicken it to a consistency similar to that of a sponge cake.
5. Bake in a lightly greased cake dish in a medium oven (Gas mark 4, 180°C, 350°F) for approximately 20 minutes or until cooked.
6. Serve in small cubes.

Can be frozen once cooked. (Abi)

RATTIE SCONES
Ingredients:
200g self raising flour
2 tbsp soya margarine
2 to 4 tbsp selected ingredient from:
- EMP
- Mashed avocado
- Grated apple
- Grated carrot
- Peas
- Mashed banana
- Dried fruit
- Cheese
Soya milk to mix

METHOD:
1. Rub the margarine into the flour until it resembles fine breadcrumbs.
2. Add selected ingredient.
3. Add enough soya milk to form a dough.

4. Just add more flour if the dough is too sticky.
5. Work dough for a minute or two until smooth.
6. Roll out and cut into shapes, or roll onto a rectangle and cut into cubes when cooked.
7. Bake in preheated oven Gas Mark 8, 230°C until turning golden.

Freeze in usable quantities depending on the number of rats you are feeding. (AC)

RAT BISCUITS - PLAIN
Ingredients:
3 cups wholemeal flour
¼ cup extra virgin olive oil
1 beaten egg
¾ cup soya milk

METHOD:
1. Beat the egg and then whisk in the soya milk and oil.
2. Stir in the flour until you have a soft dough.
3. Knead a little then roll into sheets that are around 1 cm thick.
4. Place onto a baking tray and cook for about 50 minutes at Gas Mark 3, 170°C, 325°F. When cooked and hardened, cool a little then cut into small squares. Keep in an airtight container.

VARIATIONS:
Add 2 cloves garlic chopped finely.
Add 3 tbsp peanut butter (beat into the olive oil and then add to other fluids).
Replace 1 cup of flour with a cup of rolled oats or oatmeal. Also add a tbsp honey.
Replace ½ a cup of flour with ½ a cup of EMP, pre-moistened in boiling water.

Pizza Swirls

Ingredients (18 swirls):
150g plain wholemeal flour
50g olive oil spread
40g hard cheese
½ teaspoon garlic powder
½ teaspoon mixed herbs
1 teaspoon tomato puree
25mls (approximately) cold water
Milk (optional)

Method:

1. Sieve flour into a bowl and mix in olive oil spread so that mixture resembles breadcrumbs.
2. Mix in garlic powder, herbs and cheese.
3. Gradually add in the water to form a soft, but non sticky dough.
4. Roll out dough (quite thin) on a floured surface.
5. Spread the tomato puree over the surface of the dough.
6. Roll up the dough tightly (like a Swiss roll).
7. Seal joining edge with a little milk.
8. Slice with a sharp knife to make circles around 7 mm thick.
9. Place on a greased baking tray and brush the top of each 'pizza' with a little milk.
10. Bake at Gas Mark 4, 180°C, 350°F for around 12 minutes, till golden.

Allow to cool completely, then they can be stored in an airtight container or the freezer, either whole or cut into quarters first. (Vicki)

Banana heart rat cakes

Ingredients:
2oz soya spread, melted
1 egg
1 small banana, mashed
1 tbsp of runny honey
2oz wholemeal self-raising flour

METHOD
1. Preheat oven to 180°C (a bit lower for fan ovens)
2. Mash the banana with the honey until it forms a smooth paste
3. Whisk the egg until light and fluffy.
4. Add the mashed banana and whisk until well mixed.
5. Gradually add the flour and melted soya spread, folding in gently
6. Carefully spoon the cake mixture into cases (I used heart-shaped silicone ones; don't fill these any higher than half-way).
7. Bake in the top of the oven for 10-15 minutes until golden and a skewer comes out clean.

You can add a tablespoon of finely chopped almonds or hazelnuts to the mixture at the flour stage for extra calories and flavour

For these I used Miniamo mini heart shaped silicone cake cases – they're a great size for rat treats and really cute too! We got ours from Steamer Trading but you can get them online from quite a few places (make sure you get the pastel coloured set of 12 – Miniamo make other cases that are much bigger). You could use paper mini muffin cases instead but with the silicone moulds you don't need to faff about peeling off loads of paper case before feeding time. Makes about 36 hearts. (Trudy Hurdman)

RATTIE TRUFFLES
Ingredients:
Yoghurt drops
Sunflower seed kernels
Crisped rice
Raisins
Banana chips (crushed)

METHOD:
1. Melt down the yoghurt drops and stir in the other ingredients.
2. Spoon small blobs of the mixture onto a sheet of greaseproof paper over a baking sheet or board.
3. Leave to cool and set.

When we celebrated Lily and her brother, Vic's 3rd birthday I made some of these treats and I hadn't seen either of them move so fast as when we served them up! (Jane)

MILKY PUDDINGS

KIDNEY FRIENDLY RICE PUDDING
Ingredients:
1 apple - grated
1½ cups uncooked white rice
Multivitamin powder or other supplements
2 eggs
Pint soya milk

METHOD:
1. In a large oven-proof dish mix the apple with the rice.
2. Sprinkle over a little multivitamin powder.
3. Beat 2 eggs into a pint of soya milk and pour over the rice mixture.
4. Stir .
5. Bake at Gas Mark 4, 180°C, 350°F for 1 hour or until set.
6. Cool and serve.

READY BREK DELIGHT
Ingredients:
3 cups of Ready Brek or unsweetened instant porridge
½ can of coconut milk
1-2 bananas
1 large avocado
Nutrical

METHOD:
1. Mix the Ready Brek and coconut milk together.
2. Microwave for 1 minute.
3. Mash up the bananas and avocado.
4. Mix this in with the Ready Brek.

5. Finally add a dollop of Nutrical for extra nourishment. (Belinda)

READY BREK WITH COMPLAN
Ingredients:
Ready Brek
Complan
Soya milk or Lactol
Nutrical

METHOD:
1. Spoon out the required amount of powdered Ready Brek into a bowl.
2. Make up a jug of hot Complan using the milk.
3. Mix that into the Ready Brek to a sloppy consistency.
4. Finally add a pea sized blob of Nutrical. (Belinda)

PORRIDGE
I make up instant hot oat cereal or Ready Brek with either hot water or (if I have ill rats), coconut milk - which I add after making the porridge to a stiff consistency with hot water so that the coconut milk loosens it up.

To this mix I then add a variety of different things: bananas, avocado, blueberries, peaches or a teaspoonful of honey (roguez).

MISCELLANEOUS

EASY YOGGIES
Ingredients:
1 mug of powdered milk (or soya formula)
100 ml infant apple juice
2 teaspoons corn flour

METHOD:
1. In a small pan mix the milk and juice over a medium heat until it becomes a thick paste.
2. Add corn flour, turn down heat to low, and continue stirring for about

3 more minutes.

3. Remove from heat and place in an icing bag.
4. Squeeze out drops onto trays and refrigerate until cool.
5. Remove from fridge and lay out for a couple of hours till they dry.
6. Store in the freezer (my rats will eat these cold!) (Vicki)

ROASTED CHESTNUTS

The sweet chestnut is the one nut that can be fed freely to rats. They are low in saturated fat, and very low in cholesterol and sodium. They are also a good source of vitamin C and copper, and a great source of manganese. If you can get hold of fresh sweet chestnuts, you can dry roast them and they will go down well with your ratties. To roast chestnuts, split the pointed ends and lay on a baking tray. Roast in a hot oven (Gas Mark 6, 200°C, 400°F) for about 20 minutes until the shells split open and the chestnuts are deep brown.

Tested by Jackie Skidmore and the Buck House Crew. Verdict - very tasty!

"The preparation of good food is merely another expression of art, one of the joys of civilised living"

Jean Kerr

CHAPTER THIRTEEN - OVERVIEW

Antinutrients and other naturally occurring compounds
    Antinutrients
    Phytates
    Enzyme inhibitors
    Amines, nitrates and nitrosamines
    Oxalates
    Glucosinolates
    Alkaloids
    Goitrogens
    Oestrogens
Fillers and other unhelpful ingredients
    Fillers
    Sugars by any other name
    Preservatives
    Artificial colours
Foods to treat with caution
    Food that is high in fat
    Food that has added salt
    Food that is high in sugar
Forbidden foods lists
    Blue cheese
    Raw sweet potato
    Corn
    Green bananas
    Fruit pips and stones
Foods that should be excluded
    Carbonated drinks
    Mango, citrus juice from concentrate, or citrus flesh on the skin
    Raw dry bean and raw peanuts
    Green potato
    Avocado skin and stone

Chapter thirteen
Antinutrients and food to feed with caution

ANTINUTRIENTS AND OTHER NATURALLY OCCURRING COMPOUNDS

ANTINUTRIENTS

An antinutrient is a compound that is found in food (often occurring naturally), that interferes with the absorption of nutrients. Although almost all foods are affected to some degree, levels of antinutrients vary a great deal and in a varied died should not present too great a problem. However, there are certain antinutrients that may have implications for rat diet, especially where diet is primarily *unprocessed* plant material (grains, seeds, legumes, vegetables).

Grains lack a variety of nutrients, including vitamin A, C, D and B_{12}, and while they do contain reasonable levels of many minerals, these are not necessarily readily available in their entirety. Vitamin A (or its precursor, from which a rat can manufacture the vitamin) is available in good amounts in other vegetables, notably carrots, red peppers, sweet potatoes and green leafy plants. Rats can manufacture their own vitamin C and can re-claim some of the vitamin B_{12} that is produced in their intestine by bacteria, through the practice of coprophagy (eating their faeces). Vitamin D remains an issue in many rat diets that aren't based on a commercial feed (these have added vitamin D).

The presence and bio-availability of minerals such as iron, magnesium, zinc, calcium and copper within plant crops, depends on a variety of factors including:

- the type of plant;
- the quality of the soil in which it was grown;
- levels of antinutrients;
- degree of processing;
- quality of the plant part selected;
- fibre content;
- the ability of an animal to digest the plant in the form it is presented.

PHYTATES

In many grains the phosphorus is held in the form of phytate which renders it inaccessible, because non-ruminant animals (those who have a single stomach and do not regurgitate and re-chew food) lack the enzymes needed - entirely, or in sufficient quantity - to separate all of the phosphorus from the phytate. It is held within the insoluble fibre of the bran coating. This is not the husk (chaff) of the whole grain which is inedible and discarded by the rat; it is the brown surface layer of the grain itself.

Phytates also bind with other minerals in the gut to significantly reduce their absorption. Most greatly affected are zinc, iron and calcium, though the availability of other minerals such as magnesium and copper can also be decreased.

Since phytates in high grain human diets (mainly in the developing world) are an issue, some low phytic acid mutations of grain plants have been developed already to reduce the amount of phytate present, and therefore increase the availability of phosphorus.

Phytates are broken down in the gut by the enzyme phytase, which comes from three sources:

- the diet;
- the lining of the gut (primarily in ruminants);
- bacterial action within the gut.

Rats do produce some phytase (more so than humans) within their gut, but the action of this is not thought to be their primary means of breaking down phytates. Rather, they have the ability to utilise some of the phytase that occurs naturally in some cereal grains, notably wheat, rye and barley, during germination. These enzymes will be destroyed by heat processing (e.g. micronization), and will be dormant in dry, stored grain. This is why soaking and sprouting (where the enzymes are activated) will improve the grains' digestibility and reduce phytate load. In a diet free of dietary phytase (made up of dry or processed grains), rats benefit to a large degree from phytase producing bacteria in the intestine, and this becomes their main way of breaking down phytates.[1] The net effect of all of this is that whatever the diet, rats are able to break down some of the phytate in whole cereals and seeds, but this is not sufficient to negate all of the negative effects of a high phytate diet.

Some studies have been conducted to observe the effects of phytates in the diet of growing rats, and it would seem that at levels similar to those in a diet comprised mainly of whole grains and seeds, there was significant impact on the absorption of the mineral measured (magnesium), and as a result, growth potential was reduced.[2]

Cooking, processing, soaking (especially in water with some lemon juice or vinegar added) and sprouting, all reduce phytates and break down fibre, allowing the phosphorus and other minerals to be more readily absorbed.

The intake of meat effectively counteracts the negative effects of phytate, whereas dietary fibre and polyphenols (often high is an unrefined rat diet; see page 169) increase them, partly because the fibre itself reduces the absorption of minerals during digestion. This is no doubt one of the evolutionary reasons why a wild rat does not live entirely on grains, seeds and plant material. Wild rats eat invertebrates, eggs, small vertebrate animals like mice and frogs, scavenge off larger carrion (or MacDonald's), and even eat the faeces of other animals. Not only do these sources supply more readily available minerals, but they will counter some of the negative effects of phytates on mineral absorption.

So, where does this leave us in feeding our rats? It would be wise to consider that an omnivorous diet is probably the most effective way of ensuring that a rat's diet is balanced. Vegetarian diets are possible, but do require more thought, especially in terms of supporting reproduction and meeting the needs of the elderly or ill rat. If a diet is primarily composed of grain, seeds, legumes and other plant material then it is almost certainly going to be beneficial to your rats to take one of two approaches, or (preferably) a combination of both. Firstly, include some processed grains in your mix. These can include commercial feeds such as grain based vegetarian dog kibble (e.g. Benevo), dog biscuits (e.g. Dene's wholegrain vegan dog biscuits), rabbit food that includes extruded wheat biscuits, or human grade cereals (whole grain and low sugar), such as rolled oats, Shredded Wheat, puffed wheat and flaked barley. Secondly you can look to soaking and sprouting some parts of your diet. For more details see page 184. Sprouting wheat groats and naked barley in particular, will increase the amount of phytase available, as well as reducing the amount of phytate in the grains themselves. Bearing in mind that *all* generic rat and rabbit feeds are supplemented to some degree, if you are unsure of the adequacy of the mineral content of your diet (and its availability during digestion) supplementation is a good idea, especially where straight grain mixes are used.

ENZYME INHIBITORS

Grains, seeds and particularly legumes often contain lectin and enzyme inhibitors, which can interfere with the process of digestion. Not only can they inhibit the action of some digestive enzymes, but may also prevent the healing of damaged mucosa (the lining of the gut), and therefore lead to reduced immunity, malabsorption and allergy. These enzyme inhibitors are proteins that are denatured by heat, and even legumes (e.g. kidney beans) with lethal levels of lectin phyto-haemagglutinin, which causes blood cells to clump together, are rendered safe by a cooking process that includes a short period of vigorous boiling. Kidney beans, soya, and other large beans should not be fed raw, even when sprouted. The following legumes: peas, lentils, chick peas, adzuki beans and mung beans are all safe raw, if soaked and sprouted. All other beans (except for green beans) should be cooked before feeding, and where they are sprouted, should still be boiled after sprouting. Micronization involves cooking with infra red energy before rolling the grain or legume into a flake, and reduces the antinutrients in the end product.

AMINES, NITRATES AND NITROSAMINES

Foods are often quoted as being 'bad' for rats because they contain either amines or nitrates, as these can theoretically combine in the stomach into carcinogenic compounds.

Amines are naturally occurring substances, some of which can have detrimental effects. The main health issue (as far as humans are concerned), is that they can build up in the body and cause allergic type symptoms. Some people seem to be more sensitive and symptoms are generally similar to migraine. Many of the foods that are high in amines are not really fed in quantity to rats anyway (smoked or pickled meat and fish, many types of cheese, dark chocolate) but a few are fed fairly frequently (banana, avocado, grapes, tinned fish) although I think it highly unlikely to be any cause for concern. If amines produce the same symptoms in some rats as they do in humans (quite possible), then it is unlikely those particular rats would continue to eat the food. Rats quickly become aware of foods that cause them to feel ill, and avoid them in future. This seems to be an ability that helps them to make decisions about unknown foodstuffs, to avoid food poisoning and toxins, as they cannot vomit.

Nitrates are essential for healthy plant growth so tend to be found in all plant foodstuffs, but higher levels can be found in foods such as turnip greens, beets, celery, rhubarb, spinach, radish, parsley and lettuce.

There is some evidence that ingesting nitrates and nitrites may make animals more susceptible to converting these nitrogen compounds into dangerous nitrosamines, which have long been suspected of causing cancer. Primary sources in human food are the preservatives that are added to meat products (smoked sausage, cooked meats, hot dogs etc) but these would not be part of a healthy rat diet. Whilst it is certainly possible that nitrosamines can form in the stomach if a nitrate-rich vegetable and an amine-rich food are eaten in the same meal, this scenario is limited by the presence of other nutrients such as vitamin C or vitamin E, which both help to prevent nitrosamine formation.

In humans there was thought to be a link between cancer of the digestive tract and increased nitrate intake; however, all of the recent research points to decreasing levels of gastric and bowel cancers despite increasing intake of nitrates in the diet. The same green vegetables that contain the nitrates, also provide a protective effect against cancer via antioxidants, and it seems that the positive benefits of eating vegetables far outweigh any cancer producing potential.

OXALATES

Oxalic acid is a naturally occurring acid found in a large number of plants. Some (non-food) plants contain extreme amounts and are responsible for human deaths from poisoning (usually young children). But in smaller amounts, such as are found in foods, oxalic acid does not generally cause problems in a normal and varied diet.

Oxalic acid combines with calcium, sodium, magnesium, potassium and iron, to form less soluble salts known as oxalates. These oxalates also occur naturally in plants. Oxalates form tiny little insoluble crystals with sharp edges, which are irritating to body tissue and may also contribute to the formation of kidney stones. As oxalic acid can bind with many minerals and render them inaccessible to the body, feeding foods that contain large quantities on a regular basis can cause deficiencies, most notably, of calcium.

Foods that are high in oxalic acid and oxalates should generally be fed in moderation, however, if your rat suffers from kidney disease, it would be sensible to avoid such foods for the most part. These foods include chocolate, cocoa, most nuts, peanuts, beans (not peas or chick peas), beets, parsley, rhubarb, spinach, Swiss chard, summer squash, sweet potatoes, star fruit, poppy seeds, ginger, cabbage, mango, aubergine and lentils.

Interestingly, some of these foods like spinach and Swiss chard, have excellent nutritional qualities and are a healthy addition to any diet. Once again, it is sensible to limit amounts rather than exclude completely and happily, these nutrients are also present in other green leafy vegetables such as kale, spring greens, dandelion leaves and broccoli, so substitutes are easily found.

GLUCOSINOLATES

Plants 'protect' themselves against being eaten by secreting various natural pesticides known as glucosinolates, (which account for their bitter taste), and although harmless in themselves, are quickly broken down into toxic derivatives by digestive enzymes in the stomach. Amounts of glucosinolates vary from plant to plant and some of those with high levels that are pertinent to a rat's diet are Pak-choi, cabbage, Brussels sprouts, broccoli, cauliflower, kale, kohlrabi, watercress and radish.

Toxicity would only be expected if vegetables in this group formed a large percentage of the daily diet, and symptoms would include reduced growth, reduced fertility and hypothyroidism.

However, it should be noted that these vegetables, and indeed the glucosinolates themselves also have beneficial effects. Glucosinolates have been shown to have a protective effect against cancer in humans, and all of these vegetables are excellent sources of a wide range of micro-nutrients (see Chapter 1).

So rather than exclude these foods from a rat's diet, feeding them should probably be encouraged! Glucosinolate levels are reduced by cooking, but these vegetables can also be fed raw, providing that they don't make up a significant proportion of a rat's daily intake. Fed in moderate amounts as a supplementary food (even daily), vegetables such as broccoli and kale are an excellent addition to any rat diet.

ALKALOIDS

There are several thousand known alkaloids and some are present in around 10% of all plants. Alkaloids are small organic molecules, which act on the nervous system to disrupt neurotransmitters at synapses (nerve junctions), and this effect (depending on the alkaloid) can either enhance nervous transmission or prevent it. Some well known alkaloids are nicotine, atropine (given with a relaxing pre-med before human surgery to dry up secretions/saliva), caffeine, LSD, cannabis and quinine.

Alkaloids tend to have addictive properties and they can be responsible for outbreaks of food poisoning in humans and domestic animals, for example, solanine (potatoes), tomatine (tomatoes) and dioscorine (yams). Serious poisoning is rare, but subclinical alkaloid intoxication occurs all the time. Some food plants like potatoes, tomatoes and peppers are especially rich sources, with cabbage, and many other foodstuffs are not far behind, but probably the most relevant source of alkaloids to feeding rats is the green skin of potatoes which contains solanine. Symptoms of solanine toxicity include drowsiness, hallucination, headache, stomach irritation, painful joints and shaking. Where the skin of a potato is green it should not be used as the flesh as it will also contain solanine.

GOITROGENS

Goitrogens are substances causing thyroid enlargement or goitre. These chemicals are primarily found in plants belonging to the genus Brassica, such as Brussels sprouts, turnip, broccoli, cabbage, swede, cauliflower, mustard seed, kale and rapeseed, but are found in other plant sources such as millet, strawberries and spinach. Soya-beans also contain goitrogens, and enlarged thyroid glands have been seen in some human infants fed entirely on soya formula. High dietary iodine is known to counter this effect and is now added routinely to soya baby formula to prevent such problems.

The goitrogens act by suppressing the function of the thyroid gland or the release of the hormone it secretes (thyroxin), however, at the levels they occur in foods, the diet would have to comprise primarily these foodstuffs in order to cause problems. Nevertheless, whenever a rat slows down, gains weight and develops a thinning coat for no obvious reason (symptoms of depressed thyroid function), or has an existing thyroid condition, these issues should really be considered.

OESTROGENS

Many plants contain oestrogenic compounds, called phytoestrogens, which are not destroyed by heat, and at high levels have been shown to cause feminization of rats in experimental conditions. Levels vary in different plants with notable amounts being present in foods such as soya, linseed (flax), oats, barley, sesame seed, rice and legumes. The effects of these phytoestrogens are not yet fully understood, but it is thought that they may have a positive impact on health (for instance in protecting against some forms of cancer and in boosting immunity), as well as negative hormonal effects. Soya is one food that is often singled out for attention in this regard, and there is further comment on this subject on page 141.

FILLERS AND OTHER UNHELPFUL INGREDIENTS

FILLERS

Some food manufacturers use low quality starchy fillers to bulk out their products, mainly because they are cheap to source. These tend to be 'waste' products from the human food industry and are often hard on the digestive system, sometimes causing irritation and digestive upset. They generally not only have very little food value or readily accessible nutrients, but are often high in fibre and can therefore actually reduce the absorption of nutrients from other parts of the feed. Common fillers include: rice hulls, soya bean hulls, dried cellulose, peanut hulls, wheat middling, beet pulp, dried beet pulp (sugar removed), wheat bran and brewer's rice.

SUGARS BY ANY OTHER NAME

Pet food labelling can be confusing and it is important to study packets if you want to be sure that you know what you are feeding your animals. The following are sometimes seen in pet foods and despite the variety of names used, are all basically types of sugar: sucrose (cane sugar), corn syrup, dried plain beet pulp (sugary filler), maple syrup, molasses, glycerine (used as a humectant to keep food moist), caramel (or caramel colour), cane molasses. Excess sugar in the diet can lead to a variety of issues and illnesses including hyperactivity, weight gain, diabetes, increased cancer cell multiplication, blood sugar imbalance and reduced nutrient assimilation.

PRESERVATIVES

Preservatives are often classed as either artificial or natural, however, this can sometimes be misleading. For example some forms of vitamin E used as a natural preservative are entirely synthetic. Synthetic vitamin E is often less active (less nutritive) than naturally occurring vitamin E, but it is still a usable form.

Artificial preservatives are often included only in the animal fat or digest component of a food, and as such are not always included in the list of ingredients. Manufacturers are legally only required to list the ingredients that they add to the food, so if (for instance) they buy in chicken fat which already has a preservative added, they do not need to include this on the labelling. Even more confusing is that they are then still able to say "no artificial preservatives *added*" which can mislead the customer into thinking the product does not contain these additives. If you are concerned about artificial preservatives, look for products that actually say "contains no artificial preservatives". There is further confusion over descriptions such as "EC permitted antioxidants," which is often just another way of saying that artificial preservatives have been added.

At their worst (and at doses that are much higher than those permitted in animal feed by UK legislation)[3] some of the commonly used artificial preservatives, such as Ethoxyquin, Butylated hydroxytoluene (BHT) and Butylated hydroxyanisole (BHA), can potentially cause major health issues like kidney disease, cancers and stillbirths/neonatal deaths. In perspective, the same could be said of many other substances that are safe to ingest in small quantities.

Ethoxyquin deserves special consideration because its primary toxic effect seems to be on the kidneys of (particularly but not exclusively) male rats, and this is probably the male rat's most vulnerable organ in terms of common disease processes. Whilst having some positive antioxidant properties, Ethoxyquin, is recognised to hasten kidney degeneration and aging in rat studies.[4] Doses used in these studies were well in excess of normal dietary levels, but were found to cause "*severe damage*" in male rats, or to greatly exacerbate existing renal degeneration in geriatric rats. A World Health Organisation document[5] cites long term studies on rats that involve much lower levels, and reveal physiological changes (such as greatly enlarged kidneys) in male rats given amounts only just in excess of the permissible levels for pet food.[5] Interestingly, some veterinary groups have already called for a halving of the current maximum level allowed (150mg per kg of feed).

On a personal level I try to avoid these preservatives in most of what I feed, but I don't worry about them too much in the few processed animal products that I use. Pretty much all EMP, most dog kibble and the like, will contain at least one of these preservatives, though they are often not listed on the packaging because they are added to ingredients at source. Artificial preservatives include: Ethoxyquin, BHA, BHT, sodium tripolyphosphate, propyl gallate, propionic acid and sorbic acid.

ARTIFICIAL COLOURS
Yellow 5 (tartrazine), yellow 6 (sunset yellow), blue 2 (indigotine), red 40 (allura red) amongst other artificial colours are often used in pet foods. Colours are added entirely to make the feed look more appealing to humans, and are most often added to the extruded wheat biscuits in rat and rabbit food. When tested on rats, some of these colours are implicated as carcinogens (causing tumour growth), but in much greater amounts than are found in food. In people, they are also linked to allergies and some behavioural problems. Where feeds rely on a lot of artificial colour we have to remember that our rats are eating this every day throughout their lives, and while it may seem unlikely that we would see the effects of this at the levels involved, it could be wise to err on the side of caution, in what is already a tumour prone species.

FOODS TO TREAT WITH CAUTION

A small number of foods should never be fed to rats and these are listed towards the end of this chapter. However, within the principle of a mixed and varied diet, there are also groups of foods that are best fed in small quantities only, if at all. An occasional small amount of an 'unhealthy' food is unlikely to cause any problems for your rats. It is the diet as a whole that should uphold the principles.

FOOD THAT IS HIGH IN FAT

Generally speaking, high fat foods should not be routinely given to rats. A high fat diet can lead to health problems such as obesity, diabetes, skin problems, hair loss, birthing issues and mammary tumours. However, some nutritious high fat foods (such as seeds, avocado and coconut) can be useful, especially as part of the diet of growing, lactating, undernourished and sick rats.

Some fats are essential in the diet in as much as the body is unable to manufacture them. These are called essential fatty acids and include omega 3 fatty acids which are thought to have positive health benefits. Daily small amounts of these fats throughout a rat's life, are beneficial to health and will also improve coat condition. These beneficial fats can be found in foods such as oily fish (or supplements like salmon oil), flax seed (linseed) and flax oil (linseed oil), avocado, coconut, hemp seeds.

Another exception to the 'no foods that are high in fat' principle is nuts. Despite being very high in fat, nuts can be fed occasionally as treats as they have excellent food value, especially walnuts which are a good source of omega 3 fatty acids and brazil nuts which are very high in selenium.

When supplementing your rats' diet with a beneficial oil do not worry too much about exact amounts, and drizzling a little oil over some fresh food once or twice a week should be sufficient. Occasional oily fish, avocado or coconut can be given alongside this. If you are feeding a diet that is low in vitamin D (see page 152), you may want to consider also using a drop or two of high strength (and vitamin A extracted) cod liver oil a couple of times a week. If you are using standard cod liver oil preparation, do not use to often or you may run into problems with vitamin A toxicity. Fish flesh oils like salmon oil are less likely to cause this issue, as vitamin levels are lower and the ratio of vitamin A to D is less.

FOOD THAT HAS ADDED SALT

A high salt diet can lead to high blood pressure and exacerbate kidney disease. Rats don't need salt to be added to their food, though a reasonable amount of some foods with added salt (such as breakfast cereals) will not be harmful, as rats are generally tolerant of more salt in their diet than their bodies actually need. High salt foods however, should be avoided.

FOOD THAT IS HIGH IN SUGAR

High sugar intake not only leads to obesity, but has also been linked to many other health problems, including some metabolic abnormalities, suppression of the immune system and tooth decay. Tooth abscesses and tooth loss in rats can have serious implications for the rat's future health, and for this reason alone, a low sugar diet is advisable. Fruit contains sugar (fructose) and should not be fed too liberally – but it would be undesirable to exclude fruit from the diet because of the nutritional benefits it provides.

Be careful of hidden sugars. Food labelling of human products, now requires that sugar is listed (usually as grams per 100 grams, which can easily be converted into a percentage). Breakfast cereals, biscuits, crackers, rusks, and the like often have large amounts of hidden sugar. It is helpful to get into the habit of checking packaging. If a label states that a food has 25g of sugar per 100g of product that means the product is 25% (or one quarter) sugar, and that is a lot!

As a guideline I prefer to feed a diet that contains virtually no added sugar, and the majority of ingredients that I choose are in their natural (dried) or minimally processed form. I do use some human cereals, but choose predominantly those with no added sugar, and the only other sugar in my mix is from dried cranberries and the fruit in the 'no added sugar' muesli. I also occasionally feed small amounts of fresh fruit. Ideally, the sugar content of the diet should be between 0 and 5%, and closer to zero if possible.

Forbidden food lists

Most forbidden food lists for rats are versions of the same list, though I have no idea of the original source. Some of the foods that are listed are misrepresented, and the principles involved to help you make an informed decision have already been discussed above. A few individual foods fall outside of these groupings and are included below.

Blue cheese
Blue cheese is often said to be toxic to rats. While the moulds used to manufacture blue cheese can indeed produce toxins, these would only be harmful to rats (or indeed people) in much larger quantities than would ever be found occurring in blue cheese. The effects of these moulds and their toxins, have been well studied (and rats have been used in many of these experiments). The conclusion seems to be that there is negligible risk to health from these moulds (or the toxins they produce).

Raw sweet potato
Many lists state that raw sweet potato is dangerous to rats because it contains compounds that convert to cyanide in the stomach. This is untrue and I suspect the confusion has arisen because this is indeed true of another edible root, the cassava. Cassava roots are almost pure starch and when cooked and processed, become the product we call tapioca. Sweet potato is an unrelated root vegetable and the only possible effect of eating it raw is that it may contain a trypsin inhibitor which temporarily reduces the ability to utilize protein.

Corn
Corn is sometimes also said to potentially cause problems if fed in high quantities to rats. One reason for this is that dried corn (depending on storage and processing), may contain high levels of fungal contamination, which can cause liver cancer in rats. Obviously this doesn't apply to fresh corn or corn sold for human consumption. It is unlikely to be a problem with corn in branded UK pet products either, due to quality controls and

methods of processing. If in doubt flaked corn is less likely to be contaminated than whole kernels, because of processing methods.

Another reason that is often quoted, is that corn is high in nitrates - but it is actually the lower parts of the plant that this applies to and not the ear of corn. Only in animal feeds where the green part of the plant is used (farm animals) would this potentially be a problem.

GREEN BANANAS

These are often quoted as containing an enzyme that inhibits starch digestion. I can find no scientific source for such an idea. In fact everything I have read states that green bananas contain amylase (an enzyme that digests starch). There may be some confusion because generally the term 'green bananas' has more than one specific meaning. Rather than simply referring to unripe bananas of the kind we see in our supermarkets, it also refers to a host of other varieties of banana, used in savoury cooking in other areas of the globe.

FRUIT PIPS AND STONES

These contain cyanide but only in very small amounts. Put in context cyanide occurs naturally in plants and animals, and we ourselves, both manufacture cyanide and excrete it in our breath and urine. Cyanide is easily detoxified and there is no accumulative effect, meaning that ingesting small amounts does no harm, and there is no build up over time. So, whilst apple pips and peach kernels both contain cyanide neither will cause harm if eaten occasionally. In order to give some kind of comparison, a human would need to eat about 2 kg of peach kernels in one sitting to consume enough cyanide to be dangerous. Of course, if you are concerned you can avoid these things, but giving a group of rats a whole apple, or an apple core now and again, really isn't going to cause any harm. The only fruit stone that could potentially cause illness if eaten in smaller volumes is the avocado pit, which contains a toxin called persin. I have as yet been unable to find a definitive toxicity level for persin for rats. Some references say that the lethal dose is relatively low in rat studies, so I would err on the side of caution and not allow rats to chew on avocado pits.

FOOD THAT SHOULD BE EXCLUDED

There are really very few foods that are worthy of absolute exclusion from the rats diet, though there are many that I personally wouldn't include on a regular basis (based on the principles outlined). I have not included alcohol and drugs below on the assumption that any responsible owner would not be seeking to supply these to their pets.

CARBONATED BEVERAGES

These are probably best avoided as rats can't burp! Ingested gases can be absorbed or passed from the intestine along with the rat's droppings, however, large quantities of gas in the stomach would cause distension and discomfort.

MANGO, CITRUS JUICE FROM CONCENTRATE, OR CITRUS FLESH ON THE SKIN

D-limonene in mango flesh and the skin oil of citrus fruits, can cause kidney cancer in male rats only. They have a male-specific urinary protein, which binds with the d-limonene and results in the accumulation of protein clumps in the renal tubules. This can eventually result in nephropathy and tumour formation. It has been argued that the amount of d-limonene in an orange or mango is only a small percentage of that needed to induce tumours in male rats, and this is true. The research was done to find out what amount of d-limonene needs to be given to male rats, in order for 50% of them to develop renal tumours. The amount in a glass of orange juice is approximately a 40th of this amount, while a mango contains about a 20th. D-limonene is also well excreted, and the protein binding is a reversible process. However, theoretically *any* d-limonene in the body of a male rat has the potential to bind with the urinary proteins thus resulting in protein clumps and the potential for disease. In a species where males are already prone to kidney problems, I personally feel this is an extra risk factor that is easily avoided.

Raw dry beans and raw peanuts

These contain lectins and other agents that cause disruption of cell membranes and clumping of red blood cells. Many peanuts bought in their shells (monkey nuts) have already been roasted, but always check the packaging; this should make it clear that the nuts have been roasted. Beans (other than adzuki, mung and green) should always be soaked and boiled vigorously prior to simmering until cooked.

Green potato

As mentioned above green potato contains solanine, which is toxic. Symptoms of solanine toxicity/sensitivity include drowsiness, hallucination, headache, painful joints, stomach irritation, shaking. If the skin of a potato is green it should not be used as the flesh will contain solanine too.

Avocado skin and stone

These contain potentially lethal toxins, whereas the flesh is perfectly safe to feed to rats.

References

[1]British Journal of Nutrition (1985), 54, 429-135 429
A comparative study of phytate hydrolysis in the gastrointestinal tract of the golden hamster (Mesocricetus auratus) and the laboratory rat
P. J. Williams and T. G. Taylor
[2]Nutrition Research, Volume 18, Issue 6, June 1998, Pages 1029-1037
Dietary phytate reduces magnesium bioavailability in growing rats
Josef Pallauf, Manfred Pietsch and Gerald Rimbach
[3]European Union - Community Register of Feed Additives pursuant to Regulation (EC) No 1831/2003
[4]Carcinogenesis, Volume 8, Number 5, Pp. 723-728
Ethoxyquin alone induces preneoplastic changes in rat kidney whilst preventing induction of such lesions in liver by aflatoxin B1
M.M. Manson, J.A. Green and H.E. Driver
[5]World Health Organisation and Food and Agricultural Organisation of the UN/ food add./70.38, 1969 Evaluations of some pesticide residues in food. Ethoxyquin.
(Throughout section on phytates)

Journal für Ernährungsmedizin 2006; 8 (3), 18-28
Phytate - an undesirable constituent of plant-based foods?
Greiner R, Konietzny U, Jany K-D

"He that takes medicine
and neglects diet wastes
the skills of the physician."

Chinese Proverb

APPENDIX 1
NATIONAL RESEARCH COUNCIL NUTRIENT REQUIREMENTS

Estimated nutrient requirements for maintenance, growth and reproduction (rats)
Source - Nutrient requirements of laboratory animals, fourth revised edition (1995)
(Amounts are parts per kg of diet).

NUTRIENT	MAINTENANCE	GROWTH	REPRODUCTION
Fat (g)	50	50	50
Linoleic acid (g)	*	6.0 as part of fat	3.0 as part of fat
Linolenic acid (g)	Required but	quantities	unknown
Protein (g)	50	150	150
Calcium (g)	*	5	6.3
Chloride (g)[1]	*	0.5	0.5
Magnesium (g)	*	0.5	0.6
Phosphorus (g)	*	3.0	3.7
Potassium (g)[1]	*	3.6	3.6
Sodium (g)	*	0.5	0.5
Copper (mg)	*	5	8
Iron (mg)	*	35	75
Manganese (mg)	*	10	10
Zinc (mg)	*	12	25
Iodine (microg)	*	150	150
Selenium (microg)	*	150	400
Vitamins			
A (mg)[2]	*	0.7	0.7

D (mg)[3]	*	0.025	0.025
E (mg)[4]	*	18	18
K (mg)	*	1	1
Biotin (mg)	*	0.2	0.2
Choline (mg)	*	750	750
Folic acid (mg)	*	1	1
Niacin (mg)	*	15	15
Pantothentate	*	10	10
Riboflavin (mg)	*	3	4
Thiamin (mg)[5]	*	4	4
B6 (mg)[1]	*	6	6
B12 (microg)	*	50	50

Listed nutrient concentrations represent minimal requirements. Higher concentrations of many nutrients may be warranted in natural ingredient diets (tables are based on purified diet).

*Separate requirements for maintenance have not been determined. Requirements presented for growth will meet maintenance requirements.

[1] Estimate represents adequate amounts rather than true requirements.

[2] Equivalent to 2,300 IU/kg

[3] Equivalent to 1,000 IU/kg

[4] Equivalent to 27 IU/kg

[5] Higher requirements needed with low protein, high carbohydrate diet.

Appendix 2
Fruit and vegetable list

All listed fruits, vegetables and legumes are suitable for rats within the parameters described.

A
Aduki beans (sprouted, raw, canned or boiled)
Apple (pips removed if you're a purist but they really won't do them any harm unless you feed by the cupful!)
Apricots (no stone - as for apple, dried are usually preserved in sulphur)
Asparagus
Aubergine (eggplant, bitter when raw)
Avocado (flesh only, no skin or stone – this one matters)

B
Bamboo shoots
Banana (fine for oldies in moderation, yes they are high in potassium but the kidney failure suffered by rats causes fluid and electrolyte loss through increased urine productions – so low potassium is a potential problem)
Bean sprouts (make your own from all varieties of beans and peas that can be eaten without cooking)
Beetroot
Bilberry
Blackberries
Blackcurrant's
Blueberries
Bok choy (Pak choi) (great alternative to kale and dandelion)
Broad beans (canned or boiled)
Broccoli
Brussels sprouts (raw is fine)
Butternut squash (more palatable cooked)

C
Cannellini beans (canned or boiled)

Cantaloupe melon (great moisture source for shows)
Carrots
Cauliflower
Celeriac
Celery
Cherries (without stone – as for apple)
Chick Peas (roasted, sprouted, canned or boiled)
Chicory
Clementine (girls only)
Clover leaf
Coconut
Collard greens
Courgette (Zucchini, bitter when raw)
Cranberries
Cress
Cucumber (great moisture source for shows)

D
Damson
Dandelion leaves (great ratio of calcium and phosphorus for bone health)
Dates

E
Eggplant (Aubergine, bitter when raw)
Elderberry
Endive (in moderation)

F
Fennel
Figs (small amount)
French beans (raw or cooked)

G
Gala melon (great moisture source for shows)
Garlic (more palatable cooked)

Globe artichoke
Gooseberry (cooked)
Grapes
Green beans (raw or cooked)

H
Haricot beans (canned or boiled)
Honeydew melon (great moisture source for shows)

J
Jerusalem artichoke

K
Kale (curly) (great ratio of calcium and phosphorus for bone health)
Kohlrabi
Kidney beans (canned or boiled)
Kiwi (small amounts, without skin)
Kumquat (girls only)

L
Leek (cooked)
Lemon (girls only)
Lentils (all varieties raw, sprouted, cooked)
Lettuce (small amount)
Lime (girls only)
Loganberry

M
Mandarin (girls only)
Mange tout
Mango (girls only)
Marrow (more palatable cooked)
Melon (great moisture source for shows)
Mulberry (leaves can be eaten too)
Mung beans (sprouted, raw, canned or boiled)

Mushrooms

N
Nectarines

O
Okra
Olive
Onion (more palatable cooked)
Orange (girls only)

P
Pak choi (bok choy) (great alternative to kale and dandelion)
Papaya
Parsnips (more palatable cooked)
Passion fruit
Peach (no stone - as for apple)
Peas (frozen or fresh)
Pears
Peppers (all colours)
Persimmon (sharon fruit)
Physalis (chinese lantern fruit)
Pineapple
Plums (without stones – as for apple)
Pomegranate
Pomelo (girls only)
Potato
Prunes
Pumpkin (more palatable cooked)

R
Radish
Raisins
Raspberries
Redcurrant

Red cabbage (small amount, more palatable cooked)
Red onion (more palatable cooked)
Rhubarb (small amounts and cooked only)
Rocket
Runner bean (cooked)

S
Savoy cabbage
Shallot (more palatable cooked)
Sharon fruit (Persimmon)
Soya beans (canned, boiled or fermented)
Spring greens (spring cabbage, useful alternative to dandelion and kale)
Spring onion
Spinach (small amounts – high oxalate greens)
Squash (more palatable cooked)
Strawberries
Swede
Sweet chestnuts (more palatable cooked, may cause digestive upset raw)
Sweet corn (frozen or fresh, on cob or off)
Sweet peppers
Sweet potato (more palatable cooked
Sugar snap pea
Swiss chard (small amount – high oxalate greens)

T
Tangerine (girls only)
Tomato
Turnip

W
Water chestnuts
Watercress
Watermelon (great moisture source for shows)

Z

Zucchini (Courgette) - can be quite bitter fed raw.

Unless otherwise stated all foods can be fed raw or cooked, but might be more palatable one way or the other, and preference may vary from rat to rat. The fruits that are only suitable for girls are those that contain d-limonene, a compound that can cause a male specific protein to clump together in the rat kidneys, which may affect long-term kidney health.

"Never leave a rat
to guard your dinner."

Anon

INDEX